Religion of the Heart

Essays Presented to
Frithjof Schuon on His Eightieth Birthday

Edited by
Seyyed Hossein Nasr and William Stoddart

First published in the United States of America in 1991 by
Foundation for Traditional Studies
1633 Q St., N. W., Washington, D. C.

Library of Congress Cataloging-in-Publication-Data
Nasr, Seyyed Hossein
Stoddart, William (eds.)
Religion of the Heart

ISBN 0-9629984-0-0
1. Religion – Miscellaneous   2. Metaphysics
91-72798

Printed in Malaysia by
Art Printing Works Sdn. Bhd.
29, Jalan Riong,
59100 Kuala Lumpur

The cover design by Frithjof Schuon is
the Feathered Sun, Plains Indian
symbol of the universe

Frithjof Schuon. Photo by W.N. Perry

Contents

Preface

On the occasion of the eightieth birthday of Frithjof Schuon, a number of scholars from many different lands expressed the desire to participate in a *Festschrift* to celebrate this joyous event. We as editors feel honored to be able to make possible the presentation of this volume which reflects to some extent the vast and profound influence of Schuon. Our efforts, and those of the contributors, are an expression of our gratitude to one of the foremost intellectual and spiritual figures of the century, whose writings, whether in the field of metaphysics, cosmology, comparative religion, traditional science, sacred art, or the criticism of the modern world, contain a transforming light and presence unparalleled in this day and age.

For over fifty years, Schuon has expounded the truth of various aspects of traditional doctrine and practice in a way which annihilates the errors contained in the mind and helps to overcome the obstacles which prevent the soul from embarking upon the spiritual journey which is the very *raison d'être* of human existence. At the heart of this monumental opus resides the *Religio perennis,* which Schuon himself has often referred to as the "religion of the heart". This is the very essence of religion, as well as the truth which resides in the heart – the "Throne of the Compassionate" and the locus of the Kingdom of God. May this volume, entitled *Religion of the Heart,* be accepted as a token of appreciation by those who have been led from the circumference to the Center, from the periphery to the Heart, by the luminous message of Schuon, which is itself a clarion call from the Heart-Intellect.

Seyyed Hossein Nasr
William Stoddart

The Biography of Frithjof Schuon

Seyyed Hossein Nasr

Frithjof Schuon is the foremost expositor today of traditional doctrines or what is also called *philosophia perennis et universalis.* His works, most of which were originally written in French, have been translated into most major European languages, especially English. They have also been rendered into the major Islamic languages, such as Arabic, Persian, Malay and Urdu, while one of his books was originally published in India. His thought is known not only on both sides of the Atlantic but throughout the world, from Malaysia to Morocco, from South Africa to Brazil, not to speak of Europe and North America. Yet little is known of the life of this most remarkable spiritual teacher and metaphysician who has preferred to remain outside the gaze of the public eye while for over a half century he has elucidated, in an incomparable manner, that eternal wisdom or *sophia perennis* which lies at the heart of every authentic religion and by which human beings have lived and died over the centuries and millennia of normal human existence.

While his works have found an ever greater and more perceptive audience as the years have gone by, Schuon has personally remained aloof and secluded from public scrutiny and has preferred not to have anything written about himself, always referring those interested to his message as contained in his prolific output in the form of books and articles. It is therefore not easy to provide a detailed biography of this sage whose eightieth birthday is celebrated in this collection

1

of essays by his admirers.

Frithjof Schuon was born in Basle, Switzerland, in 1907, in a German family and was nurtured in an artistic ambience, his father having been a musician. In addition to music, other forms of art, especially literature, were cultivated in the household and it was at this stage of his life that the future master of metaphysics and comparative religion gained his acquaintance, not only with European, but also with the Oriental literature which was available at that time in translation.

The early years of Schuon were spent in Basle where he had his first schooling. It was only after the death of his father that his Alsatian mother moved the family to Mulhouse where subsequently Schuon became a French citizen, Alsace having become French. He was therefore able to master French as well as German. That is why while his mother tongue was German and his first book *Leitgedanken zur Urbesinnung* and two volumes of poetry *Tage- und Naechtebuch* and *Sulamith* appeared in German, Schuon wrote all his subsequent books in French. His literary output is in fact reminiscent of his compatriot Meister Eckhart who wrote in both German and Latin. One can see in Schuon's style of writing and thinking a wedding between the metaphysical quality of the German language and the lucidity of Latin so well reflected in French, which is the most important vehicle of the Latin heritage in European civilization.

Schuon was a remarkably precocious student who had read and understood the main works of German philosophy while he was still in his early teens. Moreover, at a tender age he became acquainted with the classical works of Western philosophy, especially the dialogues of Plato, as well as certain classics of Oriental metaphysics and spirituality such as the Bhagavad-Gita and the Upanishads. It was also at this young age that Schuon discovered the works of René Guénon whom he was to meet later in life and whose exposition of traditional knowledge he continued and expanded on an unprecedented scale. In contrast to what he was learning through these sources, the rigid and lifeless educational curriculum at school which was anti-traditional in both nature and style had nothing more to offer Schuon and so at the age of sixteen he left school and began to support himself as a textile designer. He turned to art which he had loved since childhood but in which he had not as yet received any training. This activity marked the beginning of his artistic life which has continued over the years in parallel with his intellectual activity for Schuon is a remarkable painter and poet as well as metaphysician.[1]

Shortly after this period of activity as a textile designer, Schuon joined the French army in which he served for one and a half years. Upon finishing his service, he settled in Paris where he continued his work as a designer. At the same time, he also began to study Arabic at the Paris mosque and was able to gain first hand experience of Islamic as well as other non-Western forms of art which he had always loved and about which he was to write so many luminous pages in later life. The rich museums of Paris provided the possibility of his being exposed to various forms of traditional art including that of Japan which he has always deeply admired.

Paris also afforded him the possibility of becoming more familiar with the intellectual aspect of various traditional worlds before he set out on his first journey into such a world in 1932. In that year he visited Algeria which, like Morocco, was still at that time witness to the living presence of traditional life. Here, Schuon experienced his first direct encounter with the Islamic world and was able to gain intimate knowledge of the Islamic tradition from within. This knowledge included not only the art and thought of Islam, but especially the inner dimension of the Islamic tradition or Sufism whose truths he was later to present in such a brilliant manner to the West. Here also he was able to meet some of the important living representatives of Sufism, including one of the foremost figures of Sufism in this century,

Shaykh Aḥmad al-'Alawī. Some of the most beautiful German poems of Schuon reflect the deep impressions received during this journey, which was not only a physical journey but a spiritual one as well.

Schuon returned to Europe where his spiritual and intellectual powers began to manifest themselves in his first essays. He returned to North Africa in 1935, visiting this time not only Algeria but Morocco as well. In 1938 he was to visit North Africa a third time, on this occasion travelling to Egypt where he met René Guénon with whom he had corresponded for many years. A year later Schuon decided to visit India, whose traditions of wisdom had attracted him since his boyhood. He stopped in Egypt once more where he again spent some time visiting Guénon. He then continued his journey to India where he could not, however, stay long because of the outbreak of the Second World War. Consequently he was forced to return to France to join the French army and participated in the War until he was captured and imprisoned by the Germans. Soon the Germans decided to induct prisoners of Alsatian origin into the German army. Realizing that he would soon have to join the battlefront on the German side, Schuon fled, reaching Switzerland where he finally settled becoming eventually a Swiss citizen.

The next forty years of Schuon's life were to be spent in Switzerland mostly in Lausanne. It was here that in 1949 he married a German Swiss who had received a French education. She was deeply interested in metaphysics and religion and was also a painter. Together they travelled from time to time to the unspoilt Alpine regions where Schuon experienced more than ever before in his life the grandeur and beauty of virgin nature. They also travelled to other European countries as well as Morocco. Moreover, in 1968 they visited the House of the Holy Virgin near Ephesus in Turkey.

It was in Lausanne that Schuon wrote most of his magisterial works, starting with his first book in French, *De l'Unité transcendante des religions* which established him immediately as an outstanding metaphysician and seer and the most spiritually efficacious expositor of traditional doctrines. Although keeping away from public gaze, Schuon became known to an ever greater degree by those attracted to the inner life and to perennial wisdom. Many of the outstanding intellectual figures from both East and West came to visit him in his home overlooking the Lake of Geneva, while he carried out extensive correspondence with both spiritual authorities and aspirants from many parts of the globe.

Schuon had always harbored a great love for the North American Indians, especially those of the Plains, in whom he saw something of the nobility and majesty of the Primordial Tradition. In 1959 he and Mrs. Schuon came to America for the first time, visiting the Sioux and Crow Indians of South Dakota and Montana. A second visit followed in 1963. The Schuons were received as members of the Sioux tribe and made contact with some of the important traditional authorities who had survived among the North American Indians despite all the tragedies that had befallen them. The special love of Schuon for the traditional American Indian world is manifested not only in his penetrating exposition of their metaphysical and cosmological teachings, but also in his paintings of singular beauty, most of which are devoted to American Indian subjects.

These visits to America seem to have been the prelude for the last phase of Schuon's life, for in 1981 he and Mrs. Schuon migrated to America where they have now settled. Here Schuon has continued to be active both intellectually and artistically. Several major works have flowed from his pen since his residence in America while he has also continued his activities as a painter. And it has been in America that Schuon has celebrated his eightieth birthday.

On this occasion several among his numerous admirers have
contributed the essays comprising this volume in order to
express their gratefulness to a man who has touched their
lives on the deepest level both intellectually and spiritually.

It has been well over a half century since Schuon, this
remarkable sage, began to expound the profoundest wisdom
to be found in a contemporary medium. His dazzling light
still continues to illumine the intellectual and spiritual scene
shining upon the landscape near and far. He continues to
enjoy the vigor of that "youth" which emanates from the
eternal spring of the world of the Spirit. We pray for his long
life and hope that he will continue to shed light upon the
path of a world lost in unprecedented darkness and in
need as never before of that light which is neither of the East
nor of the West.

[1] See S.H. Nasr (ed.), *The Essential Writings of Frithjof Schuon* ,
Warwick (N.Y.), Amity House, 1986, which contains colored
reproductions of some of his paintings and an extensive introduction
to his thought by S. H. Nasr.

The Sun in the Tree

With Some Reflections on "Faith and Works"

Kurt Almqvist

**Being and Consciousness are
one – in God and in His
Manifestation**

It is well known that the question whether "justification" can
be achieved "by faith" or "by actions" played an important
role in Martin Luther's conflicts with the Catholic Church.
In this essay we will not enter into these discussions, but will
try to see the question in the light of the universal wisdom
which abides timelessly in the nature of things, and which –
for that very reason – forms the metaphysical core of every
revealed religion. In so doing, we follow the example of the
eminent author to whom this book is dedicated.[1]

We will also follow his example in choosing, as starting
point for our essay, the principal distinction, "Being-Consciousness-Bliss" (*Sat-Chit-Ānanda*), which according to the
Vedanta exists within Divinity and which is often mentioned
by Frithjof Schuon. As Being, God is the Object of Himself as
Consciousness, and the Unity which binds these two elements together – and which in reality they never leave – is
Bliss. Now, this supreme Polarization and Unity cannot but
reflect Itself in universal Existence by the intermediary of
the divine Word, which represents absolute Divinity on the

7

level of Manifestation.[2] And since "all things were made by Him" (John 1,3), it follows that everything in existence shares – be it indirectly – not only in divine Being, but also in divine Consciousness. In the final analysis, Existence is a tapestry made out of these threads, and the Beauty of the tapestry – the Unity of the Poles in the depths of all creatures – is Bliss.

Thus, Being and Consciousness are inseparable from each other everywhere in the substance of things. On the one hand, in one way or another, there is in everything a conscious element: total and active in man – at least in principle – passive and indirect in animals and plants, for instance in flowers directing themselves towards the sun; finally, in a purely symbolical way, inanimate things: in that their forms and other qualities reflect the divine Intelligence – a property, in fact, which they have in common with everything corporeal: "Not only men, but all things and all beings pray to Him continually in differing ways", as the Red Indian sage Black Elk expresses it.[3] On the other hand – as a consequence of the same inseparability of Being and Consciousness – a contemplative vision evoked by the symbolism of created things is not, as a rational understanding, a "merely abstract" occurrence, in the modern, derogatory sense of the expression, but it is the beginning of an existential or substantial merging of the contemplated object in the cognitive subject. Without this inseparability of the "Poles" – in Existence as in God – there would be no foundation, in cognition, for that identification of subject and object which the scholastics called *adaequatio rei et intellectus*. In other words, without this, no identification with a created being or thing in its essence, nor any degree of mindful or "reminiscential" unification, with the Divine in contemplating Creation would be attainable. That which brings about this unification is, in the words of Meister Eckhart, that "something in the soul which is uncreated and uncreatable; and this is Intellect", unification, but in reality unveiling and realization, with God's Help, of the hidden Unity of Being and Consciousness.

Actions : Elements of Our Inner Life

Earthly phenomena are partly forms and partly events, and among the latter are the actions of men. Consequently, these must also have a living relation with the cognitive subject and, by its intermediary, with Truth and Reality. And since "the Truth shall make you free" (John 8, 32), actions must be able to contribute to the "freeing".

As a matter of fact, faith means the acceptance of Truth with one's whole being. In this function it is one with love. The supreme Commandment of Love, proclaimed in Deuteronomy, is introduced by a statement of the divine Unity. Enumerating the elements in man with which this realization should be accomplished, the Old Testament begins with the heart, abode of the Intellect and therefore the innermost subject of the act. The assisting elements, according to Deuteronomy, are "soul" and "might". Frithjof Schuon has noted that, according to the three synoptic Gospels, Christ, when citing this passage, adds "mind", whereas "strength" – corresponding to "might" in Deuteronomy – is to be found only in Mark and Luke. Schuon interprets the different versions of the two Testaments in the following way: "[The difference] may indicate a certain change of accent or perspective with regard to the 'Old Law': the element 'mind' is detached from the element 'soul' and gains in importance over the element 'strength', which refers to works; and one may see in this the sign of a tendency towards interiorization of activity." [4] This interpretation gives us an extra clue to understanding how actions, which in themselves seem to be something external, may have a living relationship to the innermost core of man.

To be able to follow this clue, let us consider a parable told by Christ, a parable typical of his Message of Inwardness. During his farewell speech, he likens himself to "the vine" and his disciples to "the branches" (John, 15). As a matter of fact, in his quality as Logos or Universal Spirit, Christ represents the World-tree in its entirety, including its branches; he is then *the whole* "vine". But considered in the Center of Manifestation and in relation to it, he is *the trunk* of the Tree. The latter aspect is dominant in the parable, since Christ speaks of the opposing attitudes which may be taken by his disciples towards him: the one open, receiving, "abiding" in him, as he says, and the other closed, rejecting, "not abiding" in him.

Seen as including all of Manifestation, the "vine" is the World-tree. But this has also a microcosmic aspect: every human being may be seen as a tree, a "little world-tree". In principle, man is indeed capable of reflecting within himself the totality of Creation and, in its center, the light which "shineth in the darkness". This amounts to saying that the trunk of the "little world-tree", just as that of the great one, is the Logos or the Intellect. Analogously, the branches are the different psycho-physical elements which together make up the particular individual envisaged: in the first instance reason, will and emotion; then memory, imagination and the five senses. This becomes especially clear if one imagines a cross-section of the trunk. The circle formed by this section and the branches emanating from it are like the sun and its rays. The sun in the center, which conveys life to the tree, corresponds to the Intellect, and the rays correspond to the purely human faculties.[5]

This image may be given a meaning similar to that expressed by Christ in his parable. All the individual faculties of man should, as a matter of fact, strive to "abide" in the potentially divine Center, be attentive to its nature and commandments, serve it, conform themselves to it, and in the final instance, "extinguish" themselves in its presence, as the stars in the presence of the rising sun. Then they contribute each in its place and according to its nature – to a state of affairs where this miniature society bears the stamp of heavenly Order and Harmony and avoids being a "kingdom divided agsinst itself", and thus "brought to desolation" (Matthew 12, 25). In other words, by means of this "abiding in the vine", a spiritual and psychic state is established which is a reflection in man of divine Unity.

The necessity for the spiritual wayfarer to have this general attitude of *vacare Deo* or "poverty in spirit" has probably not been more strongly and convincingly stressed more by anyone than by the man who is celebrated by this book; and nobody has more wisely and completely described its different aspects, that is, the realm of the Virtues.

In a general way, a tree may appear to one as a spiritual model, an *upaguru* or "occasional instructor", to speak in Hindu terms.[6] Its immobility suggests incorruptibility and impassibility, and especially if it is tall and straight – it expresses noble detachment, royalty. Its network of branches bespeaks generosity and grateful joy of existence. This existence is granted the tree, from above by the sunlight and the rain, and from below by the soil. These elements symbolize Truth, Grace and the interplay of the Virtues, respectively. For the last mentioned are life-giving forces,[7] which have their analogies in the "Great Cosmos". Their Archetypes are the divine Qualities, which implies that, in the final analysis, they too have a transcendent origin. Thus, together they constitute the very soil in which the spiritual tree has its roots.

Another psychic element indispensable for growth in the Spirit is the will of man, the *bona voluntas*. It might be said to correspond, in our image, to the rising movement by which the sap, the quintessence of the "forces", penetrates into the trunk. This rising sap may be seen, by inverse analogy, as a counterpart of the descending elements, sunlight and rain, a circumstance, in turn, which may symbolize the relation between the Virtues and the other heavenly Gifts, Truth and Grace.

We should not forget that it was a tree that grew in the middle of Paradise.[8] This "Tree of Life", which was the Norm and Heart– the Logos – of the Earth, remains so in a potential way even after the Fall. Every incarnation of the Logos has come to restore the function of the Tree, and in the case of Christ, this is traditionally suggested by seeing and representing the Cross as a stylized tree, with which the body of the Crucified is one.

The Tree of Life is the representative on Earth of the "Great Cosmic Tree" of the Universe; and since both, in essence, are the Logos, it follows that the Logos is both the Center and the Circumference of Creation.

Intentions: Mediators between Actions and the Soul

It is easy to understand that the actions of man are connected with the virtues – or their contraries, the vices –, namely as their expressions: "Ye shall know them by their fruits" (Matthew 7, 16).[9] But there is also a movement in the opposite direction: from the outer manifestations of the personality to its inner state. It cannot, for example, be indifferent for an artist's or a writer's state of soul, whether he – or she – does or does not give form to it by thoughts or images. In other words, his creations do not only express his inner state, but they also exercise a reaction upon it, just as they have influence upon his public. In a similar way, in liturgy, movements such as the sign of the cross, genuflections and bowing have importance, not only as manifestations of piety but also as means to keep such a state alive, in the one who performs them and in others. But of course, an inward effect of such movements presupposes that they are not done mechanically, but that they emanate from an already present inner state.[10]

This means that there must be a sufficiently important *intention* behind an action for it to exercise a notable reaction on its performer. The intention that a person has with an action is a necessary connecting link between his mental or moral state and the act that manifests it. The intention is the "soul" of the act; it is an integral part of man's very personality. And since God, in the end, judges us according to what we *are*, this is a confirmation of the words of the Apostle James: "By works a man is justified, and not by faith only" (2, 24); and, in the same spirit: "By works was faith made perfect [in Abraham, when he had offered his son Isaac upon the altar]" (2, 21-22). The moral elements that we call "intentions" and that represent our works before God, have effects, not only outwardly, as the immediate causes of these works, but also inwardly, as an influence upon our hidden world of virtues and vices, the world where our existential substance is formed – in accordance with, or in opposition to, the Light of the divine Spirit.

Prayer: The Most Essential Work

Poverty in spirit is a poverty *for* Spirit, with the purpose of preparing its dominion in man; and since the Spirit or Intellect is the center of the human being, our attention to it is a concentration in the highest sense of the word. However, this attention or openness has a passive or static character, and in order to have a real and lasting effect, it must be "rounded off" by a dynamic element, an inner activity or, precisely, "work"; and that is prayer. Prayer – in principle "unceasing" prayer or invocation of God's Name – is the work that comprises all others, and without which no work whatsoever can have real substance. For this reason, there is if one sees more deeply into things, only a difference of degree and not of kind between a *via activa* and a *via contemplativa*. All spiritual ways are, as such, rooted in prayer and piety – in *faith*; and the difference between them, from the point of view of "works", consists only in different proportions between inner deepening and outward acts. It is consequently quite correct that it is "by faith" that "man is justified", but if our outward activities proceed from faith and return to it, they are able to assist it in the saving of the soul.

Let us add that if prayer is the highest and deepest of works, this is so because, in prayer, the *adaequatio rei et intellectus* is – in principle and to very varying degrees – a direct participation in the Unity of " Being-Consciousness-Bliss" and not only an indirect one, as is the *adaequatio* in cases of "reminiscence" by contemplating reflexions in Creation of divine Archetypes.

Acting In God's Name

Thanks to the invocation of God's Name, the performance of all actions "in God's Name" acquires a particularly concrete significance. However, we would like, in conclusion to enter a little more fully into the common, broad meaning of this expression. Essentially, all of one's contacts with, and relations to the outer world and one's own ego can be seen in the light of the great pilgrimage to "the Kingdom within". As noted above, the intermediate field between outer and inner, where the intention of acting in this or that manner arises, is also the sphere of dominion of poverty in spirit. This virtue may then also, in its own way, be called an "intention", as the divine Irradiation which gives rise to it may be called God's "Intention" with man. As a reflection of this Irradiation, man's "introspective intention" has a positive character, since in itself it signifies an inward aspiration. But it also has a negative aspect, in the service of the positive one, namely the will to detach one's mind from everything external, including one's own ego. In the former respect, the inward intention coincides with love of God and the neighbor, in the latter with "fear of God".

In relation to the world, this fear consists in not letting "care and trouble about many things" (Luke 10, 41) tie one's soul to the multiplicity with which it is in contact; and in relation to one's own ego, the fear of God consists in not permitting oneself to be blinded by solicitude about one's earthly welfare: "Except a corn of wheat fall into the ground and die, it abideth alone... He that loveth his life shall lose it" (John 12, 24-25). He loses it, because circling around the individual self makes the hard shell around one's heart still harder, so that it chokes its content: the Real Self, the Spirit, which is the germ of eternal life.

It was said at the beginning of this essay that the Divinity with which the germ in the heart is potentially identical, has two sides or poles: Being and Consciousness. Further on, speaking about the manifested plane, we said that the Logos, representative of God on this plane, has a similar polarity: it is, symbolically speaking, both the all-embracing Macrocosmic Tree and the Tree of Life, which in turn is the essence of man, the "Microcosmic Tree". Now, the two Poles have, in both cases, their indirect correspondences in the two aspects of the "fear of God". Divine Being, or – from the standpoint of Manifestation – the "Great Cosmic Tree", is the all-inclusive *Totality* to which one grants admission in oneself by shunning identification with worldly multiplicity. Divine Consciousness, or – again from the standpoint of Manifestation – the "Little Cosmic Tree", is the all-penetrating *Center* which one keeps alive in one's heart by shunning its hardening.

When the earth gets dry, it becomes hard, and it cracks; the two effects go together. But when the rain comes, the soil is turned into a totality which is both undivided and alive. The role of works might here be likened to the plowing and harrowing by which the farmer prepares the coming of the rain, thereby "prefiguring", as it were, the rebirth and deliverance in the very structure of the soil. Because of this spiritual aspect of works, the following statement of Martin Luther – although true in itself – requires an additional comment: "Just as little as the dry earth by itself can do in order to obtain an abundant and refreshing rain, can we men, by our own strength and works, do in order to procure this divine, heavenly and eternal righteousness, unless we obtain it through God's unmerited awarding, as His ineffable Gift".[11] In a wider, sapiential perspective, it must be added that, by being conscious – thanks to God – of the nature of the Merciful Rain, we have the possibility of participating in its "Being"; and further, as a consequence of this, that we have the capacity of breaking ground, by different spiritually directed works, for the arrival of the Rain, and the capacity of assimilating its water. Thus Luther is not correct, without further comment, when he limits what he calls "the active righteousness" to the horizontal, worldly plane, the realm of the Law, of the "flesh", of the "old man".

It is in this spirit that the words of the Apostle James must be understood, that "it is [also] by works that a man is justified, and not by faith only", and that "by works... faith was made perfect". This might also be formulated as follows. By virtue of faith, the positive essence of man's works is brought back to the Divine Word: "Without him was not anything made that was made. In him was life, and the life was the light of man".

[1] Concerning the various aspects of Martin Luther's personality and spiritual position, see Frithjof Schuon, *Christianity/Islam, Essays on Esoteric Ecumenism* (World Wisdom Books, Bloomington, Indiana, 1985) in the chapter "The Question of Evangelicalism"; and *In the Face of the Absolute*, (Bloomington, Indiana: World Wisdom Books, 1989) in the chapter "Christian Divergences". In particular, the question of "faith and works" is treated in the former book (pp.35ff., and 50). See also the author's most recently published work, *Survey of Metaphysics and Esoterism* (World Wisdom Books, 1986), pp.184 and 219.

[2] The position of the Logos in what Schuon calls the "onto-cosmological chain" is indicated in *Survey of Metaphysics and Esoterism* in the chapter "Summary of Integral Metaphysics".

[3] *The Sacred Pipe: Black Elk's Account of the Seven Rites of the Oglala Sioux, recorded and edited by Joseph Epes Brown* (Norman: University of Oklahoma Press, 1953), p. 75.

[4] In *Esoterism as Principle and as Way* (London: Perennial Books, 1981), p. 151.

[5] The annual rings of the trunk might be said to symbolize a hierarchic gradation within the Intellect itself: different degrees of its capacity to reflect the divine Sun, with different objects of

illumination. Thus they correspond to the different worlds of angels which in fact together form the Logos or the macrocosmic Intellect, and whose analogy is the human Intellect.

[6] See René Guénon in *Etudes Traditionnelles* (Paris), January 1948, and Marco Pallis, *The Way and the Mountain* (London: Peter Owen Ltd., 1960) chapter 4. On p. 79, Marco Pallis writes: "It may even happen that the office in question [that of *upaguru*] will devolve, outside the circle of human relationships, upon an animal, plant or even an "inanimate" object that becomes, at that moment, a substitute for the human instructor in bringing enlightenment to someone in need of it."

[7] In fact a virtue, even etymologically, is a "force". In the first Commandment of Love, cited above, the word "strength" – in Mark and Luke – is represented in the Vulgate by *virtus*: "*ex tota virtute tua*". The Latin word also means "virtue", as do its descendants in the Romance languages and English. In a similar way, the German *Tugend* and the Swedish *dygd* are cognate with *taugen* and *duga* respectively, which mean "to be capable".

[8] There is probably no better way of understanding the cosmic and spiritual symbolism of the tree than by listening to the Red Indians. In the book by Black Elk cited above, on p. 74, one finds the following passage in Black Elk's account of how the Sun Dance first came to the Oglala Sioux. The cottonwood tree, which has been chosen "in a sacred manner" for the rite, is thus addressed: "Of all the many standing peoples, you, O rustling cottonwood, are about to go to the center of the people's sacred hoop, and there you will represent the people and will help us to fulfill the will of *Wakan-Tanka*. You are a kind and good-looking tree... From the tip of your lofty branches down to your roots, the winged and four-legged peoples have made their homes. When you stand at the center of the sacred hoop you will be the people, and you will be as the pipe, stretching from heaven to earth... You will stand where the four sacred paths cross – there you will be the center of the great Powers of the Universe. May we two-leggeds always follow your sacred example, for we see that you are always looking upwards into the heavens... For all beings and all things you will bring that which is good. *Hechetu welo!*"

Furthermore, the following words, spoken during the "Releasing of the soul", may be related to the role of the Virtues in the "soil" of the spiritual tree: "You, O soul, ... are the root of the *wakan* tree which is at the center of our nation's hoop. May this tree bloom! May our people and the winged and the four-legged peoples all flourish!"(p. 27).

[9] Spiritually inspired acts may also be likened to the flowers of a tree; a blooming linden, for instance, spreads a honey-like fragrance of holiness. On the other hand, if – as we have done here – the tree is seen theoretically from above, as a glory of rays around the "sun" of the trunk, this might bring to mind certain ancient Egyptian paintings, where the rays from the Sun God are terminated by hands.

[10] With this background, the everyday, "profane" greetings between people are also meaningful: a bow or a curtsy signifies indeed that one "makes oneself small" before the other, and to what should one abase oneself if not to the divine spark that exists in everyone of us, even if very few think about it? That these gestures are now vanishing is therefore a sign that the secularization of our time is far advanced.

[11] *The Big Commentary on the Epistle to the Galatians.*

Robert Carter has kindly corrected the English of this paper.

Frithjof Schuon ou la sainteté de l'intelligence

Jean Borella

*"**Quasi modo geniti infantes,**
rationabile sine dolo lac concupiscite."*
**"Comme des enfants tout
nouvellement nés, soyez avides du pur
lait de la doctrine."**
**S.Pierre, Ière épitre, II,2;
Introit du Dimanche de *Quasimodo*.**

A priori, on pourrait estimer qu'une doctrine sacrée, de nature purement métaphysique, et dont l'origine se situe dans la connaissance contemplative et directe de la vérité, ne peut que marquer ses distances, aussi nettement et aussi fermement que possible,   à l'égard de la philosophie et de sa dialectique. C'est ainsi que procède René Guénon. Dans son premier ouvrage, *Introduction générale à l'étude des doctrines hindoues*(1921), il consacre un chapitre spécial (*Pensée métaphysique et pensée philosophique*) à cette question. Il n'y reviendra plus, se contentant, dans les oeuvres ultérieures, de rappeler la condamnation sans appel qu'il avait alors prononcée. Condamnation sans appel, puisque la philosophie, selon Guénon, ou bien se ramène à quelques sciences particulières: logique, psychologie, sociologie, etc., ou bien empiète illégitimement sur le terrain de la métaphysique, en prétendant traiter, au moyen de la seule raison, des questions qui ressortissent à l'intellectualité sacrée.

On retrouve, évidemment, une telle condamnation chez Frithjof Schuon, tant il importe, avant tout, de dissiper les confusions possibles, et de bien préparer l'esprit du lecteur à recevoir la doctrine de vérité. Parmi ces confusions et ces déformations intellectuelles, les plus importantes sont celles qu'engendre ou que propage la philosophie moderne, pour la raison qu'elle occupe le lieu même où se tient la parole métaphysique. C'est là un fait "incontournable", comme on aime à dire aujourd'hui, et que chacun peut constater à sa guise. La métaphysique traditionnelle traite de l'être et de la connaissance, du vrai et du faux, du réel et de l'illusoire, de l'origine et du devenir, de l'homme et du monde, de la nécessité et de la contingence, du fini et de l'infini; la philosophie aussi. Sans doute s'agit-il d'une identité trompeuse, cachant une hétérogenéité d'objets: sous des termes semblables, philosophie moderne et métaphysique ne parlent pas de la même chose. Encore faut-il le savoir et le faire comprendre, dès lors qu'on s'adresse à des Occidentaux qui n'ont été habitués qu' à une seule sorte de discours et qui risquent de se méprendre sur la nature même de ce qui leur est dit.

C'est pourquoi les mises en garde s'imposent et Frithjof Schuon ne manque pas, dès son premier livre, de les formuler. Il y consacre même les tout premiers mots de *De l'unité transcendante des religions* qui commence ainsi: "Les considérations de ce livre procèdent d'une doctrine qui n'est point philosophique". Trente ans plus tard, dans *Sur les traces de la religion pérenne*, on retrouve une mise en garde analogue: "il ne s'agit pas de 'philosophie' au sens courant et approximatif du mot – lequel suggère de simples constructions mentales, surgies de l'ignorance, du doute et des conjectures, voire du goût de la nouveauté et de l'originalité"(p.9). Et, en note, il est précisé que ce n'est pas le mot lui-même qui est rejeté – puisque les Anciens l'utilisaient pour désigner toute sorte de sagesse – mais l'usage qu'en font les modernes.

Cette remarque, toutefois, est intéressante, parce qu'elle nous met sur la voie d'une critique de la philosophie qu'on ne rencontre pas, telle quelle, chez Guénon. Pour Guénon, les philosophes s'illusionnent beaucoup sur l'importance du rôle qu'ils jouent dans le monde moderne. Ce qu'il leur reproche, essentiellement, c'est de ne produire que des oeuvres individuelles, et donc anti-traditionnelles. Une fois posé ce diagnostic – au demeurant indiscutable – il n'y reviendra plus, se contentant d'une caractérisation extérieure, uniformément négative (sauf en ce qui concerne Aristote), et somme toute assez vague. L'attitude de Frithjof Schuon est différente. Non seulement il caractérise d'une manière plus précise et plus intime la nature de la pensée philosophique, mais encore, comme nous le verrons, il entre en discussion avec sa forme moderne pour réfuter l'une de ses thèses majeures, ou plutôt, croyons-nous, sa thèse unique et essentielle. Dans le premier cas, il s'agit du rationalisme, dans le second cas, du criticisme.

I La raison mutilée

L'erreur du rationalisme, pour Schuon, ne consiste nullement dans l'emploi de la raison. Tout au contraire, nous constaterons chez lui une vigueur et audace peu communes dans l'usage de cette faculté. Mais elle consiste à poser la raison comme source unique de la connaissance et seul critère de vérité. C'est déjà ce qu'exprime la préface de *De l'Unité transcendante des Religions*: "ce qui distingue ici essentiellement la proposition métaphysique de la proposition philosophique, c'est que la première est symbolique et descriptive, en ce sens qu'elle se sert des modes rationnels comme de symboles pour décrire ou traduire des connaissances qui comportent plus de certitude que n'importe quelle connaissance de l'ordre sensible, tandis que la philosophie (...) n'est jamais plus que ce qu'elle exprime; lorsqu'elle raisonne pour résoudre un doute, cela prouve précisément que son point de départ est un doute (...) alors que (...) le point de départ de l'énonciation métaphysique est toujours essentiellement une évidence ou une certitude".

C'est aussi ce qui s'explicitera de manière plus précise dans le chapitre "Rationalisme réel et rationalisme apparent" de *Logique et transcendance*: "Est rationaliste qui soutient la primauté, ou plutôt la valeur exclusive, de la raison contre l'Intellection d'une part et la Révélation d'autre part, toutes deux accusées d'être irrationnelles"(p.48).

Si cet exclusivisme est réputé comme une erreur, ce n'est pas en vertu d'un parti-pris infondé et sentimental en faveur du merveilleux et de la religiosité; mais c'est à cause de la nature même de la raison. Si l'on accepte de définir la raison, dans son activité, comme la faculté de lier entre eux des jugements(donc des connaissances) selon des règles ou principes, on voit que cette raison raisonnante se trouve située entre deux sortes de réalité qui la dépassent et dont elle est tributaire: les connaissances qu'elle reçoit "de l'extérieur" (perception, révélation) ou "de l'intérieur" (intellection ou inspiration) d'une part, et d'autre part les principes innés auxquels elle obéit et qui constituent sa structure dynamique. D'un côté elle mendie du savoir, c'est-à-dire du réel connu, de l'autre elle est conscience réfléchie d'une exigence d'ordre, c'est-à-dire d'une relation fondée entre un savoir et un autre, et, finalement, exigence de l'organisation générale de tous les savoirs entre eux. L'exigence d'ordre, les lois dont l'observance par le mental définit la raison même, sont l'objet d'une science qu'on appelle la logique. Or, c'est précisément cette double dépendance qui prive la raison de toute autonomie absolue, et qui rend caduques les prétentions hégémoniques du rationalisme. A quoi il faut ajouter que la dépendance logique est fonction de la dépendance cognitive. L'exigence d'ordre, l'obéissance aux lois de la logique, découlent en effet du besoin où se trouve la raison *d'assurer le passage* d'une connaissance à une autre. Si, pour établir la connexion de deux vérités, nous sommes obligés de raisonner, c'est parce que nous n'apercevons pas *uno intuitu* leur implication, et, pour tout dire, leur unité. Les saisies du mental sont fragmentaires, analytiques, discontinues. Comment dès lors être certain que les liaisons que nous sommes pourtant contraints d'établir entre elles sont fondées et légitimes, sinon en nous conformant aux règles de la logique dont ces liaisons ne sont au fond que des applications particulières? C'est pourquoi la certitude rationnelle est toujours indirecte et dépendante (ou relative). Au contraire, la saisie intellective des êtres et des choses étant parfaite et immédiate, à l'instar de la pure perception sensible, les relations qui les unissent sont, pour une telle connaissance, données d'emblée dans la saisie même, et point n'est besoin de raisonner pour les établir: il suffit de "voir". Le raisonnement, dans ce cas, ne serait nécessaire que eu égard aux exigences de la communication de la vérité perçue, le langage étant par nature dialectique. Il reste cependant que même alors les règles de la logique et les principes de la raison ne jouent plus le rôle de garants ultimes et de fondements (non fondés) de la vérité; ils jouent le rôle de symboles, de reflets conceptuels des réalités qu'ils expriment, et sont au fond des formes mentales de participation à l'Intellect universel.

Mais la raison n'est pas seulement dépendante à l'égard du mode de la saisie cognitive, laquelle, dans son essence première, ne peut, de toute évidence, être qu'intuitive, qu'il s'agisse de l'intuition sensible ou de l'intuition intellectuelle (sinon il n'y aurait connaissance de rien), elle est aussi dépendante à l'égard des contenus sur lesquels elle opère, ou encore, pourrait-on dire, dont elle fait l'experience. En réduisant tout à la raison, le rationalisme ne se condamne pas seulement à la certitude toute relative et purement formelle des conclusions de la logique, il érige aussi en dogme une véritable cécité intellectuelle. Les seules données qu'il est condamné à accepter sont celles de l'expérience sensible la plus bornée, et il se rend aveugle aussi bien à ces

révélations "subjectives" que représente toute intellection
métaphysique qu'à ces "intellections" objectives que constituent les diverses révélations. Remarquons en outre que,
la nature ayant horreur du vide, dès lors que le mental
rationnel n'est plus informé dans ses opérations déductives
par la grâce, interne ou externe, de la Lumière divine, ce
sont les données du psychisme individuel qui en prennent la
place, voire les pulsions les plus inférieures ou les sugges-
tions les plus sinistres de l'ambiance sociale. Toute logique
est évidemment tributaire des données dont elle part et que
la raison ne saurait produire par elle-même. Tout est là.
Récuser, au nom de la raison, des millénaires de sagesse, de
sainteté et de noblesse, refuser de tenir compte d'expériences que les plus profondes intelligences du passé ont
reconnues comme des certitudes, c'est s'engager à fournir
la preuve qu'on est infiniment plus intelligent qu'elles, ce
qui est à la fois impossible et absurde. (*Logique et
transcendance.*, pp.43-66)

   Mais c'est aussi s'engager à expliquer pourquoi les hommes
du passé, penseurs, artistes, prophètes, sages et saints, ont
pu croire à ce qui, pour les diverses branches du rationalisme moderne, n'est qu'illusion, fantaisie, superstition.
C'est là proprement que le rationalisme revêt la forme du
criticisme.

II La Raison Corrompue.

   Le criticisme, en effet, dont la philosophie de Kant représente le point de départ et le modèle, consiste très
précisément à provoquer dans l'esprit humain une prise de
conscience critique à l'égard de ses propres affirmations ou
jugements, de telle sorte que l'origine ou la genèse de ces
jugements étant enfin dévoilées, ils perdent du même coup
leur signification illusoire et révèlent leur signification réelle.
On voit immédiatement l'avantage d'un tel procédé. L'ad-
versaire rationaliste de la métaphysique et du sacré est dis-

pensé par là de tout effort de réfutation argumentée. L'anti-
métaphysicien "pré-critique" affronte le croyant sur le terrain de la dialectique et oppose une thèse à une autre thèse,
un argument à son contraire. "Dieu est"; "Non, Dieu n'est
pas", etc. Mais le criticisme kantien n'oppose pas une thèse à
une autre. Il veut, plus subtilement, amener le métaphysicien "dogmatiste" à prendre une conscience *critique* de ce
qu'il dit quand il dit, par exemple, "Dieu est". Ce qui signifie
que le dogmatiste ne sait pas vraiment ce qu'il dit quand il
procède ainsi à des affirmations dépassant toute expérience
sensible (méta-physiques). Il en résulte que son affirmation
n'est ni vraie ni fausse, dans la mesure où elle n'a pas le sens
que le dogmatiste lui attribue naïvement. Il n'est pas faux de
dire : "Dieu est" (et du reste, Kant, de religion piétiste, croit
sincèrement en Dieu), mais ce n'est pas vrai non plus, étant
donné que l'idée de Dieu ne correspond pas à une *connaissance* possible pour la raison: certes, la raison peut bien
penser l'idée de Dieu, mais cette idée n'est que le reflet
hypostasié du besoin d'unité absolue inhérent à la raison
elle-même. A l'égard de Dieu, nous pouvons seulement
"croire".

Toutes les philosophies dogmatistes, c'est-à-dire tous les
penseurs antérieurs à Kant, sont donc victimes d'une illusion interne à la raison elle-même (illusion d'ailleurs inévitable, dit Kant, la critique est un combat permanent), par
laquelle la raison croit connaitre quelque chose quand elle
ne fait que penser ses propres exigences. Là est la source de
toutes les affirmations métaphysiques.

On le voit, la philosophie de Kant occupe une situation
décisive dans le champ spéculatif, et du reste beaucoup
n'hésitent pas à voir en lui "le plus grand des philosophes";
Frithjof Schuon, parmi les métaphysiciens se rattachant à la
grande tradition gnostique, est l'un des rares à avoir souligné
la nature radicale de cette situation, et à ne pas se contenter
d'une condamnation expéditive: "la thèse de Kant, dit-il, si
immensément importante pour le genre humain, si elle est

vraie..."(*Logique et transcendance*, p. 45). De fait, il y va du destin de l'intelligence. Et c'est évidemment dans ce destin que s'est engouffrée la pensée moderne. Ce que Schuon appelle, à plusieurs reprises, "l' imposture du psychologisme", à laquelle on pourrait adjoindre une imposture du sociologisme, de l'économisme, du matérialisme ou du scientisme, ressortit exactement au même processus explicatif, à ce que Feuerbach appelait la "méthode génético-critique" et dont il faisait l'arme décisive contre la religion. L'illusion que Kant mettait dans une raison dogmatiste, inconsciente de la génèse par laquelle elle produit des idées qu'elle prend ensuite pour des objets à elle donnés, Freud la place dans un psychisme inconscient de la genèse par laquelle il projette sous l'aspect d'un Sur-moi religieux ou moral les échecs inévitables auxquels se heurtent les pulsions du *ça*, tandis que Marx la placera dans l'aliénation économique dont les travailleurs sont les victimes inconscientes et dont la religion n'est que le reflet et l'alibi idéologique.

Or, et l'insistance de Schuon sur ce point est un enseignement et un avertissement pour tout penseur, la méthode du criticisme, qu'elle soit kantienne ou de toute autre sorte, repose sur une thèse radicalement contradictoire et d'ailleurs explicitement revendiquée par Kant: c'est la négation de l'intuition intellectuelle (*intellektuelle Anschauung*), autrement dit,l'affirmation d'une cécité essentielle de l'intelligence. Essentielle, oui, puisque l'illusion qui en résulte est déclarée naturelle, interne, inévitable, nécessaire, par toutes ces écoles depensée. Si d'ailleurs cet aveuglement n'était pas connaturel à l'intelligence, s'il était seulement accidentel, il serait aussi momentané, et chaque homme en aurait parfaitement conscience: il s'agirait seulement de l'expérience de l' *erreur*, expérience que tous les hommes ont faite, mais qui ne met pas en cause le pouvoir cognitif essentiel de l'intelligence. Il s'agit ici d'autre chose, non d'erreur,mais d'illusion. Précisons, non d'une illusion externe, mais d'une illusion interne à l'intelligence elle-même. L'illusion externe est celle qui vient des objets eux-mêmes ou des conditions externes de connaissance. Ainsi le prisonnier de la Caverne platonicienne prend l'ombre des objets pour des réalités, non en vertu d'une perversion de l'intellect, mais seulement faute d'avoir fait l'expérience d'autres objets. Son intellect est intact, et dès qu' il est mis en contact avec les objets métaphysiques, il les *reconnait* pour véritables. De cette illusion externe, toutes les grandes doctrines traditionnelle ont parlé. Elle n'a donc rien de nouveau. Au contraire, Kant et les post-kantiens s'affirment comme des révolutionnaires. Ils se donnent pour les decouvreurs d'une illusion (illusion transcendantale chez Kant, du Sur-moi chez Freud, de l'aliénation chez Marx) dont personne jusqu'à eux n'avait eu la moindre conscience.

Or, s'il en est bien ainsi, personne non plus ne pourra jamais en avoir conscience et il est parfaitement contradictoire de vouloir nous l'enseigner, aussi bien que de prétendre y être soi-même parvenu, par le plus incompréhensible des miracles. Comme le note Frithjof Schuon en plusieurs endroits de son oeuvre, on ne peut demander à l'intelligence de prendre conscience de ses limites essentielles, car, pour apercevoir une limite, il faut se situer au-delà de cette limite, et donc précisément n'en pas être affecté. La seule thèse qu'il soit possible de soutenir est celle de l'illimitation intrinsèque ou essentielle de l'intelligence, quoi qu'il en soit par ailleurs de son actualisation effective pour telle situation existentielle. De même, comme l'a remarqué en un sens analogue le philosophe Raymond Ruyer, l'oeil ne peut-il apercevoir le bord de sa vision. Le plus extraordinaire est que, si évidentes que soient ces considérations, personne, parmi les criticistes relativistes, ne semble s'en rendre compte. On mesure par là combien radicalement ces philosophies ont corrompu la conscience intellective de nos contemporains.

On pourrait dire, en d'autres termes, qu'il n'est au pouvoir d'aucune intelligence de nier le pouvoir de l'intelligence:

qu'il s'agisse de la négation criticiste de Kant, ou de la
négation psychologiste ou subjectiviste ou relativiste d'une
manière quelconque (matérialiste ou existentialiste par exemple). Cette réfutation majeure n'est pas un fruit tardif de
la pensée schuonienne. Qu'on relise la préface de l'un de
ses premiers ouvrages, *L'Oeil du coeur*(1950 et 1974), et l'on
verra que l'argumentation est déjà parfaitement constituée
et qu'elle représente un thème constant de cette oeuvre
multiforme.

Toutefois on fausserait gravement la signification de la
pensée schuonienne si, en tout cela, on ne voyait précisément
que de l'argumentation. Il faut y voir surtout l'occasion
d'un enseignement fondamental sur la nature et la signica-
tion de l'intelligence. C'est ce que nous voudrions souligner
pour terminer, parce que là est, croyons-nous, le message
"philosophique" essentiel de Frithjof Schuon.

III Le Mystère théophanique de l'intelligence.

Certains commentateurs, au demeurant admirateurs de
l'oeuvre schuonienne, mais formés exclusivement à l'Ecole
de Guénon, regrettent de ne pas retrouver dans cette oeuvre
le style de pensée et le ton qui leur paraissent indispensables
à l'enseignement de la métaphysique. Il leur semble que,
d'une certaine manère, Schuon renoue avec le genre philosophique, alors que Guénon prend toujours bien soin de
marquer formellement les distances.

Si, par cette remarque, on croit pouvoir mettre en évidence
une quelconque indulgence à l'égard du dévergondage
spéculatif et de la perversion intellectuelle de la pseudo-phi-
losophie moderne, on se trompe du tout au tout. Sur le fond
de la doctrine de l'intellect et sur leur commun et total refus
de la pensée moderne, il n'y a aucune différence entre ces
deux auteurs, ne serait-ce que parce que cette doctrine est
tout simplement celle de la métaphysique universelle. Au
reste, on ne saurait nier que, sous certains rapports, l'oeuvre

de Schuon prolonge celle de Guénon. Mais elle doit aussi, et c'est sa raison suffisante, manifester des aspects doctrinaux et un climat spirituel différents. Nous aimerions qualifier cette différence comme étant celle d'un plus grand *réalisme*.

La présentation guénonienne de la doctrine de l'intellect (la *buddhi* de l'hindouisme), impeccable sur le fond, soulève cependant quelques difficultés liées à une suraccentuation de son caractère transcendant. De bons connaisseurs de la pensée çankarienne, en particulier, n'ont pas tout à fait reconnu dans le portrait que Guénon avait tracé de cette faculté supra-individuelle, l'image que nous en donne le texte même de Çankarâchârya (voir, par exemple, le Commentaire aux *Brahma-Sûtra*, II, 3,30; trad. G. Thibaut, Dover Publications,pp.45-47). Sous la plume de Guénon, en effet, l'intellect apparait comme une faculté de connaissance extraordinaire, lié à un haut degré de réalisation spirituelle et donc à peu prés inaccessible. Cette description offre l'avantage de rompre avec l'expérience de la connaissance ordinaire, et d'aider à saisir, au moins négativement, l'existence et la nature d'une véritable intellectualité sacrée. Mais, si l'on évite ainsi les confusions, on risque aussi de transformer l'intellect en une sorte de "mythe" noétique et de briser l'unité essentielle de l'intelligence, outre qu'on rend alors difficilement compréhensible la lecture des textes védantins ou la *buddhi* ne semble pas jouir d'une supériorité constante relativement au *manas*.

La présentation schuonienne de l'intellect nous semble éviter ce risque et, surtout, elle a le mérite de nous éveiller à une conscience directe de cette lumière intérieure. En insistant, d'une façon peut-être excessive, sur sa transcendance, Guénon "démobilise" son lecteur: la *buddhi* est donnée pour une réalité tellement surnaturelle qu'on se trouve en quelque sorte justifié de demeurer étranger à sa lumière. Pour Schuon, qui d'ailleurs – et significativement – parle plus volontiers de l'intelligence que de l'intellect, l'intelligence garde toujours son unité et son identité en chacune de ses opérations, fût-ce la plus humble. Toute saisie intuitive, toute perception d'une évidence directe et irréfragable, est, dans son essence, intellection véritable. C'est pourquoi Schuon aime à répéter, en une formule-clef, que l'intellect est "naturellement surnaturel" ou "surnaturellement naturel". Il serait souhaitable qu'on accorde la plus grande attention à cette formule et qu'on la médite longuement, particuliére-ment en culture chrétienne. Dire qu'elle est intellection véritable en son essence, c'est dire qu'elle est participation humaine à l'acte de l'Intellect divin, qui est permanente actualité de Connaissance, et qui, selon S. Jean, "éclaire *tout homme* venant en ce monde" (et pas seulement les chrétiens).

L'intellect n'est donc pas seulement un "idéal" ou un "rêve" métaphysique, il n'est pas seulement l'apanage de quelque "champion" de la connaissance, mais il est en chaque homme, qu'il en ait conscience ou non, témoignant en chacun de la même et unique Lumière transcendante. Voilà ce que nous appelons un réalisme de l'intelligence. Ainsi les expériences cognitives les plus modestes (au moins en ap-parence) ou réputées les plus naïves sont remises a leur place et honorées comme il convient, dès lors qu'elles sont des perceptions de la vérité. Il y a chez Schuon une approba-tion seigneuriale des expressions les plus simples de la foi, ou même seulement des formes élémentaires de l'existence humaine, une façon métaphysique de les saluer, qui les restitue à leur dignité paradisiaque.

Au fond, en elle-même, – non pas dans les modalités de sa manifestation – l'intelligence n'est pas "humaine". Ou en-core, et de façon paradoxale, il faudrait dire que le propre de l'intelligence humaine est précisément de n'être pas "hu-maine", c'est-à-dire limitée à la forme humaine, comme l'in-telligence du diamant, de la rose ou de l'aigle, à des digrés divers, ne fait qu'un avec la forme de leur être. Cette intelli-gence en effet connait tout être, et même l'Etre comme tel, alors que la rose ne "connaît" que la rose, ou ne "connaît" Dieu que sous la forme de la rose. C'est pourouoi d'ailleurs la forme humaine est "indépassable" en tant que telle, et que l'hypothèse évolutionniste d'un surhomme est dénuée de la moindre intelligibilité. Notre intelligence conçoit même, au-delà de l'Etre, l'Absolu sur-ontologique qui en est la Racine infinie, la Possibilité suprême. Et c'est cette connaissance de l'Absolu-Infini, laquelle est au fond de la substance intellective, qui rend compte de son objectivité et de son illimitation, c'est-à-dire de sa capacité à prendre conscience de ce qui est comme existant "en soi" et de tout ce qui est.

Ainsi commence à apparaître ce que Schuon appelle "le miracle de l'intelligence", "le mystère de la subjectivité" ou "la théophanie de la conscience" (*Du divin à l'humain*, pp.11-24). Ce miracle, qui est celui de l'esprit en nous, réfute, par son évidence éblouissante, tous les relativismes, qu'ils soient criticistes, matérialistes, évolutionnistes, en même temps qu'il prouve, par sa nature même, et l'Absolu divin, et la relativité des degrés du réel. C'est pourquoi Schuon, très justement, est fondé à rencontrer la vérité du *cogito* cartésien, "non qu'il présente la pensée comme la preuve de l'être, mais simplement qu'il énonce la primauté de la pensée – donc de la conscience et de l'intelligence – par rapport au monde matériel qui nous entoure" (*ibidem*, p.11), et sans oublier évidemment que l'une des tendances erronées de cette philosophie peut conduire au rationalisme.

Le miracle théophanique de l'intellect constitue la base de la voie de la gnose. C'est à nous éveiller à la conscience de ce miracle que visent tous les livres de Schuon, à rendre possible son actualisation, en nous faisant entrevoir sa simplicité transcendante et son immédiateté fulgurante. Le pire obstacle à cet éveil, ce sont tous les assassins du *Logos*, tous ceux qui anéantissent "la science, la pensée claire et l'intelligence" comme dit Platon dans la plus longue et peut-être la seule citation que Schuon en ait donnée (*Résumé de métaphysique intégrale.* p.78), hommes qu'il faut "combattre avec toute la puissance du raisonnement" (*Sophiste*, 249).

Mais il est un autre obstacle qui, sans manquer de certaines justifications extrinsèques, ruine aussi bien la possibilité de la gnose véritable, et c'est le fidéisme, le refus de la logique au nom de la transcendance, le prétendu droit du divin à l'absurdité. Ici s'affirme l'une des plus fortes thèses de la doctrine schuonienne, thèse que résume excellemment le titre de cet ouvrage "radical" qu'est *Logique et transcendance* et qu'on peut énoncer ainsi: aucune révélation, si transcendante soit-elle, ne peut contredire aux exigences fondamentales de la pensée humaine, puisque la pensée humaine est précisément la raison d'être de cette révélation (Dieu ne se révèle pas aux êtres dépourvus d'intelligence). Certes, la raison, coupée de ses racines intellectives ou aveugle aux données de la révélation, ne saurait, par définition, acceuillir et reconnaitre les dimensions les plus transcendantes et, en apparence, les plus paradoxales du divin. Mais, justement, il s'agit d'une raison mutilée. En réalité, et dans son régime normal, la raison prolonge l'intellect (les lois et les principes de l' activité rationnelle expriment sur le plan de la dialectique mentale ce qu'est evidence sur le plan de la perception intellective) et en traduit (fragmentairement) la lumiére indivise dans les coagulations formelles du langage. La rançon (le "choc en retour") du fidéisme, c'est la pseudo-gnose rationaliste (celle d'un Hegel par exemple), tant il est clair qu'on ne peut impunément mépriser la raison.

Ainsi se dessinent les traits de ce que Frithjof Schuon n'hésite pas à appeler une "épistémologie sacrée" (*Du Divin à l'humain*, p. 31), épistémologie dont il élabore les éléments principaux et qu'il a illustrée à plusieurs reprises , en particulier à propos de la question du mal. L'exigence et la réalisation de cette épistémologie sacrée nous parait l'une des entreprises les plus originales et les plus fécondes de l'oeuvre schuonienne, et peut-être ne s'en est-on pas suffisamment avisé. A l'homme d'aujourd'hui, Schuon en est visiblement persuadé, il ne suffit pas d'apporter des convictions, il faut apporter aussi des évidences. Du même coup, on répondra aux objections contre la religion que les philosophies modernes tirent soit des données de la révélation (difficultés scripturaires, théologiques, spirituelles), soit des données de l'existence humaine (le mal et la souffrance, la sexualité, l'affectivité, les vertus), ou soit encore des résultats ou des affirmations de la science contemporaine (évolutionnisme, physique quantique, astronomie copernicienne et newtonienne, etc.). Entreprise originale, oui, car bien souvent dédaignée des métaphysiciens, enclins à traiter ces questions par une fin *a priori* de non-recevoir, alors que pourtant elles se posent inévitablement à tous les croyants. Nous retrouvons ici ce que nous avons appelé le réalisme schuonien, cette capacité de voir les problémes tels qu'ils se posent effectivement, à l'encontre éventuellement des habitudes de pensée ou de certaines "convenances" traditionnelles, et d'aller directement et froidement au but, au centre de ce qui est en question. L'essentiel, pour lui, n'est pas de savoir quelle étiquette il convient selon tel ou tel, d'accoler sur les réponses apportées (philosophie ou logique ou théologie ou métaphysique "cataloguées"), mais, dans la seule soumission à la vérité, de fournir à la pensée inquiète ou déconcertée de nos contemporains les quelques évidences, clefs et repères qui leur permettront, Dieu aidant, de retrouver le chemin de leur propre religion et d'accèder à sa lumière et à sa joie.

De ce point de vue, c'est l'oeuvre schuonienne elle-même qui apparaît comme un miracle. La plus haute métaphysique est mise par elle, en cette fin d'un monde, au service des interrogations les plus élémentaires, mais aussi les plus urgentes. En une série de brefs traités, dont la longueur parfois ne dépasse pas quelques pages, et dont la langue et la dialectique se simplifient au fil du temps, Frithjof Schuon,doué du génie de l'essentiel et de la force de la vision intellective, vient en aide à l'homme d'aujourd'hui en lui restituant sa vérité de toujours. Ici, on ne se paie pas de mots, ni de réveries occultistes. La foi qui anime cette oeuvre n'est pas seulement foi en Dieu, elle est aussi foi dans la noblesse sacrée de l'intelligence humaine, fût-ce celle de la présente humanité. C'est à la porte de ce coeur-intellect qu'elle vient frapper, afin de l'éveiller à sa propre béatitude, de la part de Dieu.

Le Rapport "Moi-et-Toi" en Métaphysique Universelle

Jean Canteins

Le rapport *moi-et-toi* est un rapport privilégié puisqu'il a pour effet d'en exclure tout tiers. Qu'est-ce qui lui donne ce caractère privilégié? C'est l'amour existant entre "moi" et "toi".

Mais la phénoménologie de l'amour se transpose dans la métaphysique de l'Etre car son accomplissement, lors de l'union sexuelle, retrace l'expérience de l'Unité exprimée au moyen d'un riche symbolisme érotique.

Cette "érotique métaphysique" n'est nulle part mieux formulée pour notre propos que dans la Brihadâranyaka Upanishad. En mettant en regard ce texte sacré avec celui d'Ibn 'Arabî et de quelques autres, nous ne perdons nullement de vue la doctrine du *Tawḥîd* de la *Shahâdah*[1].

Deux passages de la Brihadâranyaka Upanishad sont à citer: I.4.1-3 et IV.3.21.

Le passage I.4.1-3 décrit la genèse du premier couple à partir de *Puruṣa*, manifestation "individualisée" d'Âtman, l'Esprit universel, le Soi:

1- "*L Âtman*' était seul, à l'origine, sous l'aspect de *Puruṣa* ... Il prononça d'abord : "Je suis", *aham asmi*, d'où son nom : "moi", *aham* ,..."

3- "Il n'avait pas non plus de plaisir, *râma*, c'est pourquoi le plaisir n'est pas pour qui est seul. Il souhaita un second. Or, il était tel qu'un homme, *pumâṃs* et une femme, *strî*, étroitement enlacés (*sampariṣvaktau*, de *sampariṣvañj* : é-

treindre, embrasser) [2]. Il fit se diviser cet $\hat{A}tman$ en deux; de
là furent le mari et la femme. C'est pourquoi Yâjnâvalkya a
dit : "Nous sommes chacun [des deux] une moitié". C'est
pourquoi le "vide" *âkâsha* [d'une des deux moitiés]   fut
rempli (*pûryata* racine *pṛ*) par la femme. [3] Il s'unit à elle, de
là naquirent les hommes ..."

D'après la tradition hindoue la manifestation d'$\hat{A}tman$ –
qui n'est autre que Brahman, Dieu – dans l'homme est
appelée *Puruṣa,* la "Personne". La Bhagavad-Gita (XV.16)
précise qu'il faut distinguer un *Puruṣa* "périssable", *kṣara*, –
qui correspond à *jîvâtman*, "l'âme vivante" – et un autre
"impérissable", *akṣara,* qui est proprement $\hat{A}tman$. *Jîvâtman*
est le reflet du Soi, c'est-à-dire le moi se distinguant illusoire-
ment du Soi et se confondant avec celui-ci dès lors que
l'illusion de la dualité cesse. C'est pourquoi la "Personne" est
définie sous deux aspects qui sont les aspects transcendant et
immanent de l'unique Réalité.

La Brihadâranyaka Upanishad décrit *Puruṣa* comme une
entité ressemblant à celle formée par un homme et une
femme accouplés et la "création" du premier couple comme
la division de cette entité androgyne en deux moitiés : les
deux premières individualités. Ainsi a pu commencer le dialogue – et le rapport amoureux – entre "Je" et "Tu", c'est-à-
dire entre "moi" et *autre-que-moi–pour-moi.* Des deux moitiés
divisées l'une est "moi"; l'autre est "toi", c'est la moitié où le
vide,*âkâsha,* a été rempli par "toi" ou *autre-que-moi-pour-moi.*
La première moitié est le mari et la seconde est la femme,
conformément à l'antériorité principielle de l'homme. Or,
la mention du vide, *âkâsha,* rempli par la femme, suggère
que les deux moitiés de la Personne n'ont pas été identiques.
La présence d'*âkâsha* implique que la moitié du "toi" est, à
l'instar d'*âkâsha* impérissable, *akṣara,* et en rapport avec
$\hat{A}tman$.

La corrélation :

âkâsha = *akṣara* = $\hat{A}tman$

est un lieu commun dans les Upanishads, notamment Mandukya Upanishad, (*sûtra* 8 à 12) (cf. *Phonèmes et archétypes*, p.82).

La moitié du "toi" comporte donc un reflet d'*Âtman*, du Soi et l'union de *moi-et-toi* a, sur le plan érotique, la même force symbolique que celle du moi et du Soi sur le plan métaphysique.

C'est ce qu'exprime le passage de la Brihadâranyaka Upanishad (IV.3.21) qui reprend le fait de l'étreinte amoureuse pour définir les rapports de *Puruṣa* et d'*Âtman* : "De même que, dans les bras [littéralement "enlacé par", c'est le même terme qu'en I.4.3] d'une femme aimée, on ne sait plus rien du dehors *(bâhyam)*, ni du dedans *(antaram)*, de même *Puruṣa*, embrassé par l'*Âtman* omniscient *(prajñâtmanâ)*, ne sait plus rien du dehors ni du dedans. C'est pour lui la condition même où tout désir, *kâma*, est comblé, où il n'est de désir que pour *Âtman*, où il n'est même plus ni désir ni chagrin *(soka)*".

Durant l'étreinte de "moi" et "toi" il n'y a plus de dehors ni de dedans, non seulement les deux moitiés se sont accolées comme dans l'état où elles étaient dans le *Puruṣa* primordial mais elles se sont interpénétrées de telle sorte qu'il n'est plus possible de distinguer un dehors d'un dedans. Selon l'érotique c'est "moi" (l'homme) qui est dans "toi" (la femme), le mari pénètre en sa femme qui l'enlace et le serre contre elle – n'est-ce pas de l'homme qu'on dit qu'il est dans les bras d'une femme? L'homme est "dedans", physiquement : dans le sexe féminin, et la femme est "dehors", physiquement : elle contient le sexe masculin; l'homme est le contenu et la femme le contenant. Dans le rapport de "Je" et "Tu", c'est donc "moi" qui est "dedans" et "toi" qui est "dehors". Or, pour "moi", le dedans est l'aspect immanent et le dehors l'aspect transcendant de la même Réalité et ce n'est qu'au moment de l'union que cette différence disparaît, que "moi" réalise qu'il est "toi".

Le rapport de *Puruṣa* et d'*Âtman* est le rapport

métaphysique du "moi" individuel (c'est l'aspect relatif de *Puruṣa* qui est alors considéré par rapport à *Âtman*) et du "Soi" universel. Le "moi" a le même rôle que l'homme et le "Soi" le même rôle que la femme. C'est le "Soi" qui contient le "moi". En réalité il s'agit de l'union du "Soi" avec lui-même ou encore avec son reflet, le "moi", et cette union aboutit à la même prise de conscience de l'Unité que, sur le plan de l'expérience érotique, l'union de l'homme et de la femme.

Le mariage – à travers l'expérience de l'union conjugale – s'accomplit dans la "mort du moi" et cette "mort" induit la "mort du toi" : il ne reste rien d'*autre-que-moi-pour-moi* lorsque "moi" a lui-même cessé d'être en tant qu'individualité. Le mariage s'accomplit dans l'unification de moi et toi et dans la réalisation qu'il n'y a ni moi ni toi mais Lui, le Soi. Le mariage parfait est réintégration de la dualité *moi-et-toi* – qui n'est autre que la dualité *moi-et-Soi* – dans le Soi et la formule: "Ni moi ni toi mais Lui" n'est au fond qu'une variante de la *Shahâdah*.

Nous avons évoqué ailleurs le paradoxe de l'équation *Alif* x *Alif* = *Hâ*[=>*HuWa*]. En dépit de sa difficulté au regard de la symbolique ce paradoxe est signifiant du mystère de l'identité du "moi" (et par voie de conséquence de sa parèdre: le "toi", autre manifestation ou reflet du "moi" dans le couple) et du "Soi". L'*Alif* d'*anâ* (moi) et l'*Alif* d'*anta* (toi), en s'annulant réciproquement, génèrent le *Hâ* de *HuWa*, Lui, le Soi du *Tawḥîd*. Le voile obscurcissant de l'ego pris dans le dilemme du moi et du toi se déchire sur la réalisation qu'il n'y a que Lui, *HuWa*. Le mariage a pour effet de faire cesser la dualité – forme particulière de la multiplicité – et notamment celle du rapport *moi-et-toi*, de la résoudre en Unité, celle de l'Etre et du Soi. Sa consommation est un acte de "déification" (cf. note 42) et là réside la clé de la spiritualisation de l'"oeuvre de chair". Comme il est dit dans l'*Aitareya Âraṇyaka* (II.3.7) : "Ce Soi se donne à ce moi et ce moi à ce Soi : ils deviennent [réciproquement] l'un l'autre. Avec la "forme" du premier celui [en qui ce mariage a été consommé] est uni à l'autre monde; avec celle du second il est uni à ce monde-ci".

C'est dans le même contexte qu'il faut comprendre cette phrase de la Première Epître aux Corinthiens (6.17):"Quiconque est uni au Seigneur est un seul Esprit". Dans cette union en l'Esprit toute bipolarité ou toute bi-unité divine (qui correspond pourtant à une saisie de la Réalité conforme à la nature des choses) apparaît comme une vision provisoire ou approximative lorsque la réalisation de l' "Identité suprême" – dont la *Shahâdah* affirme avec tant de vigueur la possibilité – est obtenue.

En nous référant à l'une des plus importantes Upanishads nous constatons que la doctrine ésotérique du *Tawḥîd* n'est pas métaphysiquement différente de celle du Vedânta. En raison de l'unanimité transcendante des doctrines, nonobstant des formulations forcément particulières et appropriées, nous aurions cependant pu tout aussi bien faire référence à d'autres traditions et puisque nous avons cité le passage IV.3.21 de la Brihadâranyaka Upanishad nous citerons le logion 22 de l'Evangile selon Thomas qui paraît être une paraphrase de l'Upanishad tellement il exprime en termes analogues et avec la même thématique la même vérité du point de vue de la Gnose : "Lorsque vous ferez de deux un, et que vous ferez l'intérieur comme l'extérieur et l'extérieur comme l'intérieur, et ce qui est en haut comme ce qui est en bas, et lorsque vous ferez, le mâle avec la femme, une seule chose, en sorte que le mâle ne soit pas mâle et que la femme ne soit pas femme ... alors vous entrerez [dans le Royaume, c'est-à-dire Dieu] ". Ce logion n'est pas isolé, comme en témoigne le logion 3 : "Jésus a dit : Si ceux qui vous guident vous disent : Voici, le Royaume [=>Dieu] est dans le Ciel, alors les oiseaux du ciel vous devanceront; s'ils vous disent qu'il est dans la mer, alors les poissons vous devanceront. Mais le Royaume est à l'intérieur de vous et il est à l'extérieur de vous. Quand vous vous connaîtrez alors vous serez connus ...".

Sans vouloir reprendre ici l'exégèse très fouillée de H.
Ch. Puech (*En Quête de gnose* II), nous citerons en raison de
leur importance les passages les plus synthétiques: "Nous
connaître nous-mêmes, c'est ... être connu de Dieu, c'est-à-
dire nous connaître tels que Dieu nous connaît, tels que
nous sommes en Lui et par Lui; c'est connaître ... notre être
tel qu'il est en soi, reprendre conscience ... de notre 'moi' tel
qu'il existe dans l'Etre absolu... La connaissance de soi est
connaissance simultanée de notre 'moi' en Dieu et de Dieu
en nous ..." (*op.cit.*, p.104). "Avancer...que Dieu ou le Royaume
est, tout ensemble, 'intérieur' (c'est-à-dire immanent en nous)
et 'extérieur' (c'est-à-dire transcendant par rapport à nous)
revient à déclarer que Dieu ou le Royaume est en nous et
qu'en même temps nous sommes en Dieu ou dans le
Royaume ..." (*op.cit.*, p. 272). L'entrée dans ce Royaume–
définissable comme l'identification du "moi" au "toi", symbole ou reflet du "Soi" – "abolit en chacun [des deux membres
du couple] ce qui le définit et le distingue dans son opposition avec son partenaire ... [elle] efface entre eux tout con-
traste, toute distinction, ... jusqu'à les fondre ensemble, à les
assimiler l'un à l'autre au sein d'une unité indifférenciée.
L'extérieur ne devient pas simplement l'intérieur et
l'intérieur l'extérieur, mais ils s'identifient l'un avec l'autre
au point qu'il n'y a plus, en fin de compte, ni extérieur ni
intérieur..." *In principio* ou encore *in divinis*, "le dehors et le
dedans s'équivalent. Le Royaume n'est que relativement
intérieur et extérieur ... Il n'est en soi, en réalité, ni l'un ni
l'autre ... Il se situe par delà la dualité qu'implique [cette]
distinction... Parce qu'il n'est ni extérieur ni intérieur ... Le
Royaume ne peut être atteint que lorsque 'intérieur' et
'extérieur' deviennent ... réductibles l'un à l'autre ..., une
fois dépassée, abolie toute différence entre un point de vue
'subjectif' et ... 'objectif', une fois transcendée et ramenée à
l'unité la dualité qui nous constitue en un être double du
fait de la division... entre subjectivité et objectivité ..., lorsque
nous ne nous percevons plus comme pur sujet ni en tant

qu'objet, lorsque nous serons devenu absolument 'un' (pp.278-9)

"Faire de deux un, c'est remonter de l'ordre charnel à l'ordre spirituel ... retourner à un état antérieur ou primitif" (pp.281-3) Cet état primordial est très peu différent de l'état "androgynique" de *Puruṣa* déjà décrit. Cet état "implique ... la réunion ... des deux sexes ... mais aussi, ou par delà, la sublimation de la sexualité, la transformation de la dualité sexuelle à un plan supérieur où ... elle se résoud en indistinction". L'entrée dans le Royaume est conçue comme un retour à un état d'innocence, "innocence... qui est celle du petit enfant mais aussi bien celle d'Adam avant le péché et la chute". La description de l'état paradisiaque peut seule donner une idée de cet état qui, pour les hommes d'après la chute que nous sommes, est métaphysiquement représenté par la Réalisation de l'Unité de l'Etre, et, initiatiquement, par celle de l' "Identité suprême". Comme on le voit, cet excursus dans la Gnose ne nous a pas écarté de notre propos puisqu'il nous ramène à la doctrine ésotérique du *Tawḥîd*.

*

En Islâm même, Rûzbehân Baqlî (XIIº) a pareillement exprimé cette doctrine et son évocation nous rapprochera de la symbolique de la *Shahâdah* dont son exposé est forcément imprégné. Cette imprégnation se traduit de plusieurs manières. L'union sexuelle (explicite dans la Brihadâranyaka Upanishad, implicite dans le logion gnostique[4]) est transposée et sublimée en une contemplation ou réflexion réciproques de l'aimant et de l'aimé, l'un étant à l'autre son propre reflet. Ce phénomène du miroir – si fortement marqué dans la *Shahâdah* – est concrétisé par le fait qu'il s'agit moins ici des rapports de l'homme et de la femme (époux et épouse, aimant et aimé, moi et toi, ...) que du "contemplant" et du "contemplé" que Rûzbehân désigne par les termes de *shâhid* et *mashhûd* : mots de la même racine que *Shahâdah* qu'on peut comprendre par conséquent en filigrane de cette dernière.

Dans sa perfection, l'amour est l'expérience de l'identité, en Dieu, de l'amour de l'aimant et de l'aimé. La *Shahâdah* témoigne de l'Unité de Dieu par une multiplicité de réflex-ions, conformément à la formule du théophanisme le plus radical : *Où que vous vous tourniez là est la face d'Allâh, (faaynamâ tuwallû fathamma wajhu'Llâhi)* (Coran II.115). La *Shahâdah* est un miroir aux mille facettes qui, toutes, renvoient le reflet ou l'image de Dieu. Dans l'amour, la même théopha-nie par réflexion a lieu mais il s'agit alors d'une *réflexion sans miroir.* Ce n'est pas dans un miroir que "moi" voit Son reflet ou Son image mais dans "toi", c'est-à-dire dans *autre-que-moi-pour-moi.* Ce stade n'est encore que celui de la vision indi-viduelle : l'amour opère seulement une projection de la subjectivité de "moi" dans l'objet de cet amour : "toi". Dans sa perfection, l'amour réalise une véritable transmutation qui fait cesser la dualité moi aimat-contemplant et toi aimé-contemplé. Au sein de la conscience de l'objectivité de "toi" perce la conscience de l'identité que toi est Lui, le Soi. Dès lors, "moi" voit dans "toi" non plus le reflet de "moi" mais le reflet de Lui ou du Soi et en vertu du lien d'amour entre "moi" et "toi", "moi" réalise que le Soi qu'il reconnaît dans "toi", loin d'être le *reflété* par rapport au "moi", est au con-traire le reflétant.

Il s'en suit un brutal basculement de la vision de "moi"; de reflétant-en-toi le "moi" se reconnaît comme reflété-du-Soi et ce reflété-du-Soi qui est "moi" fait de "toi" le reflétant-en-moi. La perspective est complètement retournée. La vision se perd dans une vertigineuse suite de réflexions qui sont autant d'inversions précipitant la conscience de celui qui a réalisé cet état dans une Réalité nouvelle où toutes les mani-festations sont théophanies ou transparences. Ou bien le miroir est traversé ou bien il a perdu son tain et s'il ne reflète plus c'est qu'il n'y a plus d'opacité.

Il n'est pas question d'entrer dans le détail de l'irruption de la phénoménologie de l'amour humain dans l'amour divin telle que la décrit Rûzbehân; H. Corbin (*En Islâm* *iranien,*III.iii) l'a traitée de facon exhaustive. Nous nous contenterons de citer quelques notations essentielles.

"Le secret de l'amour humain est dans le mystère de l'Amour divin et en est l'accomplissement ... la perspective est renversée : 'l'en bas devient l'en haut, l'en haut devient l'en bas... C'est, dit encore Rûzbehân, se jeter dans la mer du non-être mais afin d'être anéanti au néant [ou d'anéantir en soi le néant] ... Désormais le mystique voit *sans* soi-même (c'est-à-dire *hors de* soi-même) Dieu *par* Dieu'. Il voit, certes, et pourtant... c'est Dieu qui voit *par* lui. Il est l'oeil par lequel Dieu se contemple soi-même. C'est ce que veut dire 'l'en haut devient l'en bas' et réciproquement ..." (pp.131-2).

Rûzbehân dit à l'interlocutrice de son traité. "... Médite cette chose étrange : c'est moi-même qui sans moi-même [autrement dit en toi] suis l'aimant de moi-même. Je ne cesse de me contempler moi-même, sans moi-méme, dans le miroir qui est la 'présence' de l'aimé. Alors moi qui suis-je donc?"

"Le regard que l'aimant contemple ... est son propre regard; simultanément ce n'est pas lui puisque c'est le regard de l'autre, et pourtant cet Autre est lui-méme ..." (p.133). C'est ce que redit la glose 95 : "Lorsque le mystique atteint la perfection en amour il totalise en lui-même les deux modes de l'étre : celui de l'aimant et celui de l'aimé. Alors il s'écrie: 'Je suis celui que j'aime et Celui que j'aime est moi, nous sommes deux esprits "immanents" en un seul corps[5]' ... c'est Dieu même qui par son propre regard éternel contemple son propre visage éternel. Alors l'existence de ma propre réalité humaine n'intervient plus ..." (p.134).

On peut exprimer cette spiritualité de l'amour par une paraphrase de la *Shahâdah*

Dans l'amour il n'y a pas d'aimé si ce n'est par l'aimant et il n'y a pas d'aimant si ce n'est par la vision de l'aimé. Dans l'amour de l'aimant pour l'aimé c'est Dieu qui s'aime Lui-méme. L'amour spirituel est contemplation. L'aimé est la contemplation de l'aimant, qui est Dieu, se contemplant soi-

même dans l'aimé. Le visage de l'aimé est la Face de Dieu
mais le visage de l'aimé est aussi le miroir reflétant le visage
de l'aimant; c'est donc que l'aimant est Dieu Lui-même se
contemplant dans un miroir lui renvoyant son image; mais il
n'y a pas de miroir et cette image est l'image de l'aimé. On
passe de l'amour humain à l'amour divin par une double
identification avec Dieu et cette identification n'est autre
qu'une prise de conscience de l'Unité de l'Etre : 1- l'aimant
est l'aimé, 2- la beauté de l'aimé est la Beauté de Dieu, d'où
l'aimé est Dieu (première identité), 3-.1'aimant voit le visage
de Dieu dans le visage de l'aimé (théophanie), 4- la contemplation est réflexion : dans le miroir qu'est l'aimé l'aimant
voit réfléchi son propre visage comme visage de Dieu, autrement dit l'aimant est Dieu par le moyen (ou l'intermédiaire)
de l'aimé (seconde identité).

Cette "déification" réciproque[6] :

aimant → DIEU ← aimé

hausse l'amour et le mariage parfaits au niveau d'une voie
initiatique. L'aimant et l'aimé se reconnaissent comme deux
polarisations de Dieu qui se voient mutuellement dans l'autre
par l'oeil de l'autre. Or, l'autre c'est "toi", c'est l'image de
Dieu pour "moi" et puisque "toi" est mon reflet je suis Dieu
se contemplant Lui-même dans "toi".

Rûzbehân concentre le rapport amoureux dans le regard
et le choix d'un contact dépouillé de tout érotisme doit être
ressenti chez lui comme l'indice d'une authentique imprégnation de la métaphysique de la *Shahâdah*. Bien que, dans cette
ambiance sublimée, le symbole trop concret de dedans et de
dehors soit absent, il nous faut y revenir cependant en raison
à la fois de son importance et de son ambivalence.

L'intérieur et l'extérieur doivent être compris désormais
comme les deux "transformations" d'un seul et même état,
celui de l'Identité suprême. Leur distinction et leur opposition ne constituent qu'une étape provisoire vers la réalisation de cet état et ils n'ont eux-mêmes de sens que par lui.

En d'autres termes l'intérieur et l'extérieur ne se définissent que par rapport à l'Unité de l'Etre universel.

Dans les textes cités (Brihadâranyaka Upanishad et Evangile selon Thomas) l'intérieur et l'extérieur sont synonymes d'immanent et de transcendant. Une telle correspondance n'est cependant valable que du point de vue subjectif. Est immanent ce qui est en moi; est transcendant ce qui est autre que moi et hors de moi, ce qui dépasse le moi. Du point de vue objectif, par contre, l'intérieur, qui est le caché, l'ésotérique, est supérieur à l'extérieur, la simple apparence des choses, l'exotérique. L'intérieur est la réalité, l'extérieur n'en est que le reflet. L'intérieur est l'infini, l'inexprimable et à la limite le silence; l'extérieur est le fini ou le défini, l'exprimé – autant de notions qui se réfèrent à la parole. L'intérieur est encore l'Unité, le point unique du centre; l'extérieur est la multiplicité, la circonférence formée d'une indéfinité de points.

Bien d'autres corrélations pourraient être énoncées (cf. Coomaraswamy, *Selected Papers*, II.199n) mais nous nous limiterons à celles-là.

Elles suffisent à nous montrer toute l'ambiguité – faite de réversibilité – des deux termes concernés. Cette ambiguité se projette sur les notions qu'elles expriment : qu'il s'agisse du mari et de la femme[7], de l'homme et de Dieu ... En termes de connaissance, se connaître soi-même c'est connaître l'intérieur et cet intérieur est Dieu – ou plus exactement Dieu en nous, mais connaître Dieu c'est tout aussi bien connaître l'extérieur inhérent dans la désignation de Dieu comme le Royaume (logion 3), c'est-à-dire Dieu tel qu'Il est en lui-même.. Connaître Dieu c'est être connu de Dieu. En termes de *Tawḥîd* c'est se connaître tel que Dieu nous connaît ou encore tel que nous nous connaissons en Lui et par Lui. Or, connaître c'est être et la même conclusion vaut dans une formulation ontologique.

Dieu en nous – ou, pour conserver la terminologie déjà employée, Dieu "en moi" – et Dieu "en Soi", que symbolisent

les deux *Puruṣa* immanent et transcendant dont il est parlé
dans la Bhagavad-Gîtâ, sont séparés par un voile, une paroi
et cette paroi opaque est faite de toute l'opacité des choses
et en premier lieu de l'opacité du "moi", de l'opacité de
cette contrepartie individuelle du Soi qu'est l'ego. C'est dire
que la paroi n'est opaque qu'en fonction de la qualité de la
vision du "témoin", de sa capacité de discrimination. Quand
l'oeil s'éveille à la vision de la Réalité il "voit" les choses
comme des théophanies et, en fonction de son sens de
l'analogie, il les "reconnaît" comme des reflets de l'Etre
universel. Cette paroi devient miroir : la vie est des lors un
spectacle ininterrompu de miroirs renvoyant en toutes choses
la même image et cet "Infini Spectacle" est Dieu. Toute la vie
peut être ainsi conditionnée par une vision des choses comme
miroir de Dieu.

Cependant, il existe, *Deo volente*, un degré d'unité encore
supérieur lorsque, la paroi ne faisant plus miroir et n'étant
plus opaque, les choses ayant perdu le tain de *Mâyâ* mon-
trent dans leur transparence la Réalité divine. C'est souvent
par la perfection de l'amour pour l'être aimé que ce tain de
l'illusion peut s'écailler et tomber et c'est ainsi que la dualité, abolie le temps d'une étreinte pour le commun, devient
unité permanente pour le spirituel. Le moi se réalise comme
faisant un avec le Soi et cette identité est ce qui est
appelé l' "Identité supréme" : "Si nous nous représentons la
Divinité, objectivement, comme lointaine, elle est là de l'autre
côté (du voile, de la paroi); si nous nous La représentons
tres proche elle est en nous. Mais ces deux natures de Dieu,
tel qu'Il est en Soi et tel qu'Il est en nous, sont en réalité une
seule" (Coomaraswamy, *op.cit*, 393)[8].

[1] La symbolique des lettres tient compte à sa facon de cette relation de la problématique du mariage et de la métapbysique de la *Shahâdah*. Dans la formule, le mariage est représenté par le *Wâw* rattaché au triple *Hâ – lâ ilâha illâ Huwa*, Germe des Noms *HuWa*, *ALLâH* et *Lâ ilâha illâ ALLâH*. Nous avons rappelé l'identification de *Wâw* comme symbole de l'homme; nous avons laissé de côté sa fonction conjonctive en vertu de laquelle *Wâw* est encoré appel *ḥarf al-wadd*, "lettre de l'amour" (ou de l' "attachement") et cette qualité "hiérogamique", est confirmée par sa valeur numérique six, le "nombre du mariage" (cf. notre *Phonèmes et archétypes*, p.15 n).

[2] Cet état correspond à ce que le Vedânta définit par *bhedâbheda* (litt. "distinction sans différence"); on peut lui appliquer encore la formule eckhartienne : "fondus mais non confondus". De son côté Al-Ḥallâj a célébré cette bi-unité dans le distique fameux (*Dîwân*, pièce 57): "Je suis [devenu] Celui que j'aime et Celui que j'aime est [devenu] moi /Nous sommes deux esprits 'in-fondus' (*ḥalalnâ*) en un (seul) corps."

[3] Cette description de la création de l'homme et de la femme n'est pas sans évoquer celle de la création du monde que propose la Kabbale avec la notion de *zimẓum*, "contraction". Il s'agit non de l'enseignement midrashique selon lequel Dieu s'est contracté *en* Lui-même ou *en* un lieu déterminé mais de la doctrine du *retrait* de Dieu qui a pour conséquence de ménager une sorte de "vide" d'où procède ce monde. Pour comprendre que ce "vide" apparent puisse être à l'origine du monde il faut savoir que Dieu est identifié à En-Sof, le Non-Manifesté de sorte que le monde, manifesté résulte de l'effacement d'En-Sof (ou du Non-Etre, de l'Infini). Ibn 'Arabî n'enseigne pas autre chose qui, à propos du symbole du *Wâw*, definit de même ce monde-ci comme le *ghaybu' l-ghayb*, l'effacement du Non-manifesté.

Un tel effacement ne peut s'entendre que de facon analogique et est tout aussi "inconcevable" que la doctrine kabbalistique. Dans les deux cas la difficulté tient à ce que, contrairement à la logique, le Non-Etre, l'Infini est symbolisé par le "plein" ce qui, par voie de conséquence, fait du "vide" le symbole du contraire : le fini, le manifesté, l'existentiel.

Cette genèse ou manifestation n'est possible, selon la Kabbale, que par "l'entrée de Dieu en Lui-même", c'est-à-dire par un acte de contraction au cours duquel Dieu se rétracte sur Lui-même et permet ainsi à quelque chose qui n'est pas Lui ou En-Sof d'exister.

Tout se passe comme si une "part" de Dieu se retirait, "laissant place" (une telle formulation n'est acceptable que comme un pis aller car Dieu est omniprésent, unique et sans partie) au processus de la création. Ce retrait de Dieu précède forcément toute manifestation ou émanation. Quant au lieu d'où Dieu se retire, il n'est qu'un point comparé à son Infinité mais c'est le point primordial qui comprend tous les degrés d'existence.

Pour en revenir à la Brihadâranyaka Upanishad remarquons que la "moitié" de *Puruṣa* d'où émane la femme est dite "vide" par rapport à la "moitié" de l'homme qui, comparativement, est "pleine". Cette différenciation cosmogonique se retrouve transposée dans l'ordre physiologique où l'homme et la femme font respectivement figure de "plein" et de "vide" d'où leur correspondance avec les modalités de contenu et de contenant, de dedans et de dehors mises en évidence dans le rapport amoureux. La femme, qui procède du "vide" laissé par le retrait d'une moitié de la "Personne divine", est elle-même "vide" par rapport à l'homme, son partenaire issu de la moitié "pleine", et c'est pourquoi il est dans la nature des choses que l'un comble le "vide" de l'autre.

A ce propos il est un autre passage de la Brihadâranyaka Upanishad qu'il convient de citer ici, bien qu'il se rapporte au *Brahman* suprême ou non-manifesté (*adas* : Cela là-bas) et au *brahman* non-suprême ou manifesté (*idam* : ceci, ici-bas), car la parabole dont il s'agit est suffisamment suggestive pour illustrer ce qu'a d'illusoire, dans le Principe, la différenciation de "plein" et de "vide" dont l'homme et la femme sont les expressions sensibles : "Cela (*adas*) est "plein" (*pûrna*, qui signifie aussi "complet", "total" et par extension peut être synonyme d'"infini"); ceci (*idam*) est "plein". Le "plein" procède (*udañc*) du "plein" de sorte que même en lui ôtant (*âdâ*) le "plein", le "plein"reste (*avasish*) [plein] (Brihadâranyaka Upanishad, V.1.j).

[4] En mettant l'accent sur le "connaître" le logion 3 n'exclut pas l'aspect sexuel, conformément à la périphrase biblique pour désigner l'union conjugale: Adam *connut* Eve (*Gen.* 4.1).

[5] Le second vers du distique, non cité, complète l'idée : "Aussi me voir c'est Le voir et Le voir c'est nous voir" (Al-Hallâj, *Dîwân*, pièce 57). Citer Rûzbehân c'est faire allusion aux Fidèles d'Amour dans le cadre de la *Shahâdah* En fait la même formulation existe chez les Fidèles d'Amour occidentaux. Pour ne citer qu'un exemple on lit dans un poème de Cecco d'Ascoli :

"Donqua io so ella ..." et L.Valli (*Il linguaggio segreto di Dante et dei Fedeli d'Amore*, p.84) rapporte cette affirmation unitaire dans le même sens que ci-dessus : "l'amante si assimilava con l'amata e finiva col dire come Cecco d'Ascoli : 'Dunque io son Ella'", en précisant plus loin (p.252) : "Perchè il poeta dica 'Donqua io so ella' ora si puo ben intendere. Egli è immedisamato con la 'intelligenza attiva' come la figura 'moglier et marito' del Barberino e secondo la frase di Averroè 'la massima beatitudine dell'animo umano è nella sua suprema ascensione. E discendo ascensione intendo il suo perfezionarsi e nobilitarsi in modo che si congiunga con la intelligenza attiva e *siffatamente uniscasi a quella che diventi uno con essa'* ... "

[6] Cette "déification" fait de deux un : le "moi" individuel et divisé réuni au Soi indivis (l'Esprit ou l'Essence); cette "déification" est décrite comme un mariage, cf. la Brihadâranyaka-Upanishad (V.3.21)

L'opération inverse, selon laquelle l'un devient multiple, est la "génération".

[7] Ainsi, à propos du couple, nous avons vu que dans l'acte sexuel l'homme est "dedans", contenu, la femme "dehors", contenant. Néanmoins, en soi, c'est la relation inverse qui est vraie : la femme est l' "intérieur" et l'homme l' "extérieur"; sur le plan de la sexualité cette relation est confirmée par l'extériorisation du sexe masculin et l'intériorisation du sexe féminin. Non seulement l'union unit mais inverse les pôles et elle unit dans la mesure de cette inversion des pôles : l'homme, en soi supérieur à la femme, la rend – en s'unissant à elle – supérieure à lui en l'identifiant à Dieu. "Moi", *subjectivement* supérieur à "toi", rend ce "toi" *objectivement* supérieur en l'identifiant au Soi. Telle est la clé de la réalisation de l'Unité de l'Etre par l'Amour.

[8] Et en paraphrasant un autre passage : "Tel qu'il est en lui-même" le moi *est* phénomène, "tel qu'il est en Dieu" il *est* essence. Dans ces deux sentences le verbe être a deux sens différents : dans le premier cas celui de "devenir", dans le second celui d' "être" (*op.cit.*,p.425).

Pour son "objectivité" on peut mentionner ici la description que donne le Pr. Izutsu de l' "expérience spirituelle" de Hakuin : "lorsque Hakuin fut éveillé de sa méditation par le tintement de la cloche d'un temple, c'était le son de lui-même, dans ce tintement, qu'il entendit. Tout l'univers était le son de la cloche et Hakuin lui-même était le son de la cloche écoutant le son de la cloche" (*Towards a Philosophy of Zen Buddhism*,Teheran 1977).

A Sufi Approach to Religious Diversity

Ibn al-ʿArabī on the Metaphysics of Revelation

William C. Chittick

The *philosophia perennis* as expounded by Frithjof Schuon holds that the revealed religions are transcendently one, yet necessarily and providentially diverse in their historical actuality; they represent particular manifestations of a single, universal Truth. Schuon often writes about Islam, which provides many clear and explicit texts that support this position. The Koran itself declares that the essential message of every revelation is the same, while each message is unique. All believing Muslims affirm the universality of religious truth, though many if not most of them would take the position that this pertains to the historical period preceding Islam; it is true that all religions have come from God with a common underlying message, but religions other than Islam later became corrupted, which explains why the Koran often criticizes the People of the Book.

Among the Sufis one would expect to find a clear exposition of the universality of Truth without the reservations expressed by other Muslims. But the Sufis "walked on exoteric stilts", to use Schuon's expression, so they had to take into account the beliefs of their contemporaries. Even an Ibn al-ʿArabī, who was not afraid to attack the limitations of the exoteric mentality, often supports a literal reading of the

Koranic criticisms of the People of the Book, without suggesting that by "Christians" or "Jews" the Koran means anyone other than the contemporary practitioners of those religions. But this perspective has to do with the "particularity" of religious truth, the level where one doctrine conflicts with another; in the context of traditional Islamic civilization, Ibn al-ʿArabī could hardly speak as a person unattached to the Koran's uniqueness.

Like most other Sufis, Ibn al-ʿArabī had little if any contact with Christianity or Judaism other than in various popular forms; he probably never met a saintly representative of either of these traditions, and he almost certainly never read anything about them except what was written in Islamic texts. So there is no reason to expect him to accept the validity of other revealed religions except *in principle*. But this is an important qualification. To maintain the particular excellence of the Koran and the superiority of Muḥammad over all other prophets is not to deny the universal validity of revelation nor the necessity of revelation's appearing in particularized expressions. Since all revealed religions are true in principle, the particular historical circumstances which lead one to suspect that they have been corrupted may change. This is what happened when Sufis like Dārā Shukūh met Hindu saints in India.

In what follows a tiny portion of Ibn al-ʿArabī's arguments that support the universality and particularity of revealed truth are gleaned from the *Futūḥāt al-makkiyyah* and the *Fuṣūṣ al-ḥikam,* two of his major works. To the extent possible I have tried to employ Ibn al-ʿArabī's own methodology in presenting traditional metaphysics, without any attempt to correlate this with contemporary expositions; anyone familiar with the *philosophia perennis* will certainly recognize a number of its basic teachings.

Islamic dogmatics is usually divided into three broad categories that reflect the content of the Koran: divine unity, prophecy, and eschatology. By "prophecy" is meant not just the mission of Muḥammad, but a universal dimension of the relationship between man and God, a dimension illustrated most strikingly by the series of Semitic prophets beginning with Adam and ending with Muḥammad himself, the last prophet before the end of time.

In the Koranic view, revelation is a message delivered by God to a prophet (*nabī*) or "messenger" (*rasūl*). It is universal, since "Every nation has its messenger" (Koran 10: 47) and the fundamental content of the message is always the same: "There is no god but I, so serve Me" (21: 25: cf. 16: 36).[1] Muslims must have faith in all the messengers, since each is but a confirmation of what came before.[2] Even so, every message is unique, since each is given to a prophet "in the tongue of his people" (Koran 14: 4).

God sent the prophets to remind human beings that they were created to be His servants (*ᶜabd*) and vicegerents (*khalīfah*) and to warn them of the consequences of shirking their responsibilities. According to the Koran, when God sent Adam down from Paradise, He said to him,

> If there comes to you from Me guidance, then whosoever follows My guidance shall not go astray, neither shall he be wretched; but whosoever turns away from My remembrance (*dhikr*), his life shall be a life of narrowness, and on the Day of Resurrection, We shall raise him blind. (20: 123-124)

Here, quoting as it were from the primordial revelation given to mankind, the Koran makes clear that revelation is sent for the purpose of guidance; ignoring it will lead to wretchedness (*shaqāʾ*) a term that is employed to describe the state of the inhabitants of hell, as opposed to the "felicity" (*saᶜādah*) of the blessed.

The Koranic teachings on prophecy just outlined have been studied and amplified by generations of Muslim authorities representing all the perspectives of Islamic intellectual life.[3] The present paper surveys the views of one of the foremost spokesmen for Islamic esoterism, Ibn al-ʿArabī (d. 1240), whose legacy has dominated the theoretical exposition of Islamic metaphysics down to recent times;[4] it describes his theory of revelation within the context of his comprehensive teachings on the nature of existence, the possibilities of human perfection, the parameters of knowledge, and the constraints of belief; and it concludes by showing how he upholds the necessity for religious diversity without relativizing the absolute Truth.

The One and the Many

Ibn al-ʿArabī is known primarily for a teaching that later thinkers came to call the Oneness of Being (*waḥdat al-wujūd*). The brief reviews of this doctrine that are found in various textbooks, whether in the West or the Islamic world, usually ignore the fact that Ibn al-ʿArabī devotes most of his incredibly voluminous corpus of writings[5] to accounting for and explaining the nature of multiplicity, which, like Being's Oneness, is an intrinsic attribute of reality.

In discussing the relationship between God's unity and the world's multiplicity, Ibn al-ʿArabī constantly makes use of the Koranic concept of the Names (*asmāʾ*) of God. (He also employs the term "attributes" [*ṣifāt*]: if God's "Name" is Merciful, He possesses the "attribute" of Mercy.) Traditionally the Names or attributes are said to number ninety-nine, though closer to 150 are mentioned in or implied by the Koran, and sometimes they are said to number 1001. For Muslim thinkers in general, the Names, much like the Platonic ideas, provide the prototypes for all created reality. Thus, for example, God is the Living, the Knowing, the Willing, the Powerful, the Speaking, the Generous and the Just; for Ibn al-ʿArabī and others, these seven Names are the "Seven Mothers" (*al-ummahāt al-sabʿ*) who jointly give birth to the cosmos. Some of God's Names denote meanings that are diametrically opposed to each other (*mutaqābil*), e.g., the Abaser and the Exalter, the Life-Giver and the Slayer, the Forgiving and the Vengeful; the properties (*aḥkām*) or effects (*āthār*) of such Names help account for much of the change, opposition, and strife that are found in the world.

All the Names refer back to a single Reality, which is sometimes called Being (*al-wujūd*) or True Being (*al-wujūd al-ḥaqq*). The Koranic delineation of the Divine Names reveals the universal modes (*iʿtibārāt*) of Being's external and internal operations. Each Name gives news of a manner in which Being can be correctly viewed and understood. Many Names allude to different types of relationship which Being establishes with the multiple existents of the cosmos. For example, Being may be called the Creator of the world, the Light of the heavens and the earth, the Manifest and the Unmanifest, the First and the Last, etc. Yet Being Itself remains a single Reality, since the Names are only providential specifications of possible modes in which It may be envisaged. In the last analysis, they are merely relations (*nisab*) posited by revelation to explain what can be known of Being in Its self-manifestation.[6] As Ibn al-ʿArabī remarks,

> He is the First and the Last in a Single Entity... Zayd refers to you as "he", ʿAmr says to you "you", and you say "I". So "I" is the same as "you" and "he", even though "I" is not the same [in another respect]. Hence the relations are diverse. (*Futūḥāt* II 278.13)[7]

Though all the Names refer to a single Reality, none denotes Its true nature. From this point of view even the Name Allāh, which is called the "all-comprehensive Name" (*al-ism al-jāmiʿ*) since it is the referent of all other Names, is said to denote that Reality only inasmuch as It makes Itself known. In Itself, in Its very Essence, the single Reality is unknowable. The Prophet used to pray, "Oh Allāh, I ask Thee by every Name by which Thou hast named Thyself, taught to one of Thy creatures, or kept exclusively to Thyself" (cf. II 619.18). These "exclusive" Names, says Ibn al-ʿArabī, are "the Names outside of creation and relation" (II

69.31). They pertain to Being in Itself, which Ibn al-ᶜArabī often refers to simply as the It-ness (al-huwiyyah)[8] or the Essence (dhāt; originally "possess or of," i.e., that which possesses or is named by the Names).

In discussing the Essence's unknowability, Ibn al-ᶜArabī likes to cite the Koranic verse, "Allāh is independent of all the worlds" (3: 97, 29: 60). Here it should be noted that the Name Allāh is taken, as it often is, to refer to the Essence, although from another point of view, even such terms as It-ness and Essence are considered provisional.[9]

> In Itself, the Essence has no name, since It is not the locus for effects, nor is It known by anyone, nor is there any name that could clearly designate It in Its state of being devoid of relations. The reason for this is that "names" serve to make known and to distinguish, but this door is shut to everything other than Allāh, since "None knows Allāh but Allāh." (II 69. 34)

If the Essence possesses attributes that denote It in any real sense, these are negative (salbī). One of these, "nondelimitation" (al-iṭlāq), is worth considering in some detail for the light it can throw on Ibn al-ᶜArabī's understanding of the nature of revelation: The Essence or Being in Itself, "independent of all the worlds," is free of any limitation and confinement whatsoever. Moreover, the Essence is not delimited by nondelimitation; in other words, It is not only free of all limitations, It is also free to assume all limitations, on pain of being limited. Or again: God viewed as the Essence is not only infinitely transcendent, He is also immanent in all things, since these are nothing but the possible delimitations that He assumes because of His nondelimitation. Ibn al-ᶜArabī's many summaries of these points sometimes sound like paradoxes, and he himself will often end them by speaking of the "bewilderment" (ḥayrah) that marks the great saints in face of God's self-manifestation. The following passage is more straightforward than many:

> Allah possesses Nondelimited Being, but no delimi-

tation prevents delimitation. Rather, He possesses all delimitations, so He is nondelimited delimitation, since no single delimitation rather than another rules over Him. So understand what it means to attribute nondelimitation to Him! He who is such a Being is nondelimited in the attributions [that are made to Him]: so nothing is to be attributed to Him in preference to anything else. (III 162.23)

The Divine Names, it bears repeating, represent the archetypes of the world's multiplicity: they delineate the various modes in which Nondelimited Being delimits Itself when It brings the cosmos into existence. Nondelimited Being is the Being of Allāh, while delimited Being (al-wujūd al-muqayyad) – which will be referred to here as "existence" (though only a single term, al-wujūd, is used for both Being and existence in Arabic) – refers to all the things and realities that are collectively known as the cosmos, world, or universe (al-ʿālam), i.e., "that which is other than Allāh" (mā siwā Allāh). Each thing (shay') – or "existent" (mawjūd) – manifests the properties of Being through its very existence; moreover, all the specific characteristics or attributes of a thing are effects (āthār) of the Divine Names. The relationship between Allāh (Being, the Essence) and the Names corresponds to that between the thing and its attributes. But whereas Allāh manifests all Names, no one existent can manifest all the possible attributes of existence in their full deployment. Since each existent represents a delimitation of Nondelimited Being, it will be able to manifest Being's Attributes – Its Names – only to a certain degree. This "degree" is known technically as the existent's "preparedness" (istiʿdād), a term which is closely connected to the idea of the immutable entity (al-ʿayn al-thābitah).

The infinite possibilities of self-manifestation possessed by Nondelimited Being are known by God for all eternity. In other words, every single thing or quiddity (māhiyyah) along with every one of its specific characteristics is a self-delimitation of Nondelimited Being, determined by the nature of Being Itself, and known forever by virtue of Being's unlimited self-knowledge. As objects of knowledge (*maʿlūmāt*), the things are referred to as immutable entities; they are immutable because they are eternally known by God, and entities (sing.: *ʿayn*) because they possess specific entifications (*taʿayyun*) or thingnesses (*shay'iyyah*) or delimitations *(taqyīd)* that distinguish (*tamayyuz*) them from other entities. But as objects of God's knowledge they do not exist outside of His knowledge, any more than our thoughts exist outside of our minds.

If God chooses, He can bring an entity from nonexistence (*al-ʿadam*) in knowledge into existence. But even when an immutable entity becomes an existent entity (*ʿayn mawjūd*), it never ceases to remain nonexistent, so what is termed "its existence" is in fact delimited Being; in other words, its existence belongs to God, just as all of its specific characteristics are properties of the Divine Names. In explaining the relationship between the Nondelimited Being of God and the existence of the entities Ibn al-ʿArabī demonstrates his true skill at expressing metaphysical subtleties. Here it is only possible to allude to one of the many analogies he employs to illustrate this relationship.

Nondelimited Being is Light, for "Allāh is the Light of the heavens and the earth" (Koran 24: 35), but a Light so luminous that It cannot be perceived; likewise, the entities cannot be perceived, since they are nonexistent, i.e., they are pure darkness. Once Nondelimited Light and pure darkness are mixed, a realm of visible light known as "brightness" (*diyāʾ*) comes into view, while Light and darkness remain invisible. But in the final analysis, the only thing that is seen is Light delimited by darkness; our perception of brightness results from the privation of Light. In other words, even though the entities are nonexistent, their effect upon Being is to delimit and define it in certain specific modes, thereby distinguishing it from Being as delimited and defined by other entities in other specific modes; all "existent entities" display the properties of Being, since nothing else truly exists. What appears to the eyes may be called the properties of darkness, but in fact it is the properties of Light, which alone is.

The extent to which each entity allows the light of Being to shine forth, or the capacity of each to act as a "locus" (*maḥall*) or "locus of manifestation" (*maẓhar*) within which Being displays Its properties, is known as the entity's "preparedness" (*istiʿdād*).

> Opposite the Being of God stand immutable entities, eternally described as nonexistent... His Being is effused upon these entities in accordance with what their preparednesses require. (II 55.4)

Man, made in the image of the all-comprehensive name Allāh, possesses potentially the greatest capacity to manifest the properties of Being (though the preparedness of each human individual differs). Ibn al-ʿArabī compares the "effusion of existence" (*ifāḍat al-wujūd*) to the light of the sun, and preparedness to the ability of the creatures to absorb and make use of the sun's rays:

> God says, "Thy Lord's bestowal is not confined" (Koran 17: 20). In other words, "God bestows constantly, while the loci act as receptacles in the measure of the realities of their own preparednesses." In the same way we say that the sun deploys its rays upon the existent things; it does not withhold its light from anything, but the loci receive the light in the measure of their preparednesses. Then each locus attributes the effect to the sun and forgets its own preparedness. The person of cold temperament enjoys the sun's heat, while the person of hot temperament suffers because of it. But the light in itself is one. (I 287.10)

This, in short, explains the diversity of existents in the world. The different preparedness of each entity to receive the light of Being means that each delimits Nondelimited

Being in its own fashion. But the effusion of God, His self-disclosure *(tajallī)* or self-manifestation, is One and Nondelimited in itself.

> He who discloses Himself is one entity in Himself, but the disclosures differ because of the preparednesses of the loci.(I 287.19)

Ibn al-ʿArabī summarizes his doctrine of the relationship between Being and the nonexistent entities as follows:

> We believe concerning the existents in all their differentiation *(tafsīl)* that they are the manifestation *(zuhūr)* of God *(al-Ḥaqq)* in the loci of manifestation, i.e., in the entities of the possible things, in keeping with the preparednesses of these possible things. The attributes of that which is manifest are diverse, so the existents become distinguished and plural in keeping with the plurality of the distinction of the entities in God Himself. So there is nothing in existence except God and the properties of the entities, while there is nothing in nonexistence except the entities of the possible things ready to become qualified by existence. (II 160.1)

The Two Commands

The Koran makes clear that both the universe and the prophets are revelatory instruments of God. The miracles and scriptures of the prophets, the verses of the Koran itself, and the phenomena of nature are all referred to as God's "signs" *(āyāt)*. In respect of being signs, their function is to bring about qualities such as remembrance, reflection, understanding, and intellection in human beings.[10]

> A Book We have sent down to thee [O Muḥammad], Blessed, that men possessed of minds may ponder its signs and so remember.(Koran 38: 29)

> It is He who sends down to you out of heaven water of which you have to drink, and whence come trees for

you to pasture your herds, and thereby He brings forth
for you crops, and olives, and palms, and vines, and all
manner of fruit. Surely in that is a sign for a people who
reflect. (16:10-11)

The creatures of the universe are not only God's signs but
also His servants. The mountains, the birds, the heavens, the
stars – all sing His praises. However, mankind (along with
the jinn) stand apart from other creatures, inasmuch as
some of them refuse to submit to God's authority. Although
God says, "I have not created jinn and men except to serve
(or "worship") Me" (51: 56), some men refuse to obey His
commands:

Have you not seen how to God bow all who are in the
heavens and all who are in the earth, the sun and the
moon, the stars and the mountains, the trees and the
beasts, and *many* of mankind? (Koran 22: 18)

How is it that human beings are able to disobey God? One
of the answers that Ibn al-ᶜArabī provides for this question
has to do with the nature of the command that is disobeyed.
In fact, he says, following earlier authorities, the Koran clearly
distinguishes between two kinds of command: the engendering command *(al-amr al-takwīnī)* and the prescriptive command *(al-amr al-taklīfī)*. The first brings the creatures into existence: "His only command when He desires a thing is to say
to it 'Be!' and it is" (Koran 36: 82). The second is delivered
by the prophets in the form of revelation and lays down
mankind's obligation to serve God through prayer, fasting,
paying the alms tax, undertaking the *hajj*, and so on. The
engendering command is directed at all existents, while the
prescriptive command is aimed specifically at mankind. In
virtue of the first command the Koran says, "To God bow all
who are in the heavens and the earth, willingly or unwill-
ingly, as do their shadows in the mornings and evenings"
(13: 15). In virtue of the second command the Koran can
speak of human disobedience and sin. The first command
cannot be disobeyed, since it determines a creature's very

existence; the second can be rejected, whether partially or completely.

Why does one God have two commands? There is no plurality in the Divine Essence, so the commands refer back to different Names. Specifically, the engendering command derives from the Name Allāh, while the prescriptive command relates to certain other Names such as the Guide (*al-Hādī*) and the Beneficent (*al-Munⁱim*), whose properties become manifest in the form of revelation.

The Name Allāh comprehends the properties of all other Names; its manifestation is the total universe on the one hand and the human individual, "created upon Allāh's form," on the other. Both macrocosm and microcosm reflect God; hence the world is often called the "great man" (*al-insān al-kabīr*).

> Every attribute accepted by the ontological level of Allāh (*al-ḥaḍrat al-ilāhiyyah*) is also accepted by both the small man and the great man. (II 139.30; cf. II 150.26)

When Allāh says "Be!", this command brings the universe and all things within it into existence. But when He says in respect of His Name the Guide, "Do this!" or "Avoid that!", those who follow His command become separated from those who reject it; eschatologically, this results in heaven and hell becoming filled with inhabitants, the one to reward the obedient, the other to punish the disobedient.

Since the prescriptive command derives from certain specific Names, while the engendering command derives from the all-comprehensive Name, the prescriptive command is in fact embraced and determined by the engendering command; it can be called a specific form assumed by the engendering command for the purpose of accomplishing certain definite ends, such as the separation of the people of heaven and hell. But from the point of view of the engendering command, there can be no such thing as disobedience. In other words, disobedience toward the prescriptive command always derives from obedience toward the engendering command.

The reason that disobeying the prescriptive command will lead to. wretchedness, even though it amounts to obeying God in respect of the engendering command, can best be explained by an example: In addition to being the Guide, God is also the Misguider (*al-Muḍill*). Though not mentioned in the well-known lists of ninety-nine Names, this Name is often referred to by Ibn al-ᶜArabī and is implied by thirty-five Koranic verses in which God is the subject of the verb "to misguide." For example, "What, do you desire to guide him whom Allāh has misguided?" (4: 88). In certain circumstances, God's misguidance may dominate over His guidance; as a result, the prescriptive command will be disobeyed.

The factors which determine whether an individual will be guided or misguided go back to the nature of the Divine Essence Itself, or in other words, to the properties of the various Divine Names, which determine the preparedness of each entity. For example, the Koran says succinctly, "God misguides the evildoers" (14: 27; cf. 40: 74). That is to say, when a person manifests the properties of certain Divine Names that result in his committing acts that go against the prescriptive command, he calls down upon himself God's misguidance. But on closer examination it becomes clear that here a temporal mode of explanation is inappropriate, since a person who is misguided has always been so. After all, his entity, known eternally by God, is immutable, so in fact the properties of the Name Misguider are already apparent once a person is an "evildoer," since this Name is one of the Names that has determined his entity.

To the objection that this means that "God makes the sinners sin, then punishes them for it," Ibn al-ᶜArabī replies that God does not make the sinners *do* anything, He only makes them *exist*. They are the outward manifestations of immutable entities, so "they are what they are." God cannot change their entities any more than He can change His own Essence. When He manifests the entity of the sun, it shines, and when He manifests the entity of a sinner, he sins, thus displaying within himself the properties of the Name Misguider. The sinner is the locus of manifestation for a delimited possibility of outward existence possessed by Nondelimited Being in virtue of the fact that, in a certain respect, God is named the Misguider.

Three Paths to God

Ibn al-ʿArabī explains the difference between the engendering and prescriptive commands in a variety of manners. For example, he often refers to the straight path which all Muslims ask to be guided upon in their daily prayers. He points out that in fact the Koran refers to several straight paths, each of which has different characteristics; three of them are of particular relevance to the present discussion: the Path of Allāh, the Path of the Beneficent, and the Path of Muḥammad.

All creatures walk upon the straight path of Allāh, since everything obeys the engendering command. From the perspective of the all-comprehensive Name, each thing has its own perfection which is determined by its immutable entity, i.e., by those Divine Names which it manifests. However, this perfection may appear noxious and evil from the point of view of other perfections. For example, the loci of manifestation for the Name the Forgiver will be far different from those of the Name the Avenger.

The properties of the Divine Names are diverse in respect of being Names. How are the Avenger, the Terrible in Retribution, and the Severe comparable to the All-Compassionate, the Forgiver, and the Kind? For the Avenger seeks vengeance from its object, but the All-Compassionate seeks the removal of vengeance. Each Name looks upon things in keeping with its own reality. (II 93.19)

Because all things have come from Allāh and walk upon His path, all return to Him. "To Allah belongs the Kingdom of the heavens and the earth, and to Allāh is the homecoming" (Koran 24: 42; cf. 3:28, 5: 18, 35: 18). "To Allāh belongs all that is in the heavens and the earth, and to Allāh are all things returned" (3: 109; cf. 8: 44, 22: 76, 35: 4, 57: 5).

Allāh's straight path is referred to specifically in the verse,

> "And thou, surely thou guide unto a straight path – the path of Allāh, to whom belongs whatsoever is in the heavens and in the earth. Surely unto Allāh all things come home." (42:52)

Allusions can be found to Allāh's straight path in such verses as, "He gave each thing its creation, then guided" (20:50). Ibn al-ᶜArabī comments:

> So each thing is in an actualized straightness. The straightness of a plant is that its motion should be downwards, while the straightness of an animal is for it to move horizontally....
>
> Hence there is nothing but straightness; there is no way to opposition.... "The straightness of a bow is in its curve," because of what is desired from it. So there is nothing but straightness within the engendered universe, since that which bestows existence upon it – and that is Allāh – is upon a straight path. (II 217.27)

Ibn al-ᶜArabī defines Allāh's straight path as follows:

> It is the general path upon which all things walk, so it takes them to Allāh. This path includes every divine religion and every construction of the human mind, since each one takes to Allāh; it embraces both the wretched and the felicitous. (III 410.24)

According to Ibn al-ᶜArabī, the second path, the straight path of the Beneficent, is referred to in the opening chapter of the Koran; this is the straight path upon which Muslims pray to be guided in their daily prayers.

Guide us on the straight path, the path of those who receive Thy Beneficence, not of those against whom Thou art Wrathful, nor of those who are astray. (Koran 1: 5-7)

This same path is referred to in the following verse:

He has laid down for you as religion what He charged Noaḥ with, and what We have revealed to thee [O Muḥammad], and what We have charged Abraham with, and Moses and Jesus.... (42: 13)

Having referred to these and other prophets God also says,

We elected them, and We guided them to a straight path. That is Allāh's guidance; He guides by it whom He will of His servants. (6: 89-90)

Ibn al-ᶜArabī describes the straight path of the Beneficent as follows:

This is the path that includes every prophet and messenger... Concerning it al-Bukhārī [the foremost Ḥadīth authority] included a chapter entitled "Ḥadīths on the fact that the religion of all the prophets is one."... If some of the statutes [of the various religions] differ, this [goes back to] the law which God has appointed for each one of the messengers. He says, "To every one of you We have appointed a law and a way. And if God had willed, He would have made you one nation" (Koran 5: 48). (III 413.14)

Finally, the Path of Muḥammad designates the guidance that was given exclusively to him, i.e., the Koran. It leads to the specific form of mercy and felicity that God has singled out for the followers of Islam (III 413.24).

From one point of view, the second and third paths are paths of Allāh like the first, but they differ profoundly from it in that their specific determining factors are Divine Names related to guidance and felicity. "Every path leads to God," but not every path will result in a benefit accruing to the person who follows it. In Ibn al-ᶜArabī's words,

God says, "This is My straight path, so follow it, and
follow not diverse paths, lest they scatter you from its
road" (Koran 6: 153), i.e., the road wherein is your
felicity. After all, each path leads to Allāh since He is
the end of every path– "To Him the whole matter shall
be returned" (11: 123) – but not everyone who returns
to Him attains felicity. So the path of felicity is the religious path (al-mashrū͑ah), nothing else. (II 148.11)

Names such as the Guide, the Forgiver, and the Beneficent lead directly to salvation and felicity, but Names such as
the Misguider, the Avenger, and Terrible in Retribution
lead to punishment and wretchedness. In other words, everyone follows God's engendering command whether he
wants to or not, but no special benefit results; felicity can
only be achieved by following the prescriptive command.

There is no path that does not take to Allāh, but God
says to His Prophet and to us, "Go thou straight, as thou
hast been commanded" (11: 112). He does not address
him in terms of unqualified straightness, since ... the
important thing is to which of the Divine Names you
will attain and come home: for the effect of that Name
– whether felicity and bliss or wretchedness and chastisement – will penetrate him who attains to it. Hence
the meaning of "straightness" here is motion and rest
upon the religious way or the straight path, i.e., the
Divine Law (al-shar͑ al-ilāhī). Faith in God is the beginning of this path, and the "branches of faith"[11] are its
waystations. (II 218. 14)

Guidance and Human Perfection

It was said above that one reason for the existence of the
prescriptive command is to populate the two abodes, heaven
and hell. Another way of expressing this is to say that the
prescriptive command brings about the full development of
human possibilities. Without revelation, both the highest

and the lowest human potentialities could not be actualized. Revelation allows human beings to reach both the heights of perfection and the depths of degradation, i.e., the whole range of human possibilities that are demanded by the engendering command.

Since human beings are created "upon the form of Allāh," they possess all the divine Attributes, at least potentially. They are, in effect, "little gods," and hence God appointed them as His vicegerents or representatives upon earth. But vicegerency presupposes servanthood (ʿubūdiyyah), which in turn means the submission of the human will to the divine Will(i.e., al-islām).

It can be said that the primary divine Attributes that are reflected within the theomorphic being known as man are Life, Knowledge, Will, Power, and Speech. Hence revelation is addressed to a living being who possesses knowledge, chooses among the objects of his knowledge through will, puts his will into practice through power, and grasps the divine Word while articulating his own situation through speech. By means of the last attribute in particular he actualizes an encounter between the divine and the human. Speech is the quality that sets man apart from other creatures; through it revelation descends from heaven and spiritual practice is made possible.

It hardly needs to be pointed out that these qualities are not possessed equally by all human beings and that the degree to which they are possessed determines to a large degree a person's human standing. It should also be obvious that equilibrium (iʿtidāl) among these attributes contributes to human perfection; each of the attributes supports the others, and the lack of any one will vitiate the usefulness of the others. "Knowledge without power", and even more so "power without knowledge", are conditions that seem to be well known to everyone; certainly we hear them being discussed constantly, for example, in the domain of politics.

In the Islamic view, full human perfection involves the presence of all the divine Attributes, not only these five. Moreover, equilibrium becomes the key to whether or not the attributes will lead to the felicity that is the goal of human life. In Sufi terminology, the spiritual path is said to involve "assuming the traits of Allāh" (*al-takhalluq bi akhlāq Allāh*), or "assuming the traits of the divine Names" (*al-takhalluq bi'l-asmā' al-ilāhiyyah*). The concrete psychological, moral and spiritual perfections that are achieved by actualizing these Names are known technically in Sufism as the "stations" (*maqāmāt*) of the spiritual path.

Even today human life is commonly viewed as a process of growth through which various attributes are acquired and developed. The worth of increasing one's knowledge and strengthening one's will power is universally acknowledged. What is not universally acknowledged is that human potential for growth and development is not limited by any conceivable bounds; made in the image of God, the human being can actualize all the Divine Names, each to an unlimited degree.

From this point of view, the need for revelation comes back to human ignorance of the human/divine nature. Without too much instruction, we can understand the value of knowledge and power, but to realize the value of all the divine Attributes and then to actualize each of them in proper equilibrium with all the others is totally beyond human capability, unless a divine intervention takes place. The final reason for the impossibility of achieving human perfection and the concordant human felicity through individual effort is the unknowability and nondelimitation of the Divine Being Itself, "upon whose form" man was created. The things of the universe – and in particular man's own self – cannot be known in their relationship to the unknowable Essence until God specifies their situation through revelation.

Ibn al-ᶜArabī devotes hundreds of pages to explaining the deficiencies and limitations of the human intellect, *al-ᶜaql*, a word which derives from a root meaning "to bind, to fetter, to confine." The intellect, he says, is that which, on a cognitive level, restricts the Nonrestricted and delimits the Nondefined. Hence it is barred from grasping the ultimate Origin of things – Nondelimited Being – through its own powers. Only revelation can provide it with the necessary guidance to function in harmony with the other human faculties and realize its full potential. And just as the intellect – the instrument of human knowledge – can only function correctly through accepting the divine guidance, so also the other faculties, such as will and speech, can only play their proper roles within a divine framework, i.e., the prescriptive command.

Through creation, Being manifests Itself within the infinite possibilities of delimitation demanded by Its very Nondelimitation. This means that the whole range of possible combinations of divine Attributes must be manifested not only in the creatures of the macrocosm, but also in the individual human microcosms. There must be a virtually unlimited number of human types and human individuals manifesting the infinite possibilities of Being's delimitation, or the whole range of possible interactions among the Names. Ibn al-ᶜArabī writes in great detail about the vast range of possible human perfections as actualized in the different degrees of faith and sanctity. He also devotes a good deal of space to the various possibilities of deviation and disequilibrium that result when the properties of the Names fail to produce a harmonious human being.

From one point of view, the destiny of each person is determined by his immutable entity, or the particular possibility of ontological deployment that he represents. But from another point of view, each person participates actively and freely in shaping his own fate, since he is a divine image possessing the attribute of free will. Hence he chooses to accept or reject revelation and is held responsible for his choice. From the human point of view, we choose freely many of the Attributes of God that we actualize within ourselves. By following revelation, a person opens himself up to the full range of human possibilities and is able to actualize them – always in keeping with his own preparedness, of course – such that those that lead to felicity outweigh those that lead to wretchedness. Human perfection as such involves a full realization of all the ontological possibilities represented by the Divine Names. Hence it is said that the "Perfect Man" (al-insān al-kāmil) – he who truly actualizes the divine form – stands at the "center of the circle of existence," equidistant from all possibilities of manifestation and displaying each in proper harmony and equilibrium with all the others. In contrast, when a person rejects the guidance of the prophets, he precludes the possibility of realizing all human potentialities and is therefore condemned to remain in disequilibrium and disharmony, a state that will lead to wretchedness in the next world.

One way to explain the concept of human perfection as the function of an equilibrium among the divine Attributes is to refer to the two Attributes of Mercy and Wrath. Although God is both Merciful and Wrathful, His Mercy – according to the well-known prophetic statement – "precedes His Wrath." This means that God Himself is essentially Mercy, while Wrath is a secondary attribute that comes into play only when certain creatures are taken into account. The Koran affirms that "God's Mercy embraces all things" (7: 156; cf. 40:7), while it states that His Wrath is directed only toward those who have strayed from the straight path of the prophets.

The Divine Names are often divided into two categories, those of Mercy (or Gentleness, or Beauty) and those of Wrath (or Severity, or Majesty). The principle of Mercy's precedence means that the Merciful Names possess a certain priority over the Wrathful Names. The former include Names such as the All-Compassionate, the Forgiver, the Pardoner, the Gentle, the Guide, and the Beneficent, while the latter include Names such as the Avenger, the Terrible in Retribution, the Mighty, the Severe, and the Misguider. It will be perceived immediately that guidance pertains to Mercy and misguidance to Wrath; felicity is related to the first group of Names and wretchedness to the second.

Ibn al-ʿArabī develops a complicated cosmology based largely on the interplay of Mercy and Wrath.[12] He demonstrates that the ontological priority of the Merciful Names means that these attributes pertain to the divine Nature as such, while the second group comes into play within the cosmos. Thus, for example, the Koran states that "The All-Merciful is seated upon the Throne" (20:5), while the traditions of the Prophet make clear that the Throne encompasses the Footstool upon which God's "two feet" are placed. According to Ibn al-ʿArabī, these are the foot of Mercy and the foot of Mercy mixed with Wrath. And since "His Footstool encompasses the heavens and the earth" (Koran 2: 255), Mercy and Wrath enter into the very fabric of the created universe, while beyond the Footstool there is only the all-Merciful.

Since Mercy is an Attribute that pertains to God Himself without taking creation into account, it is closely connected with those Attributes that result from "proximity" (qurb) to God, such as knowledge or illumination, union, unity, and equilibrium; in contrast, Wrath is manifested only within the creatures, so it has a certain connection with ignorance, separation, multiplicity, and deviation. To the extent that a human being is dominated by attributes connected to Wrath, he remains in separation and dispersion; only by seeking out God's Mercy and Forgiveness is he able to ascend to the realm of union and unity.

Wrath has a necessary role to play within the cosmic harmony, though it is subordinate to Mercy; in the same way, separative existence performs a positive function, since through it the full manifestation of all the divine Attributes is achieved. Even the Names of Mercy depend in a certain respect upon the Names of Wrath for the entire range of their possibilities to be actualized. Ibn al-ʿArabī likes to quote a prophetic tradition in this connection:

> By Him in whose hand my soul is, if you had not sinned, God would have removed you and brought a people who do sin, then ask God's pardon and are forgiven.[13]

Through these words, says Ibn al-ʿArabī, "The Prophet alerted us to the fact that everything which occurs in the cosmos takes place only to make manifest the property of a Divine Name" (II 96.12).

In the same sort of context, Ibn al-ʿArabī relates the story of one of the faithful who complained to a saint about the corruption of the times. The saint replied,

> What business have you with God's servants? Do not interfere between the Master and His slaves! Mercy, Forgiveness, and Charity are seeking them [the sinners]. Do you desire that the properties of the Divinity should remain ineffectual (*muʿaṭṭal*)? Busy yourself with yourself and pay no heed to such things! (II 177. 11)

But it is especially the Names of Wrath that achieve the full deployment of their properties through those who reject the prescriptive command. For example, God is "Tyrannical, Proud" (Koran 59: 23). When these two Attributes are actualized by the saints within the context of Mercy's precedence, they are accompanied by the necessary humility appropriate to the fundamental human situation, which is that of servanthood. But these two attributes must also possess loci of manifestation wherein they can dominate over the properties of servanthood, and the result will be pride and arrogance of the worst sort. Since the effects of the Merciful Names will be almost totally nullified in such cases, disequilibrium, spiritual blindness, and ultimate wretchedness will be the result. Hence the Koran says, "God sets a seal upon every heart that is tyrannical, proud" (40:35). The disequilibrium produced by the manifestation of such Names, says Ibn al-

ᶜArabī, can lead a person to claim divinity, as in the case of
Pharaoh (II 244.35). Hence even extreme forms of human
imperfection display the properties of certain Divine Names,
albeit in a mode that will lead to wretchedness and chastisement.

But wretchedness is not separate from Mercy, since Mercy
precedes Wrath and must exercise its effects even upon the
objects of Wrath. This is a constant theme of Ibn al-ᶜArabī's
writings and it leads him to insist upon the limited duration
of the chastisement of hell.[14] Aeons and aeons may pass, but
eventually the fires of hell will be quenched and Mercy will
embrace all of its inhabitants.[15]

The Gods of our Beliefs

Revelation is a self-delimitation of Nondelimited Being
with a view toward human perfection and felicity. To reject
revelation is to reject the possibility of attaining to the perfection of the human state and to delay the arrival of felicity
for aeons if not "forever". To accept it is to acknowledge its
truth *(taṣdīq)*, to commit oneself to its demands *(īmān:*
"faith"), and to put one's commitment into practice. To the
extent that the individual conforms to the norm provided by
the religion *(al-mīzān al-mashrūᶜ)*, he will be led to the actu-
alization of the potentialities of human nature, which are determined and defined by the full range of the divine Attributes, latent within him by virtue of his having been created
"upon Allāh's form."

The degree to which conformity to the divine norm will
be actualized depends upon many factors, not the least of
which is "belief" *(iᶜtiqād)*, or the manner in which one con-
ceives of the object of one's faith. Though each practitioner
of the religion will have "faith in God," what he actually
understands by this "God" in whom he has faith has far-
reaching implications. The Arabic word *iᶜtiqād* –"belief" –
derives from the root ᶜ-q-d, which means to knit, knot, or tie;

to join together, to convene, to make a contract. The word *iʿtiqād* itself, the eighth verbal form of the root, means to become firmly tied or established, literally of figuratively. "Belief", then, is a "knot" firmly tied in the heart or the mind. For Ibn al-ʿArabī, it is a binding and delimitation of Nondelimited Being that takes place within the human subject. It is a natural human state, in the sense that everyone has some concept of the nature of reality or the meaning of existence, however unarticulated this concept may be. At the bottom of everyone's heart there is a knot, a delimitation, which determines how he looks upon Nondelimited Being and how he lives his life. Hence it is not necessary for a person "to believe in God" to have a belief; in the final analysis, every knot tied in the heart is a delimitation of the Nondelimited, hence a "belief" about Being or "Allāh".

The extent to which our belief corresponds to God as He is in Himself depends upon our capacity for knowledge. In other words, an individual's "preparedness" allows him to understand what he understands, just as it allows him to be receptive (*qābil*) toward the properties of Being's Names to a certain specific degree, no more and no less. The preparedness delimits knowledge, just as it delimits Being.[16] Hence Ibn al-ʿArabī speaks of God's "ontological" self-manifestation or self-disclosure (*tajallī*) to the entity, a self-disclosure that is delimited by the entity's preparedness; and he employs the same term to refer to the "epistemological" self-manifestation of God that is perceived for what it is by the saints through "unveiling" (*kashf*) and perceived by others in a form that is delimited and defined by their own beliefs. For example, he quotes the famous answer of Junayd when asked about knowledge and the knower:"The water takes on the color of its container."

> Junayd declared that the container has an effect upon what is contained. He wanted you to *know* whom you know. Then you will understand that you only judge your object of knowledge in terms of yourself. So you only know yourself. (III 161.24)

Since man knows only himself, he also believes only in himself, in the sense that his belief is determined and defined by his own conceptual limitations. And again, this depends totally upon his preparedness.

> God bestows preparedness, as indicated in His words, "He gave each thing its creation" (Koran 20: 50). Then He raises the veil between Himself and His servant, who sees Him in the form of his own belief; so God is identical with the servant's belief. Thus neither your heart nor your eye ever contemplates anything but the form of your own belief concerning God. (*Fuṣūṣ* 121; cf. *BW* 149)

Since the object of one's worship or service (*ʿibādah*) is determined by one's belief, one never worships anything but one's own fabrication.

> It is proper for the creatures to worship nothing but what they believe concerning God, so they worship a created thing .... There are none but idol worshippers. (IV 386.17)

If the precise content of an individual's belief is determined by his preparedness, this in turn is determined by a divine Name or Names.

> Each person who conceives of God is dominated by the property of one of God's Names. That Name discloses itself to him and bestows upon him his belief through the disclosure, without his knowing it. (II 58.14)

But God in Himself is nondelimited, "so He is far exalted above entering under the sway of delimitation or being restricted to one form or another" (II 85.21). True knowledge of God demands nondelimitation by any form or belief. Hence the "gnostics" (*al-ʿārifūn*), those saints who have perfect knowledge of things as they are, never deny God in any belief.

> The eye sees nothing but the God of belief, and clearly, beliefs are variegated. So he who delimits God denies Him in that which is other than his own delimi-

tation, while acknowledging Him only in the manner in which he delimits His self-disclosure. But he who frees Him from any delimitation will never deny Him and will acknowledge Him in every form in which He undergoes transmutations. (*Fuṣūṣ* 121; cf. *BW* 149)

Here Ibn al-ᶜArabī alludes to a well-known ḥadīth which is one of the scriptural bases for his teaching concerning the "God of belief" (*al-ilāh al-muᶜtaqad*). In a long description of the Day of Resurrection, the Prophet recounted how God will appear to people in various forms, each one of which will be denied. Finally, He will transmute Himself (*taḥawwul*) into a form which they will recognize as the object of their own belief, and only then will they acknowledge His lordship.[17] According to Ibn al-ᶜArabī, the "gnostics" grasp God's nondelimitation and therefore never deny His self-disclosure in any form; all others delimit Him and therefore deny Him in the forms that do not correspond to their particular brand of delimitation (III 410.17). In the next world, the ability of the gnostics to recognize every self-manifestation for what it is will place them in the highest levels of paradise.

Look at the levels of people in their knowledge of God: it is identical to their levels of vision of God on the Day of Resurrection.... So beware of delimiting yourself to a specific knot and disbelieving in everything else, lest you lose great good; indeed, you will lose knowledge of the situation as it is in itself. So be in your soul a *materia* for the forms of all beliefs, since Allāh is greater than that He should be confined by one knot rather than another. For He says, "Wheresoever you turn, there is the Face of Allāh" (Koran 2: 115), without mentioning one place rather than another. He mentioned that "there is the Face of Allāh," and the "face" of a thing is its reality. Through this He alerts the hearts of the gnostics, lest the accidental qualities of this world prevent them from becoming aware of something so precious. (*Fuṣūṣ* 113; cf. *BW* 137)

The great saints recognize the truth of every belief; they understand that every tying, every binding, every restriction, is necessarily a delimitation of Nondelimited Being ; it is based on the properties of the Face of God, whose self-disclosures are infinitely variegated and can be seen wherever we turn. In effect, the saints recognize that – from this point of view – the whole of existence represents the dance of possibilities, the self-manifestation of the Nondelimited in the forms of the infinite entities. Each thing is exactly what it must be; every belief demonstrates the scope of the believer's preparedness at the moment of belief. All things are on the Straight Path of Allāh; every thing obeys the engendering command, and each person possesses a belief that will take him to Allāh, the end of all paths. But the exact path of return to Allāh, who is named by every Name, will depend upon the specific Name that determines the belief.

He who makes Allāh "Time" (al-dahr), will attain to Him by means of His Name Time, for Allāh comprehends all Names.... When a person believes that He is Nature, He will disclose Himself to him as Nature. Whenever a person believes anything about Him, whatever it may be, He will disclose Himself to him in the form of that belief. (III 411.23)

Ibn al-ʿArabī encourages the seeker of God to expand his own beliefs in order to have a greater "share" (ḥaẓẓ) in the vision of God in the next world. Speaking of the beatific vision granted to the saints in paradise, he points out that its scope depends upon the variety of beliefs concerning God that they are able to encompass.

If a saint achieves all forms of belief, he will possess the shares of everyone. He will be in general bliss and will delight in the joy of every believer.... But if he limits himself to a thing single, his share will be in that to which he has limited himself, nothing more. (II 85.26)

The saints who realize all beliefs are known as the Folk of Allāh, since they witness God in respect of this all-compre-

hensive Name and contemplate His never-ending self-disclosures in respect of each one of the Names embraced by it.

It is incumbent upon the Folk of Allāh to know the
doctrine (ʿilm) concerning God of every sect (niḥlah)
and every religion (millah), so that they can contemplate Him in every form and never stand in the position
of denial. For He permeates existence, so none denies
Him but someone who is delimited. But the Folk of
Allāh follow Him whose folk they are, so His property
flows over them. And His property is the lack of delimitation, for He possesses all-pervading Being; so His folk
possess all-pervading vision. When someone delimits
His Being, he delimits his own vision of Him; such a
one is not of the Folk of Allāh. (III 161. 14)

All beliefs – i.e., all views that delimit and define Nondelimited Being in any way whatsoever – are true; all of them
"lead to Allāh," since this Name comprehends all other
Names. In this respect there is no difference between the
belief of the world's greatest theologian and that of a mad
man. But not all beliefs lead to human perfection or to
immediate felicity in the next world, since any belief, by
definition, delimits the object of belief and thereby restricts
the share of the believer in the vision of Nondelimited Being.
If the delimitation follows the guidance of revelation, then
the Names which define the delimited object of belief will be
Names of Mercy that draw the believer in the direction of
unity, harmony, and equilibrium and result in felicity after
death; but if the delimitation rejects the proffered guidance
and instead follows the confining view of the individual, the
Names ruling over the situation will be Names of Wrath that
will result in disequilibrium, dispersion, disintegration, and
wretchedness.

The gnostics or Folk of Allāh accept the truth of every
belief, yet they walk upon the Path of the Beneficent, or
more specifically, the Path of Muḥammad, since these paths
provide the means to integration and unity, or to a fuller

share of the vision of God. In other words, they "believe" in all religions and all constructions of the human mind, but they have "faith" only in God as He has revealed Himself to mankind through a particular prophet; their "practice," therefore, is based totally upon prophetic practice, and more specifically, upon the practice of Muḥammad, whose way is viewed as embracing the ways of all the prophets.

The gnostics' understanding that all beliefs are true is intimately connected to their vision with the "eye of the heart" that all existent things are controlled by the engendering command. In no way does their acceptance of all beliefs negate their understanding that all men are called to follow the prescriptive command, since there is no other path to felicity. This is why Ibn al-ʿArabī writes,

> It is incumbent upon you to practice the worship of God set down by revelation and established by tradition (al-samʿ) ... "So worship thy Lord" who is described in revelation "until certainty comes to thee" (Koran 15: 99). Then the veil will be lifted and your sight will be piercing (cf. Koran 50: 22). (III 311. 23)

Ibn al-ʿArabī summarizes this whole discussion in a passage that explains some of the properties of the divine Name "He who sends forth" (al-Bāʿith), the verbal root of which is employed repeatedly in the Koran to refer to God's activity in "sending forth" the prophets. The disbelievers, he says, were not totally mistaken in "taking to themselves other gods apart from Allāh" (Koran 19: 81):

> Nothing made them do this except a correct principle: They saw a diversity of opinion concerning Allāh, in spite of the general agreement on His Unity, or on the fact that He is one and that there is no other god but He; so they differed as to what this God is. Each person with a theory spoke of what his theory led him to; it became established that "God" is He who possesses this property. What he did not know is that this "God" was nothing but his own fabrication. Hence he

only worshipped and believed in a God created by himself .... Then the people differed widely, though the Single Thing does not differ in Itself.... Since this was the situation, they were easily induced to take stones, trees, planets, animals, and other such creations as their gods, each group and follower of a doctrine about God doing this in accordance with the views that dominated over him..... So man created in himself that which he worships and about which he judges.

But Allāh is the Judge; He cannot be restricted by intellect, nor can judgements be made about Him. Rather, His is the command in His creation, from before and behind. There is no god but He, the God and Master of all things....

Now Allāh is "He who sends forth," so He sends forth the messengers – thoughts – to peoples' minds (*bāwāṭin*) and they speak in accordance with these messengers and believe in them. In the same way, He sends forth the messengers known as "prophets" to the outside world.... So the intelligent person is he who abandons what he has in himself concerning God for that which has come from God concerning God. If that which the prophets have brought agrees with what the thought-messengers have brought to their minds, so be it – and let them thank God for the agreement. But if any difference appears, it is incumbent upon you to follow the outside messenger. Beware of being led astray by the messengers within the mind! Then you will attain to felicity, God willing. This is a piece of advice from me to every receptive person who possesses a sound intellect. "And say, 'My Lord! Increase me in knowledge!'" (Koran 20: 114). (IV 279.7)

Summary and Conclusion

True Being, or God, is one in Itself and many in Its self-manifestations. The cosmos as a whole – "that which is other

than God" – in the totality of its spatial and temporal exten-
tion, is Being's self-manifestation, while the innumerable
existents encompassed by the cosmos represent the differen-
tiated deployment of the One Being's ontological possibilities; the universal categories of these possibilities are referred to as the "Divine Names". By virtue of its existence,
each thing follows the engendering command, and in this
respect everything is exactly what it must be.

A human being is no different from any other existent in
respect of the engendering command. Every person follows
the "Straight Path of Allāh" whether he wants to or not, since
he is created by God. But in virtue of being made upon
God's form, a human being is given life, intelligence, free
will, power, and speech, attributes that manifest directly the
primary Names of God. Since each person possesses these attributes, he has no choice but to employ them in his everyday life, in effect accepting responsibility for the consequences. Every sane person knows that his actions have re-
percussions and that he would be wise to exercise a certain
care in managing his affairs. But human possibilities go
infinitely beyond the parameters of those perfections that
can be actualized without divine guidance; hence the engendering command brings the prescriptive command into existence, even though God is fully aware that not everyone
will follow it. Indeed, if everyone did follow it, one of the
purposes of its existence – to populate hell – would be
nullified.[18]

Felicity and wretchedness are two human possibilities that
go back to the domination of certain divine Names in human beings, especially Mercy and Wrath, or Guidance and
Misguidance. Which one will dominate depends ultimately
on the preparedness of the individual, i.e., the capacity of his
immutable entity to act as a receptacle for the properties of
the divine Names. Since the entities are fixed for all eternity,
God does not intervene in a person's destiny, except to
bestow existence when his preparedness demands it. This is

why Ibn al-ᶜArabī can say, "No one possesses in himself anything from God, nor does he have anything from other than
himself" (*Fuṣūṣ* 66; cf. *BW* 69); or again, writing of the
human situation in the next world, whether wretched or
felicitous: "Let them blame none but themselves and let
them praise none but themselves: 'God's is the conclusive
argument' (Koran 6: 149) through His Knowledge of them
[as immutable entities]" (*Fuṣūṣ* 96; cf. *BW* 115).

Ibn al-ᶜArabī is not asking people to be fatalistic, quite the
contrary; he wants to show why the prescriptive command
must be followed, even though God's Will shall be done.
Human freedon is real on its own level and must be utilized
to that extent. In particular, we are free to expand our
limited beliefs concerning God; this is why the Koran commands us to pray, "My Lord, increase me in knowledge!"
(20:14). The way in which we may actively seek an increase in
knowledge corresponds to the way set down by the prescriptive command. Again, God says in the Koran, "I have not
created the jinn and men except to serve/worship Me"
(51:56), and the commentators agree that here by service or
worship of God is meant gaining knowledge of Him. In the
same way the Koran commands, "Serve/worship God, until
certainty comes to thee" (15: 99). Worship, service, knowledge, certainty, felicity – all are actualized through following
the prophetic way.

If it is true that we worship nothing but our own belief, yet
it is also true that beliefs, which are the products of our
thoughts – the "inward messengers" – can be shaped and
refined through following the outward messengers, and eventually a person may be put into harmony with the Mercy that
results in felicity. Depending upon the divine guidance provided by revelation leads to an opening up of the soul toward
the mercy and grace that transform and make whole; rejection of the guidance and mercy that are offered means
cutting oneself off from the Names of Mercy and turning
oneself over to the Names of Wrath, which bar the way to
human wholeness and condemn the soul to wretchedness.

Though this essay has barely begun the task of uncovering those aspects of Ibn al-ᶜArabī's teachings that have a direct bearing upon the nature of prophecy and revelation, perhaps enough has been said to warrant a few brief conclusions. It was remarked at the outset that the Koran views revelation as a phenomenon both universal and particular. Every community has received a celestial message that is essentially the same in each case though different in outward details, the implication being that every revealed religion is true. Ibn al-ᶜArabī's purpose in writing about religious diversity is only to demonstrate why the Koranic view should be what it is.

One way to understand the implications of Ibn al-ᶜArabī's position is to place him within the context of the contemporary study of religion. Let us imagine that he were to apply his view of revelation to the current academic scene. He would probably note immediately that, broadly speaking, today's scholars take one of two approaches to the question of the "truth" of the religions. One group, who might be called the "absolutists", have firmly tied the knot of their own belief in the form of a specific religion, sect, or school of thought; there is only one true way; all others are in error or at best represent imperfect approximations of the one true path. At the other extreme, the "relativists" have loosened the knot of everyone else's belief, saying that each religion and sect presents a valid point of view, so we must abandon any notion of absolute truth. The absolutists usually conclude that, since there is only one true perspective, there cannot be any "unity" among the religions. The relativists in contrast tend to view all religions as basically the same, which generally amounts to saying that none of them has any ultimate claim to truth.

If one can presume to suggest how Ibn al-ᶜArabī might reply to these two points of view, it may be fair to say that he would agree with each on certain points and disagree on others. While agreeing with the absolutists that there is only one road to felicity, Ibn al-ᶜArabī would immediately qualify this by pointing out that the uniqueness of the path relates to the individual, not to the path itself; in other words, what makes the way "one" and therefore uniquely important is the absolute demands a religion makes upon its followers. These demands cannot be met except by total dedication to a single way.

Ibn al-ᶜArabī would agree with the absolutists that the religions represent a vast array of diverse and often conflicting beliefs and practices, but he would reject any suggestion that only one of the religions is true. The whole question of "truth," he would suggest, needs to be reexamined, since there are a number of points of view from which it can be envisaged.[19] In relation to the engendering command, every perspective is "true," since every definition delimits the Nondelimited in some manner or another, and in respect of being delimitations or "knots", all are equivalent; every formulation is valid in some respect, or else it would not exist. What is of fundamental importance is to determine the "respect" in which we want to consider a perspective. In order to judge among different formulations, we must choose some specific attribute or definable standard against which "truth" and "falsehood" can be gauged; the Absolute as such cannot be defined or conceived, since it is "no thing". Hence an absolute "some thing" is needed which can act as a point of reference. For example, we can ask which point of reference – which "relative absolute"[20] – is adequate to provide a valid formulation for the nature of "material existence" considered as an independent, self-sufficient object; and to this we might answer that the "scientific method" provides the necessary criterion for truth. "Truth," then, is the measure of conformity to some standard of reference which plays the role of an absolute. For Ibn al-ᶜArabī, the standard for truth judgements in matters of religious import must be the prescriptive command: That religion or perspective within a religion is "true" which guides us to felicity. There will be both true and false perspectives, since not every finger points at the moon. Moreover, among true perspectives some will take to a greater felicity than others, just as some will provide a more perfect image of the goal. The value of the perspective lies not only in the extent to which it is able to grasp the true human situation and to delineate the goal in accordance with the prescriptive command, but also in its ability to take the individual to the goal that it delineates. Truth works hand in hand with practice.

It needs to be emphasized that there cannot be a single "true" perspective that would preclude the existence of other true perspectives. The reason for this may be said to be the vast diversity of human capacities and "preparednesses" (*isti'dād*), or the plurality of the divine Names, which comes down to the same thing. "The water assumes the color of its container," said Junayd, and one of the meanings of this statement is that "We have sent no messenger save with the tongue of his people" (Koran 14:4). The necessity for diverse formulations of the truth is proven historically by the great number of prophets sent by God, not to speak of the diversity of perspectives within each religion.[21] In short, Ibn al-ʿArabī sees religious diversity as an intrinsic attribute of reality; religions must differ because of the plurality of the Names, or because of the "relations" (*nisab*) that exist between God and His prophets, or God and the world.

To turn to the relativist position, Ibn al-ʿArabī would agree that there are many ways and that "all religions are one," but he would immediately qualify this second statement. Religions are certainly not one on the level of form, rather on the level of the ultimate source of the religions (i.e., the prescriptive command as such, and beyond that, the Divine Essence). They are also one in that each attempts in its own way to actualize the unlimited potentialities of human nature; each represents a self-delimitation of the Nondelimited with a view toward dissolving privative human qualities and opening the "divine image" up to the Infinite Being from which it derives.

Finally, Ibn al-ᶜArabī would reject categorically the relativist idea that there is no such thing as absolute truth. The Essence – God Himself – is by definition the Absolute, and "Truth" (al-Ḥaqq) is His Name, one that Ibn al-ᶜArabī, like many Muslim authorities, often uses interchangeably with "Allāh". If the Absolute Truth which is Allāh demands that all paths lead to It – just as they derive from It as a result of the engendering command – It also demands that certain paths take on an absolute value in relation to man's felicity. Hence the Path of the Beneficent becomes an absolute standard by which the truth of human beliefs can be judged. The existence of a perspective or a belief – brought about by the engendering command – does not prove its "truth", since truth and validity depend upon providing the means to actualize human felicity. Ibn al-ᶜArabī would insist upon the existence of objective criteria for discerning between truth and error; these two must be defined in terms of felicity and therefore in terms of revelation, the only means at our disposal through which to grasp the full extent of human possibilities.

In short, there is an Absolute Truth – the Essence, It-ness, True Being – that stands beyond all possibilities of formulation but which nevertheless makes possible valid formulations of a "relatively absolute" truth through Its own self-revelation, i.e., the prescriptive command. The Absolute Truth as such cannot be defined, yet Its revealed expressions take upon an absolute value for human beings. The followers of the different revealed religions are justified in looking upon their own perspectives and ways as absolute and unique, since in fact, for its followers, each way is the only means to achieve felicity.

Thus Ibn al-ᶜArabī would choose a middle path between the extreme positions of the absolutists and the relativists. He would affirm the existence of Absolute Truth but deny the possibility of providing a formulation of Its nature adequate in every respect. He would affirm the absolute necessity of the prescriptive command for attaining to human felicity, but deny that that command could be revealed only in a single form. He would affirm the existence of both truth and error in human beliefs while judging among them on the basis of the prescriptive command. Finally he would maintain that truth is inseparable from practice; no matter how adequate a given formulation of the nature of human felicity might be, it must be accompanied by a means of realization to have any lasting value.

[1] This verse, which is preceded by the words, "And We sent never a messenger before thee except that We revealed to him, saying...", corresponds to the first half of the Muslim testimony of faith (*al-shahādah*): "There is no god but God." The particularity of revelations pertains to the domain of the second half of the testimony: "Muḥammad is the messenger of God."

[2] Koran 2: 285. Cf., e.g., 2: 136, 3: 84, 4: 150-152; 3: 3, 9: 42, 46: 12.

[3] For a survey of the various perspectives of Muslim authorities on the significance of other religions, see S.H. Nasr, "Islam and the Encounter of Religions," in his *Sufi Essays*, Albany: State University of New York Press, 1989, pp. 123-151 (also published as *Living Sufism*).

[4] On the importance of Ibn al-ʿArabī, see Nasr, *Three Muslim Sages*, Cambridge: Harvard University Press, 1964, chapter 3. Cf. W. Chittick, *The Sufi Path of Knowledge: Ibn al-ʿArabī's Metaphysics of Imagination*, Albany: SUNY Press, 1989. See also H. Corbin, *Creative Imagination in the Ṣufism of Ibn ʿArabī*, Princeton: Princeton University Press, 1969; T. Izutsu, *Sufism and Taoism*, Tokyo: Iwanami Shoten, 1983.

[5] In his study of the 850 works attributed to Ibn al-ʿArabī, Osman Yahia concluded that about 700 of these are authentic and 400 are extant (*Histoire et classification de l'oeuvre d'Ibn ʿArabī*, 2 vols., Damascus: Institut Français de Damas, 1964). A single work, *al-Futūḥāt al-makkiyyah*, contains 2580 pages in the old edition. Each volume of

the critical edition, which began appearing in 1973, contains about 500 pages of text; at the present rate, 37 volumes or 18,500 pages will be needed to publish the full text of the old edition.

[6] Cf. Chittick, *The Sufi Path of Knowledge,* Chapter Two.

[7] References are indicated as follows: Roman numerals refer to the volume number of Ibn al-ᶜArabī's *al-Futūḥāt al-makkiyyah,* Arabic numerals to the page and line numbers. *Fuṣūṣ* refers to Ibn al-ᶜArabī's *Fuṣūṣ al-ḥikam* (ed. ᶜA. ᶜAfifi, Beirut: Dār al-Kitāb al-ᶜArabī, 1946) and *BW* to its translation by R.W.J. Austin, *Ibn al-ᶜArabī: The Bezels of Wisdom,* New York: Paulist Press, 1980).

[8] *Huwiyyah* is usually translated as Ipseity or He-ness. "It-ness" may better express the nonspecificity that the Arabic term conveys. On the fact that the term is more general and all-embracing than the Name Allāh, cf. III 514.22.

[9] Since the referent of the two terms is the same, one cannot claim that the Essence is "beyond Allāh" (II 42.35), unless Allāh is defined in the specific context as referring only to the Names and Attributes of God, not to God in Himself.

[10] Cf. Chittick, "'God surrounds all Things': An Islamic Perspective on the Environment," *The World and I,* 6, June 1986, pp. 671-78.

[11] This is an allusion to a ḥadīth found in both al-Bukhārī and Muslim: "Faith has seventy-some branches, the most excellent of which is the declaration, 'There is no god but God,' and the least of which is the removal of what is harmful from the road." Cf. J. Robson (tr.), *Mishkāt al-maṣābīḥ,* Lahore: Sh. Muhammad Ashraf, 1963-66, p. 6.

[12] Cf. Chittick, "Death and the World of Imagination: Ibn al-ᶜArabī's Eschatology," *Muslim World,* 78, 1988, pp. 51-82.

[13] The ḥadīth is found in Muslim. Cf. Robson, *Mishkāt al-maṣābīḥ,* p. 494.

[14] According to Ibn al-ᶜArabī, there are two kinds of mercy (*raḥmah*), referred to respectively in two divine Names derived from the same root, the All-Merciful (*al-Raḥmān*) and the All-Compassionate (*al-Raḥīm*), Names which are found in the Muslim formula of consecration: "In the Name of Allāh, the All-Merciful, the All-Compassionate." Since the Name All-Merciful is taken as practically synonymous with Allāh (cf. Koran 17: 110), the Mercy of the All-Merciful – also called the Mercy of Gratuitous Gift (*imti'nān*) – corresponds to the engendering command; hence it is showered

down upon all creatures without restraint; it is the mercy that "embraces All things." The second kind of Mercy – the Mercy of the All-Compassionate or of Necessity (*wujūb*) – correlates with the prescriptive command, since it can only be actualized by following revelation. It is referred to in the Koranic verse, "I shall write it [i.e., Mercy] down for those who are godfearing and pay the alms..., those who follow the messenger" (7: 156). Cf. Chittick, "Ibn ᶜArabī's own Summary of the *Fuṣūṣ:* 'The Imprint of the Bezels of Wisdom,'" *Journal of the Muhyiddin Ibn ᶜArabi Society*, I, 1982, p. 62.

[15] Most Muslim theologians, not just Sufis, maintain that hell cannot be eternal. "In general it can be said that the non-eternity of the Fire has prevailed as the understanding of the Muslim community, supported by al-'Ashari's opinion that punishment is not of unlimited duration" (J.I. Smith and Y.Y. Haddad, *The Islamic Understanding of Death and Resurrection*, Albany: SUNY Press, 1981, p. 95). For Ibn al-ᶜArabī's explanation of this point, see Chittick, "Death and the World of Imagination."

[16] The essential identity of knowledge and existence is often discussed by Ibn al-ᶜArabī. For example, "The root of the world (*al-ᶜālam*) is ignorance, while knowledge is acquired; for knowledge is existence, and existence belongs to Allāh; but ignorance is nonexistence, and nonexistence belongs to the world" (III 160.21).

[17] See Muslim, *al-Ṣaḥīḥ, kitāb al-imān*, no.302 (Cairo: Muhammad ᶜAlī Ṣabīḥ, 1334/1916, I, pp. 114-117). Cf. *al-Futūḥāt*, I 314.1, II 311.25.

[18] Ibn al-ᶜArabī refers to this connection between hell and the prescriptive command with his words, "If not for the existence of the religions, there would be no disbelief in God resulting in wretchedness. Therefore God, says, 'We never chastise until We send forth a messenger' (Koran 17:15)." (II 248.3)

[19] Ibn al-ᶜArabī's works are often structured on a principle that might be called that of "perspective shift." Each Divine Name or prophetic logos establishes a distinct perspective with its own standards for judging truth and error, differing in certain respects from other perspectives. Thus his *Fuṣūṣ al-ḥikam* ("Bezels of Wisdom") deals in 27 chapters with as many different prophetic logoi and the corresponding divine Attributes. If it be asked which perspective allows a person to see the shifting perspectives, the answer would have to be the perspective of the Name Allāh, which

corresponds to that of the Prophet Muḥammad, the most perfect
of the Perfect Men. To attain to the Prophet's perspective, a person
must be his inheritor (wārith), and Ibn al-ᶜArabī clearly implies that
he himself is the last inheritor of the totality of the sciences and
spiritual degrees of the Prophet – hence his allusions to the "Seal of
Muḥammadan Sanctity".

[20] This term is not contradictory, as Frithjof Schuon has shown
repeatedly in his writings (e.g., Stations of Wisdom, London: John
Murray, 1961, p. 27).

[21] Ibn al-ᶜArabī divides human understandings into three basic
types and shows how the Koran has verses aimed specifically at each
type: Some people understand God as Nondelimited, others cannot
gain any knowledge of Him unless they delimit Him by attributes
that preclude temporality and guarantee His absolute Perfection,
and still others cannot gain knowledge of Him without delimiting
Him by the attributes of temporality and conceiving Him within
the constraints of time, place, limitation, and measure. Hence God
sent down the religions in accordance with these three levels of
understanding. "God revealed 'Nothing is like Him' (Koran 42:
11), and this is directed at those who know Him as Nondelimited.
For those who delimit Him with the attributes of Perfection, He
revealed such verses as: 'God is powerful over everything, and God
encompasses everything in knowledge' (65: 12); 'He does what He
desires' (85:16); 'He is the All-Hearing, the All-Seeing' (17: 1);
'God, there is no god but He, the Living, the Everlasting' (2: 254);
'Grant him protection till he hears the Word of God' (9: 6); 'He
knows all things' (2: 29). Then God also sent down the verses: 'The
All-Merciful sat upon the Throne' (20:5); 'He is with you wherever
you are' (57: 4); 'He is God in the heavens and in the earth' (6: 3);
'And We bore Noah upon a well-planked vessel, well caulked,
running before Our eyes' (54: 14); 'Had We desired to take to Us a
diversion, We would have taken it from Ourselves' (21: 17). In such
manner the revelations embrace that which is demanded by the
constitutions of the world's inhabitants. So the believer is always
one of these three types, except for the perfect human being, for
he embraces all these beliefs and knows their origins and contexts"
(II 219.30).

I The Synderesis

St. Albert the Great

Questio LXXI (De Synderesi) from the *Summa Theologiae* of St. Albertus Magnus, *O.P.*

II The Synderesis

Dom M. Prummer, O.P.

extracted from his
Manuale Theologiae Moralis secudum principia Sancti Thomae Aquinatis

two translations from the Latin by
Rama P. Coomaraswamy

Introductory Comments

A few years ago Mr. Frithjof Schuon invited me to write an article on synderesis from the Catholic point of view. Circumstances did not allow me immediately to fulfill this request. However it remained very much in my mind and various items were gathered together with this end in view.

It is now a great pleasure for me to offer to the present *Festschrift* the following two translations from the Latin relating to the synderesis. The first and longer one, beginning on page 93, is taken from the *Summa Theologiae* of St. Albert the Great. It is a seminal article because it summarizes scholastic opinion on the synderesis up to the twelfth century, and because St. Albert was not only the teacher of St. Thomas Aquinas, but also, in all likelihood, the teacher of (and certainly, at a minimum, a strong influence on) Meister Eckhart. The second translation, on page 108, is of an extract on the synderesis from the *Manuale theologiae moralis secundum principia Sancti Thomas Aquinatis* which was published in 1927 by Dom M. Prummer, O.P. This was a standard text on moral theology up to the time of Vatican II.

I should like to thank Father E. Urquhart for helping me with and for correcting these translations.

Both translations are now offered to Mr. Schuon with my very deepest respect.

Rama P. Coomaraswamy

FIRST TRANSLATION

The Synderesis by St. Albert the Great

Questio LXXI (De Synderesi) froom the *Summa Theologiae* of St. Albertus Magnus, O.P.

ARTICLE I

The nature and definition of Synderesis.

The first question is what is the nature and definition of synderesis?

We shall proceed in the following manner:

1) According to St. Basil, in his commentary on the beginning of the Book of Proverbs, "as we understand, there is a natural power of judgement in the soul, by means of which we discriminate between good and evil. This is a habit of the soul which is placed there naturally and is an instinctive power of judgement. And if this quality is cultivated by penetrating study, the person will have a right and equitable power of judgement and discretion." From this we can accept three things with regard to Synderesis, of which the first is the definition, that is to say, Synderesis is a virtue which the soul has grafted in it naturally, an instinctive power of judging by means of which we distinguish good from evil. Secondly, this judgement is natural to the soul. And thirdly, it is a power of the soul, and not, as some people say, a habit.

Some may say that we are speaking of reason and not of Synderesis. CONTRA: Against this I say that reason does not have the natural capability of judgement, but rather of investigation as has been shown previously. Similarly reason does not have the seeds of justice placed in it naturally, but rather learns from custom and the teachings of prudence.

2) Also, the blessed St. Augustine upholds the teaching that Synderesis is a power of the soul, on which he says, the universal law is naturally written in order that we might judge naturally. He calls this natural judgement Synderesis. Therefore as this habit is a habit only *in potentia* and is in the power of the soul, Synderesis will be a certain power of the soul.

3) Also, The Gloss of St. Jerome on Ezechiel 1:10 states "a great many hold that according to Plato, a soul is either rational, irascible, or concupiscent, which he calls logixon, thomixon and epithomixon and refers to these respectively as man-like, lion-like, and bull-like. That part of the soul which is rational and understanding, which deals with thinking and deliberation, and the strength and wisdom of them all, are situated in the organ (lit: arch) of the brain. Fierceness, anger and violence are qualities of the lion which are situated in the gall. Further, libido and luxury and all sorts of voluptuousness and cupidity are seated in the liver, which is symbolized by the bull who is used for heavy farm work. There is a fourth aspect of the soul, which is above these three and independent of them. The Greeks call this *sundereson*, which is that spark of conscience in Cain which could not be extinguished from his being (lit: chest). It is this that causes us, when overcome by pleasure or anger, or even sometimes by the appearance of acceptive reasons, to feel ourselves to have fallen into sin. And this aspect is appropriately assigned to the eagle and is not to be confused with the other three but is for the correction of their errors. "We can learn four things about Synderesis from this commentary. First, that it is a power of the soul distinct from reason, irascibility and concupisence. In this way of seeing things, reason includes knowledge, understanding, deliberation and wisdom; irascibility includes fierceness, anger and violence; and concupiscence includes libido, luxury and all aspects of the desire for voluptuousness. By this we have a

means of means of knowing of what genus Synderesis is: it is a power of the soul. The second is that Synderesis is the scintilla or spark of the conscience, and because a spark is always mixed up with a fire from which it naturally comes, we know that this power is not without its habit, as was said above on the authority of Basil. The third is that this alone among the four aspects of the soul is without an organ of any kind in the manner in which reason is placed in the brain, irascibility in the gall and concupiscence in the liver. For it is both outside and above these three. The fourth: that this power is in no way mixed with the other powers that move the soul, but is for the correction of mistakes in them.

4) Up to this point it is clear that this power of the soul is primary among the four. And this brings us to another statement of St. Jerome, namely that "Synderesis is that spirit which pleads for us with indescribable groans. For no one knows what things are in a man, unless it be the spirit which is in him. Hence Paul says 'May the God of peace himself sanctify you in all things; that your whole spirit and soul and body may be preserved blameless in the coming of our Lord Jesus Christ'"(1 Thessal., 5:23). It is proved then that this spirit (Synderesis) is a power of the soul.

5) Also, just as there is a force in us which always distorts and inclines us towards evil, which is the evil inclination of our senses, so also there is opposed to this always something present in us which inclines us to good and whispers to us to abandon evil, and this will be the power of the soul which is Synderesis. Therefore Synderesis is indeed a power of the soul.

6) Also, as we said in an earlier section, of that part of the intellect that deals with ideas (theories), there is the intellect which is always *in actu* and is always active and is called the active intellect. And this active intellect has for its object knowable truth. So also, out of the part of [us which is the seat] of motives there ought to be some similar power of the soul that has as its object the good of action. But this is not

reason which can on occasion be deceived. Therefore it will be Synderesis which is above reason.

If the above is conceded, Synderesis is a power of the soul. Against this, however, (the following points can be made):

1) Synderesis, according to its own name, means a certain cleaving to the knowledge of good and evil: for it is composed of two words in Greek, *sun* and *aerisis* which means an opinion or knowledge adhered to in some manner by means of reason. Therefore, it would seem that Synderesis is, according to its name, a habit rather than a power.

2) Also, if that which always inclines us towards evil is a habit, which is called *fomes* (*corruptio fomes*, the inclination towards evil that results from original sin), there is opposing it a habit which always inclines us towards goods. Now this opposing force is Synderesis. It follows that Synderesis is a habit.

3) Again, the deliberating will which is free will has two options: One from the lower part inclining towards evil which is the *fomes* (mentioned above), and the other from the superior part which assists us in doing good. And this latter is Synderesis. Now, since nothing helps on or hinders a power unless it be a habit, Synderesis is a habit.

If, on account of what has been said, it is demonstrated that Synderesis is without doubt a habit, then we must ask if it is one or several habits or the joining together of several powers.

It would seem that Synderesis is the same as the practical intellect. (*Editor's note:* It seems that the thesis here advanced is that Synderesis in itself is a power, but when joined to reason or intellect, can be considered a habit.)

1) In previous discussions we have seen that the Philosophers hold and teach that the practical intellect is always correct. But since this quality is attributed to Synderesis, and those things which are the same are the same in subtance, it seems that Synderesis is the same as the practical intellect.

2) The Philosophers reasonably do not hold the moving power towards good to be by means of understanding or judgement, unless it be in the practical intellect or reason. Insofar as such a power of the soul is Synderesis, this Synderesis will be a power of the practical intellect or reason.

3) Also, the same St. Jerome uses the words of the Apostle in chapter 5 of I Thessalonians, verse 23, "The whole of your spirit and soul" etc., as being about Synderesis. But the same Gloss states that the word "spirit" is used for the word "reason". Therefore Synderesis is reason.

4) Also, the same Gloss says that the Apostle in the previous quotation specified three things: spirit, soul and body, which is to say that by which we understand, that by which we live, and that by which we are seen and touched. Therefore Synderesis is that by which we understand. But that by which we understand is the intellect: therefore Synderesis is the intellect.

5) Also, it is commonly said that Synderesis is signified by that man in the Book of Job who alone escaped destruction (the falling in of the house over Job's children) and returned to tell Job what he had suffered. And in his commentary on this text, St. Gregory says that only one man escaped, that is, that the rational judgement returns to the soul and tells it all the things it has lost, in order that the soul, its mind considering what it has lost, would accept affliction. Therefore Synderesis which renounces evil would seem to be [the same as] reason.

6) The saints ennumerate the motive powers of the soul and only point out three, irascibility, concupiscence and rationality. Therefore it would seem that Synderesis, if it is a motivating power, and if it is a not to be found in concupiscence and irascibility, must be found in reason.

CONTRA: Against these: we have the authority of St. Jerome that Synderesis is outside of and above, and in no way mixed with these three, but corrects errors in them. Therefore Synderesis is neither reason nor intellect.

7) Further: It seems that Synderesis is not a single power but several: for judging and desiring are not of the same power: Synderesis however judges actions and desires the good. Therefore it would not seem to be a single power.

8) Synderesis rises up (rebels) against evil which action seems to be irascibility. Now rising up, desiring and judging do not seem to be the same power, so that Synderesis would seem to be, not one, but three powers.

9) Further: It would seem that Synderesis is a certain uniting of all the superior powers of the soul. For when mankind was corrupted by sin in his natural powers, he was not corrupted to that degree that nothing remained intact. Therefore in each of the powers something upright remained which in judgement and appetites was consistent with the primal rectitude in which man was created (i.e., before the fall) : and in this manner he has an inner murmuring against everything which is not upright. Now this is the office of Synderesis in man. Synderesis is that which holds to recti- tude in each of the virtues and their being maintained in accord with primal rectitude.

In conjunction with this we can also ask why, up to now, no Philosopher has placed Synderesis within the motive powers of the soul when many saints have done so.

SOLUTION: Without pre-judgement, I say that Synder- esis is a special power of the soul in which, according to St. Augustine, the universal law is inscribed, just as in specula- tive matters there are principles (axioms) and a hierarchy of values. A man does not learn these for they are in him by his very nature and help him to learn what is true. So also with regard to things which have to be done, there are also universals which direct us in works by which the practical intellect is helped to distinguish good and evil in moral matters, and these a man does not learn, but are, according to St. Jerome, a natural law written on the spirit of man; and as Augustine says, a universal law, such as one should not engage in fornication or murder, or that one should have compassion in the face of affliction, and so forth. And all this is the subject of Synderesis, and for this reason St. Augustine called it a natural court of law – in Greek, Synderesis – to which universal and infallible judgement adheres, and about which it is not deceived. And this is what the eagle is meant to signify in Ezechiel, for it sees things which are on high – that is, in accord with divine justice. However it does not apply this to particular issues, for that is the function of reason. Just as in speculative matters it is the intellect which deals with axioms, in it is reason which orders these principles in syllogisms for the purpose of reaching conclusions, a truly universal knowledge.

Against the first and second points: I say, first of all, that Synderesis is truly a power of the soul, but that what St. Basil said is to be noted, that in it is placed the seed of justice and the universal natural law and that it will always be upright, if this mode of justice, that is to say, of power, is cultivated with erudition. It behooves us to apply this universal law by means of positive law to particulars. Positive law is discoverd in particular cases by reason.

The same argument makes the solution to the second point clear.

Against the third point: on the authority of St. Jerome it is said that in truth Synderesis is a power of the principles of natural law joined with a habit, and it is called the spark of the conscience, and that this conscience results from the joining together of Synderesis and reason, and that as far as Synderesis is concerned, error is impossible, though it is possible to be received on the part of reason. And this will be explained better in what follows in the questions on conscience. Now when St. Jerome says that reason and wisdom reside in the brain, it is not to be understood that he is implying that reason is there as in an organ, but in the way spoken of above, namely that the power from which reason comes is situated there such as is the situation with the imagination and the ability to form phantasms. In a similar manner, concupiscence is placed in liver, not because it is said that the liver is the organ of concupiscence in the sense that it has the power of direction, but because the complex of the liver joins the appetite in act – it is the warmth and humidity of the liver that is involved. The warmth pulls the appetite along and the humidity retains it. Similarly, the power of irascibility does not reside in the gall (gall bladder) as an organ, but the complex of the bile brings anger to a head because of its warmth and dryness. This is why it is said of St. Damascene that in him the bile was evaporated. Heat in many ways moves the spirit and the blood, and dryness strongly attracts the species of annoyance.

Against points four and five: again it is said that Synderesis is a spirit in so far as as it is said to be a spirit... [*the Latin here is unclear probably due to a printing error.*] The word spirit however is used in various senses as is explained above in the questions dealing with imagination.

Against point six: To this it can be objected that Synderesis is a habit, though it is said, not a simple habit, but rather a power connected with a habit

And by this the solution to the three objections which would characterize Synderesis as (only) a habit are made clear. A power of itself does not necessarily help a power or incline it to lean towards the good, while a power in conjunction with a habit does so help and incline.

And with regard to the question as to whether Synderesis is the same as the intellect or reason.

It is said that the intellect is considered in two different ways, generally and particularly. Generally: in respect to all the powers of the rational soul which move with cognition and here Synderesis is part of this, Particularly: here a distinction is made between Synderesis and the intellect. This is because Synderesis is concerned only with universal principles. Reason deals with parts, putting things together (as in a syllogism) while intellect does not put things together (i.e. grasps the truth directly). In a similar manner, reason, as it is commonly understood by the saints, accepts for all powers that move with understanding. This is explained in a special way by St. Augustine: he divides reason into a superior part and an inferior part according to the distinction between wisdom and knowledge, as is said above. In the former, reason is under the motion of Synderesis, and in the latter it is not.

From this, the solution is clear against all those who object that Synderesis is part of reason or the intellect.

Against the seventh objection: as to whether Synderesis is a single power or several.

I answer that it is one. It can be said that Synderesis is the desire for good which it judges, and this judgment is always in a universal manner. But desire as such is not determined and when it is attracted to evil this will be by means of the senses and not by rebellion or anger. For there is no power to move without desire, for which reason the Philosopher says that the intellect moves in proportion to its appetite, and by means of this appetite. But this appetite is not for a particular thing but a general appetite affecting all movement.

The eighth objection: against this it can be said that rebellion against evil is irascibility. Now when reason finds a given thing to be evil and moves the entire body to repel it, this is not the same as Synderesis as has already been said.

The ninth objection. There is yet this last question, whether Synderesis is a joining together all the powers.

I answer no. One can say that not all men are completely corrupted. Nevertheless corruption is so far distant from being integrity that corruption is the beginning of sin and acts without integrity. Corruption could never be the effect of principle; therefore efficiency in act is an imperfect power, touched with corruption. Synderesis however is a special part of the soul much higher than all the others and far removed from the corruption of original sin (*fomes*). And being so far separated from corruption, it cannot be van-

quished. For all these reasons, there are those who say that Synderesis is part of the primal rectitude in all men.

And there is one final question, namely why do the Philosophers fail to mention Synderesis?

I answer that the Philosophers distinguish between the powers according to their general objects, and if they consider things that are to be done, do that in accord with the reasoning of human law. The saints however more specially distinguish between the divine law and the human law, i.e. the principles of law as distinguished from their application in particular cases. And therefore the saints place Synderesis at the apex and in the superior part of reason which adheres to the contemplation of divine justice according to the eternal truths – the Philosophers place it in neither one nor the other.

ARTICLE II

Whether the person having Synderesis can sometimes sin, or never.

The second question is as to whether Synderesis can be defiled by sin or error.

It would seem that such is the case because:

1) St. Jerome says, in his gloss on *Ezechiel* concerning Synderesis, that "this is the conscience which is spoken of in *Proverbs* (18, 3): 'The wicked man, when he is come into the depth of sins, contemneth, but ignominy and reproach follow him.'"Ofttimes we see, cast down headlong and slipping from his place, someone who seems to sin without shame, and of him one can appropriately say "for thou hast a harlot's forehead, though wouldst not blush" (Jer.18:3). When therefore one sees that one does not fall headlong nor slip from his place, unless by sin or error; whenever we see this, we see that Synderesis on occassion consents to sin.

2) Again, man, as he is in himself, is totally condemned to

hell. Therefore it seems that in himself he sins totally. But if, as a result of some power, some part of him did not sin, it would be unjust that that part of him be condemned. Therefore according to this Synderesis sins.

3) Again, man is totally corrupted by sin; therefore consequently Synderesis. Therefore it is seen that Synderesis is at times stained (by sin) secondary to corruption.

4) Again, Synderesis is a power of the rational soul. Therefore it deals with opposites such as good and evil. Therefore, reason sometimes is able to act in union with Synderesis and sometimes otherwise.

On the contrary, St. Basil says, according to the authority given above, that the natural judgement of the soul is, as it were, in the tribunal that resides in our mind which embraces the things that are praiseworthy and condemns the things that are vicious. But that which always condemns evil can in no way consent to sin.

Again, Chrysostom in his *Homily on John* says: "The incorruptible judgement of the conscience having been placed in us by He who made us, by the greatest grace and mercy of the ineffable one". The judgement of the conscience is incorruptible, that is, the judgement of Synderesis, and that Synderesis is called the scintilla or spark of the conscience. Therefore it follows that Synderesis is not corrupted by sin.

And further, we have it on the authority of St. Jerome as is noted above, that this Synderesis corrects errors and is in no way mixed up with the other aspects of the soul. If then its office is always to correct, in no way can it consent to sin. This we know from the authority of St. Gregory, as indicated above, who says that its function is to announce destruction and damnation.

But if we concede these points, it is at once manifestly seen that heretics, pagans and Jews set forth, to their danger, the defense of their errors without any remorse of conscience. And this being so, it would seem that Synderesis consents to error.

SOLUTION: The consensus the saints holds that Synderesis can in no way err. The reason for this is that Synderesis is nothing unless in respect to universal principles engrafted into us by nature regarding which error is impossible. Thus, for example, not to fornicate or murder.

But reason which is below Synderesis brings the universal to the particular and examines whether a particular situation involves fornication or murder. And because very great error is possible with regard to particulars, reason frequently is deceived.

To the first objection, I say that Synderesis does not fall down headlong in itself, but in what is inferior, that is, in reason, which makes a mistake in applying universal judgements to a particular situation.

To the second objection, I say that man is damned because of sin and not on account of the power of sinning. The act is totally man's as both the Philosopher and St. Demascene state. And this is why he is totally condemned. One can say that a certain power within him remonstrates against sin.

To the third objection, I say that man in himself is totally corrupted by sin but not so equally in all his parts. For he is corrupted in certain things secondary according to whether he is victorious or not, as for example the senses. He is corrupted in other things where, because of weakness, he is always overcome, despite Synderesis which is always upright. And in some things, he is partially corrupted, such as reason which sometimes is upright and sometimes is not.

To the fourth objection, I say that the power of the rational soul is to deal with opposites. Not that it deals with opposites as an end, but rather that it deals with one of the opposites, and unless it makes a mistake, it will always come to that one. But Synderesis never makes a mistake as is obvious from the principles given.

And finally I say that in heretics and other such infidels Synderesis does not say anything more than that faith must be defended and that life must be given up in the defense of faith and justice. But it does not distinguish whether this or that is of faith, or justice. And because of this it does not err, for its principles are most true. But reason which says that this or that is of faith or is erroneous, and that this or that is justice or injustice, can err and be deceived. And because these heretics and infidels suppose reason to be certain, it follows that they feel no remorse of conscience.

ARTICLE III

Whether Synderesis can in any person be destroyed.

The third question is as to whether Synderesis can be extinguished in any person.

It would seem that the answer is no.

1) St. Jerome says, as noted above, that it was unable to be destroyed in Cain.

2) Again, concerning the damned in hell, Isaiah says "Their worm shall not die" (66, 24); this worm is the worm of their conscience, rebuking them from the rectitude of Synderesis.

Again, Dionysius: "Good is given to them naturally. And we say, by no means is it changeable (mutable), but rather it is always intact and most splendid." If then Synderesis is concerned with natural good, it seems that it remains intact and most splendid, even in the damned. If, however, it is said that the same holds for free will, which, however, is perverted in the damned, it is obvious that what we said above is not true - namely that Synderesis is a habit of nature that always leads the power to right judgement.

Again, St. Bernard says that the worm of hell, (i.e., Synderesis), once rejected, burrows into the very teeth which can in no way rid themselves of it. The worm is that remorse that Synderesis perpetrates on account of sin. Therefore Synderesis remains intact even in the damned.

ON THE CONTRARY

1) St. Jeremias (II,16):"The children of Memphis and of Taphnes have deflowered thee, even to the crown of the head." In a commentory on this passage it is explained that the malignant spirit extends from the inferior members, even to the crown of the head, where it corrupts the very depth of the soul with the disease of infidelity (literally, the disease of dissenting from the thinking of the Church). However, the pure heights of the mind (or the depths of the soul) is the seat of Synderesis. Therefore Synderesis is corrupted by the disease of infidelity, and thus it is extinguished.

2) Again, *fomes* (the inclination to sin) and Synderesis are opposed in their manner of inclining the soul. But the inclination to sin in some people is totally absent as in the Blessed Virgin. Therefore, the inclination of Synderesis can also in some people be entirely extinguished by sin as in Antichrist who is the worst of men.

3) Besides, in what way would it remain in the damned, when it is unable to rescue a person from an evil will or punishment?

SOLUTION: There are some who before us have said that goodness is of two modes, natural and from grace. And evil is also of two characters, namely punishment and guilt. And if Synderesis inclines towards the good and pulls back from evil, they say that in the damned it does not incline towards the good of grace. Natural good is considered under two modes, that is, in itself: as the good of nature that the damned desire, and as not desired, but following the perverted will, and in this situation they say Synderesis is extinguished. Similarly the damned desire to sin, and here again they argue, it is extinguished. Punishment is considered in two ways, that is, in proportion to the guilt incurred and in itself. In the first mode they desire it. For they say that the damned would rather be punished for their guilt and sin than to be without guilt and without punishment. And once again on this ground they say that Synderesis is extinguished. If truly punishment is considered in itself, they do not desire it. But without prejudice we say that this appetite of the perverse will is that which resides in free will. The appetite of Synderesis is always upright in both the damned and the living and is the remorse for evil acts committed, and for good acts omitted. And because of this, it is called the worm of remorse which gnaws at the damned.

To the first objection I say that the highest mind is called the light of faith and leads to the elevation of reason, and this is what the commentary says: the disease of infidelity is this, that by infidelity the faith is corrupted.

To the second I say that grace is a greater power than sin, and because of this one can say that *fomes* (the inclination to evil) is, in someone, extinguished by grace. However, not on account of this is Synderesis necessarily extinguished by sin.

And to the third objection, Synderesis remains in the damned to their greater torment, for the gnawing of the worm is no little pain. It induces the impious inwardly to groan and make bitter repentence, as it says in the *Book of Wisdom* "they will be troubled with terrible fear, and shall be amazed at the suddenness of their unexpected salvation" that is to say, of good, "saying within themselves, repenting, and groaning for anguish of spirit, these are they whom we held some time in derision and for a parable of reproach. We fools estimated their life increased and their end without honor." (5:2-4). Synderesis remains in the damned for this reason that it might oppose those whose perverse free will is angry at the pricks of conscience of Synderesis on account of their consenting to evil.

SECOND TRANSLATION

A *discussion on Synderesis extracted from the MANUALE THE-OLOGIAE MORALIS SECUNDUM PRINCIPIA SANCTI THO-MAE AQUINATIS* by Dom M. Prummer, O.P. (published in 1927)

Synderesis[1] is a habit of the first principles of morality, and the act of Synteresis in general is to do good and to avoid evil, or as St. Albertus Magnus says: "Its action is twofold, namely, an inclination to the good and a remonstration against evil[2]." But the work of conscience is to judge in a particular case what is to be done, and what omitted. Conscience can make a mistake, but Synteresis can never make a mistake[3]. Wherefore, in a very beautiful way, St. Jerome, and especially the scholastics of the thirteenth century, called Synderesis "the spark of conscience", "the little fire". For synteresis is like a little fire lighted in our intellects by the Creator Himself. This little fire is derived from the very light of God Himself, according to Psalm 4 *Signatum est super nos lumen vultus tui Domine* ("There is signed over us the light of Thine own countenance.") It gives forth both light and heat: light in showing us the general principles of morality; heat in impelling us to good and in restraining us from evil. This spark can in no way be extinguished, neither in this life, when man soils himself in sin, nor in heaven, nor in hell. Whence St. Thomas Aquinas says[4] "the spark of reason is unable to be extinguished as long as the light of intellect remains. But intellect is never taken away by sin." This Synteresis remaining in the damned is the first cause of their so-called "worm" which never dies, for it always remonstrates againt them for the evil they have perpetrated, and impels to good, which, because of the obstinacy of their evil will, is always being rejected[5].

¹ Authors are not in agreement as to whether it should be written synderesis or synteresis. Also, they are not in agreement as to where the name synteresis comes from, which first is used by St. Jerome in his commentary on Ezechiel 1:7 [Migne, *Patrologia Latina*, 25.22]

² S. Theol. 2, tr. 16, q.99, m. 2.a.3. The same was taught by St. Thomas Aquinas, *De verit.* q. 16,a.2.

³ B. Albertus, *De cret.* 2, q. 71, c. 2; see also St. Thomas, *loc.cit.*

⁴ e, dist. 39, q. 3, a. I.

⁵ *C. S. Theol.* 1, 2, q 85, a. 2. ad 3. St. Albert the Great and Alexander of Hales teach the same, although they are not in agreement about the function of Synderesis in the next life.

Femininity, Hierarchy, and God

James S. Cutsinger

There are at least two different ways of discussing ideas. The first might be called the horizontal approach, and it is by far the more common in academic settings. The writer puts himself in the background, his own views aside, and attempts to describe what others have thought. He may if he is especially brave venture a concluding surmisal or tentative evaluation of his data, but he is careful to respect the pluralism of the scholarly world, and he therefore avoids raising suspicions that he has committed himself. We are all familiar with this method. There is, however, a second – albeit rarer – possibility, and that is to approach an idea or a set of ideas as true – one may say "as if it *were* true" (if he still wishes to be cautious), or "because it *is* true" (if he does not mind being called "dogmatic"). Here, too, the writer will wish to stay in the background; it is not after all his thinking a thing true that makes it true. But the foreground is in this "vertical" case occupied, not so much by the bibliographies and periods and academic generalities with which he is familiar, but by the ideas themselves – essentially naked, cut free from their historical contexts and considered of value only insofar as they may point us toward the Real.

My approach in this chapter is a combination of both these methods. I intend on the one hand to describe a particular school of thought, the perennialist or traditionalist school, as represented by three twentieth century metaphysical authors: Ananda Coomaraswamy, René Guénon,

110

and – especially – Frithjof Schuon. And I plan to emphasize in particular their views of the feminine and the role femininity plays in their critique of modern thought. On the other hand, it is not my intention to present their ideas simply as historical curiosities. I wish for the reader to look, not at, but through their thinking and along their claims toward a fresh recognition of certain truths. I have accordingly avoided the customary qualifications and scholarly provisos. It is hoped that this will prove useful particularly for those whose interests would not otherwise have brought them into contact with these authors or with perennialism, and for whom certain textual and biographical details might be irrelevant, but who may nevertheless be concerned with the deeper religious and philosophical issues suggested by my title. In any case, my chief intention here – like that of my fellow authors – is to provoke readers to ask, not whether what I say about Schuon and the other perennialists is in keeping with their books, but whether what they say (in this case) about femininity, hierarchy, and God is in keeping with Reality.[1]

Penetration to the heart of their thinking will be made easier by noting first that several terms so far employed are dangerously misleading. Whatever the traditionalist school may be, it is not a "school of thought"; and if perennialism is anything, it is not an "-ism." Though the writers in question themselves sometimes speak in these more familiar and more academically acceptable ways, and though the demands of a formal essay will require that I, too, continue to use such language from time to time, their distinctive and persistent intention is in fact to transcend the bounds of schools, perspectives, and opinions. For the perennial ideas that they seek to express emerge from a Source independent of the sundry schools and systems manufactured by the human mind.

Theirs, they say, is a *sophia perennis* – a perennial wisdom or philosophy – which is the substance of truth common to all the world's major religions. Words ending in "-ism" are always the derivatives of adjectives, and what they designate is therefore inevitably abstract and lacking a substance or integrity of its own. The ideas that we are considering here, however, are utterly the opposite, for the perennial philosophy – it is claimed – is the cause and origin of derivations and not in any sense their result.

The defense of this claim – this very arrogant and presumptuous claim, some may be tempted to add – depends above all upon a single, fundamental principle, which the traditionalists repeatedly emphasize throughout their prose: the principle, namely, that man is much more than a body and mind, and that his knowledge extends – *de jure* if not *de facto* – far beyond the heuristic ideas abstracted by reason from the physical senses. Anthropologies of this latter sort will of course inevitably resist as the merest dogmatism all assertions of the kind I have sketched, all claims presuming to be free from the "conditioning" of history and culture. Such is not the perennialist anthropology, however. According to Schuon, Coomaraswamy, and Guénon, man is a ternary being, tripartite in his essential structure, comprising not only the body and mind of Cartesian dualism, but also a third element, the Intellect or Spirit. This last transcends the individual person as such and is not so much a human faculty as it is a mode or a level of being, which embraces and grounds a person, together with the history of which his mind and body are parts, instead of being embraced or comprehended by him. By virtue of Intellect, man can know with certainty what truly is – he can discern and assess the full range of being – for the Intellect and Reality are in fact a single substance, a single, undivided, and indivisible plenitude.

Now to speak of a level of knowing and being that transcends the individual person is to speak, of course, of hierarchy, an idea introduced in my title, and one to which we must now turn directly. For more than any other, the idea of an ontological hierarchy, as conveyed by the image of "the great chain of being," has provided the perennialists with their essential and most distinctive teachings. These authors are agreed above all that something and nothing, being and its absence, are not the only alternatives – that "to be" or "not to be" is *not* the question – but that Reality is a matter of degrees, emerging at its highest level from a Source or Principle *so* real as to be better called "Supra-ontological" or "Beyond-Being." This divine Principle is too full of the Real to contain itself; superabundantly, it spills over its own most proper nature, first into itself and then "outside," in what St. Bonaventure called the self-diffusiveness of the Good. In their upper registers, the levels of this self-diffusion, manifestation, or emanation from the Principle are immaterial and not yet quantified. But the process of manifestation inevitably leads toward a coagulation, solidification, and division of being as lower reaches of the hierarchy are approached, with matter as we know it, hard and resisting, being the densest level of all and the terminal point of the entire movement.

The perennialists add that manifestation is at once intrinsic and extrinsic to the Principle or Source, for the Principle is both infinite and absolute, hence immanent and transcendent. As infinite, that is, having no bounds, the Source can never be removed from anything real. To exist *is* to participate in the Principle, which comprehends or contains Reality in all of its many levels, from the seraphim to stones. On the other hand, being absolute and self-caused, the Source or Supreme Reality remains above and beyond all contingencies and accidents, which is to say outside the world and totally other than everything not itself. Schuon expresses this crucial metaphysical insight in the following way:

> Esoterically speaking, there are only two relationships to take into consideration, that of transcendence and that of immanence: according to the first, the reality of

Substance [that is, the Principle] annihilates that of the accident; according to the second, the qualities of the accident – starting with their reality – cannot but be those of Substance.[2]

Or again he writes: "The universe is thus a veil which on the one hand exteriorizes the Essence [that is, the Principle] and on the other hand is situated within the Essence itself, inasmuch as it is Infinitude."[3] As the term "veil" implies, this relationship between the world and its ultimate Origin is captured best, perhaps, in the Hindu idea of *Māyā*, which both reveals and conceals the supreme reality of Brahman – which in fact veils and conceals precisely in order to reveal. For according to the perennial philosophy, the world actually manifests the Principle only insofar as attention is not diverted or attracted by the manifestation itself, that is, by the creature, whose sole function is to empty itself in the direction of God, in order to empty those who look upon it of all that separates them from their Source. As we shall be seeing, the feminine is at the very center of this recollective process. Though the Divine is fully present in creatures, it is only paradoxically so, for it makes itself most present through absence – through precisely those features of creation by which the world testifies, even in the midst of its greatest beauty, that it is not itself God. Only thus, by expressing itself best in its silence, does the Principle recall our awareness of both transcendence and immanence.

With these basic teachings in mind, treating them not of course as proofs or demonstrations, but simply as supports for further reflection, I would have us turn now to the place of the feminine in the perennial philosophy.

"Gender is a reality," C. S. Lewis has written, speaking from a traditional Christian perspective,

and a more fundamental reality than sex. Sex is, in fact, merely the adaptation to organic life of a fundamental polarity which divides all created beings. Female sex is simply one of the things that have feminine gender; there are many others, and Masculine and Feminine meet us on planes of reality where male and female would be simply meaningless. Masculine is not attenuated male, nor feminine attenuated female. On the contrary, the male and female of organic creatures are rather faint and blurred reflections of masculine and feminine. Their reproductive functions, their differences in strength and size, partly exhibit, but partly also confuse and misrepresent, the real polarity.[4]

Now according to the perennialist school, this "real polarity" is to be found, not only as Lewis suggests in creatures, however superhuman, but all the way up to and in the Divine Reality itself, in what we have been calling the Principle, which is the ultimate Source of everything else, and which is for that reason the source and paradigm of all distinctions. In its absoluteness and transcendence, the Divine is the archetype for everything masculine, while its infinity and capacity for immanence are displayed at every level of the feminine. Though such ideas will appear to the skeptic as fantasy, projection, or pathetic fallacy, the polar qualities revealed to us as sex are actually and objectively present on every plane of the ontological hierarchy, above us as already suggested, as in the relationship of sun to moon, but also below, in certain alchemical pairs, like gold and silver, or in physical states, like solid and liquid – the former term in each of these pairs signifying an expression of what the Chinese call *yang* or masculine power, and the latter of *yin*, which is the feminine energy. As Seyyed Hossein Nasr has written, "The difference between the two sexes cannot be only biological and physical, because in the traditional perspective the corporeal level of existence has its principle in the subtle state, the subtle in the spiritual, and the spiritual in the Divine Being itself."[5] To put the point in western theological terms, man and woman are both created in the divine image and are therefore equally theomorphic. "Each sex," says Schuon, "represents a perfection."[6] Or again, in a less theological and more metaphysical language, we have the words of Coomaraswamy: "'That' . . . of which our powers are measures . . . is a syzygy of conjoint principles."[7]

I have been speaking of the masculine and feminine as qualities and energies, but a note of warning is important lest these words deceive us. Qualities in this case are not "attributes"; they are not, in other words, characteristics or distinguishing features that are simply attached by convention to certain visible or tangible objects, to be then abstracted or prescinded from them. For the traditionalist, the true order is just the reverse. Visible and tangible things are said to exist only by virtue of their inherence or participation in the qualities and only by dependence on them. The nominal represents a condensation of the adjectival. Masculine and feminine, as C. S. Lewis observed, are not attenuated male and female, but veritable realities in their own right, rooted in the Divine itself. Only by keeping this teaching in mind can one begin to understand the place of the feminine in perennialism. Unlike the typical theologian of the classical West, for whom God has been primarily "He," the traditionalist repeatedly insists that both the masculine and the feminine are indispensable revelations or, as Schuon would say, "prolongations" of the Divine Source, and hence that male and female equally speak of God from within the physical and organic world of human sensibility. On the other hand, though they do speak equally, what they have to say is not the same nor hierarchically equivalent, and it is in this respect, until one looks more closely, that perennialism may appear to be unjust or chauvinistic to modern eyes. I shall return to this crucial point later.

Traditionalist doctrine includes three distinct polarities of the masculine and feminine, three patterns of relationship, of which we have so far glanced at only two. On the one hand, these twin qualities are the expression of powers or energies intrinsic to the Divine itself, for God is both absolute and infinite, just and merciful, "rigorous" and "gentle,"[8] "inviolable" and "generous."[9] Thus, as Schuon says, "The Supreme Divinity is either Father or Mother."[10] On the other hand, since the universe is the creation of God, or the manifestation of the Principle, this polarity within the Divine is ineluctably extended "outside" as well, into that universe which is both within and without its Source. Hence, the supreme complementarity is duplicated on every plane of existence, whether angelic or astrological, human or animal, vegetable or mineral. Masculine and feminine are embodied, moreover, not only among the kinds or species of creatures, but in various created forces and natural laws, and in certain pairs of human faculties: in "contraction" and "expansion,"[11] "geometry" and "music,"[12] and "knowledge" and "love."[13] We should note that in both of these first two respects, whether we consider the polarity as within the Principle or as within its manifestation, the two poles or qualities are complementary, reciprocal, and symmetric. They are, as it were, horizontally equal.

It should come as no surprise, however, that a metaphysics as hierarchical as the perennial philosophy stresses also certain vertical applications of this fundamental pair, nor perhaps is it surprising to discover that in *most* such instances – I do emphasize "most" – the feminine is subordinate to the masculine.

This third, vertical order of relationship pertains, not to complements inside or outside the Divine Reality, but to opposites that bridge this very distinction and that express in that way the union of God and creatures. Here the most distinctive characteristic of the masculine power is said to be its initiative and activity and of the feminine, its receptivity and passivity. Heaven is masculine in relation to earth, and immanence is feminine with respect to transcendence; essence or form is *yang*, substance or matter is *yin*. Indeed, this vertical relationship of the genders is an essential feature of the ontological hierarchy. According to Coomaraswamy, in fact, "The fundamental distinction in terms of sex defines the hierarchy. God himself is male to all."[14] We shall see shortly, however, that this observation is not the whole story.

As already mentioned, the concept of *Māyā*, linked by etymological associations to both *materia* or matter and *mater* or mother, is an especially important idea in the traditionalist understanding of the created universe. Says Schuon of *Māyā*, "She is the great theophany, the 'unveiling' of God.... *Māyā* may be likened to a magic fabric woven from a warp that veils and a weft that unveils; she is a quasi-incomprehensible intermediary between the finite and the Infinite."[15] *Māyā* in fact is the presence of the Infinite in the finite, the projection of the Divine's own internal femininity, that is, infinity, outside itself, an "outside" which in its dependence, contingency, and indefiniteness not only contains but constitutes the feminine.

All the characteristics normally associated with *Māyā*, those of play, relativity, and illusion, constellate, for the perennialist, around the feminine, and they may be turned, we are taught – like those of the masculine – either toward the service of the Principle or against it: either, in other words, toward recalling creatures to their Source or toward blinding, distracting, and deceiving them. As Coomaraswamy describes it, "*Māyā*... is the maternal measure and means essential to the manifestation of a... world of appearances, by which we may be either enlightened or deluded according to the degree of our own maturity."[16] It is to the former possibility, to the beneficent, "Beatrician," or "Marian" aspect of the feminine as theophany, and to its central role in the perennialist critique of modernism, that I shall soon be directing attention. The traditions warn, however, that this quality, like its masculine counterpart, does in fact possess in addition certain maleficent capabilities and deceptive extremes, which cannot but predominate if the feminine is abstracted from its proper dogmatic and liturgical contexts and considered outside the protective limits of an orthodox tradition. If I discuss here only the positive applications of femininity, it is not to forget that much else would need saying before a truly perennial evaluation of the genders could be reached.

At this point, however, I must interrupt our considerations of the feminine proper and say a few words about what is meant in this context by the term "modernism." If we are to understand the value of femininity in the perennialist challenge to modern thought, we obviously need first to be clear just what that thought is.

When authors like Guénon, Coomaraswamy, and Schuon speak of the modern worldview, which they trace roughly from the end of the western Middle Ages, what they have in mind essentially is a viewpoint that is lacking in hierarchical order. The modernist vision is a reductionist vision, a way of seeing and interpreting all reality as if it existed on a single level, and thus a tendency to ignore or reject those dimensions of being that refuse to conform to that chosen plane. It is a view of the more in terms of the less. Although one might object that modern scientific distinctions among the physical, chemical, and biological orders of existence are in one sense a function of planes or levels, these planes are nevertheless all confined to the material and empirical order. No modern scientist would ever speak, as do the perennial philosophers of their hierarchy, as though some of these organizational levels were more "real" than others. Moreover, when it comes to a consideration of mind or consciousness, the modern view has completely reversed or inverted the traditional perspective, since matter is regarded by the modern thinker, not as the result, but as the cause of mind. For the sake of this summary, I am obviously neglecting important exceptions to this rule – thinkers who, though modern by traditional measures, would nevertheless attribute to the mind more than an epiphenomenal status, and who would consider consciousness as possessing an integrity of its own. And yet surely the perennialists are right that very few even of these philosophers take the further step of realizing that consciousness is itself the cause of matter, and they are right, too, that no one who is by definition "modern" will be prepared to recognize in the human mind the echo or reverberation of yet higher, non-human modes of awareness. I should emphasize that the term "modern" is here being used, as by Schuon and others of the traditionalist school, to describe a view or philosophical perspective, and not a period or age, though certainly the word is meant to suggest that the perspective in question has been the more typical and dominant in recent times. Nevertheless, we are not to infer that a person who is chronologically modern cannot be traditional, or there would be no living perennialists.

Modernism can be characterized as the result, or better perhaps as the intersection, of several similar tendencies, all of them reflecting in various ways the assumed centrality and apparent inescapability of matter. These several tendencies may be called, following Guénon, reduction, quantification, and solidification. It is the last that especially concerns us here. According to the traditionalist assessment, the dominance of materialistic ontologies and empiricistic epistemologies in our time has resulted from a certain coarsening, hardening, or condensation in man's perception of the world. This solidification has exhibited itself both subjectively, in an excessive individualism or egoism – with man conceiving of himself as a closed and insulated entity, locked as it were within his physical body; and objectively, in a positivistic search for fundamental particles and elementary natural laws. This solidification is perhaps most strikingly obvious in the mechanistic applications of modern science. But it is also more subtly and destructively present in the conformation of man's understanding of himself to the contours and structures of empirical objects, so great is his fascination with technology and its apparent successes. According to

Guénon, "Modern man has become quite impermeable to any influences other than such as impinge on his senses; not only have his faculties of comprehension become more and more limited, but also the field of his perception has become correspondingly restricted."[17] Thinking has been identified with the belief that what we know – if we know at all – is ultimately derived from what our natural senses tell us, and that any idea worth serious consideration must in some way or at some level of practicality be applicable to the world disclosed by physical perception. All nonmaterial phenomena that are inexplicable in material terms have been reduced in this way to the domain of the subjective and psychological.

For the traditionalists, modern thought means in short the persistent preference and substitution of the opaque for the transparent and the eclipse, therefore, of quality by quantity, of the higher by the lower, and of the spiritual by matter – the eclipse, in other words, of the Divine Reality by creatures. Though he seems not to know it and usually resists the charge, modern man has become riveted upon phenomena, which he no longer even realizes *are* phenomena, that is, appearances of another Substance, but which he treats instead as integral realities. Thus according to Schuon:

> One finds in modern thinking a significant abuse of both the idea of the abstract and the idea of the concrete, the one error being evidently allied to the other. All reality not physically or psychologically tangible, although perfectly accessible to pure intellection, is described as being "abstract" with a more or less disparaging intention, as though it were a matter of distinguishing between dream, or even deception, and reality, or healthiness of mind. Substance, that which exists of itself, is regarded as "abstract," and the accidental as "concrete."[18]

We come at this point, not to the place, but to the specific operative role of the feminine in the perennialist challenge to modernism – what I have called the theophanic value of femininity and its recollective power.

It will be helpful to recall the traditional identification of the feminine with *Māyā*. Like *Māyā*, we saw, the feminine involves illusion, concealing in the midst of revealing and revealing by way of concealing. At first glance, this feature of the feminine quality may seem merely deceptive and deluding. But for the perennialist, while the negative and occluding dimensions of the divine play must always be remembered and carefully guarded against, illusions nevertheless remain of inestimable liberating value, especially in the recollection to their Principle of minds that have become too masculine, which is to say too fixed, too externalized, too heavy, too determinate and "solid." Perhaps we can now say too "modern." Unlike both accurate perceptions, on the one hand, and hallucinations, on the other, illusions are a combination of being and nothing, of something and its absence. For they register things that truly are, though never quite *as* they are. So, too, the feminine. And it is in precisely this way, because of its gift of illusion – its liquidity, flexibility, and openness – that femininity is uniquely qualified to represent the ultimate Source of things to the self-imprisoned mind. For that Source, let us remember, is both transcendent and immanent, and it is therefore always other than itself in its sameness – always beyond its creatures even while being within them.

Schuon discerns this illusory nature even at the level of the female physical form, and he therefore observes: "As symbols, the masculine body indicates a victory of Spirit over chaos, and the feminine body, a deliverance of form by Essence." For the feminine, he continues, "is like celestial music which would give back to fallen matter its paradisiac transparency, or which, to use the language of Taoism, would make trees flower beneath the snow."[19] "The key to the

mystery of salvation through... femininity," he writes elsewhere, "lies in the very nature of *Māyā*: If *Māyā* can attract
towards the outward, she can also attract towards the inward.
Eve is life, and this is manifesting *Māyā*; Mary is Grace, and
this is reintegrating *Māyā*."[20] Or again Schuon says:

> The beauty of woman appears to man as the revelation
> of the bliss of the Essence of which he is himself as it
> were a crystallisation – and in this respect femininity
> transcends man – and this explains the alchemical role
> and the "dissolving" power of woman's beauty: the
> vibratory shock of the aesthetic event – in the deepest
> sense of the word – should be the means of "liquefac-
> tion of the hardened heart."[21]

It is thus that the feminine – taking the term to mean as
always, of course, not an abstracted attribute of a certain
kind of organism, but a spiritual and supernatural power
which, though exhibited in it, is more real than the cosmos
itself – it is thus, by its expansive and dissolving power, that
the feminine may serve to awaken modern minds by drawing
their attention away from the edge and the surface of things
into their liquid heart and substance. Wishing to leave no
one satisfied with the apparent fixities and givens of corporeal manifestation, the perennialists look to the feminine, as
Coleridge would have said, "to arouse and emancipate the
soul from this debasing slavery to the outward senses"[22] – in
other words, to liberate the human intelligence from its
complacency and from the arbitrary constraints of seeming
solids. Says Schuon, "Woman... in her highest aspect... is
the formal projection of merciful and infinite Inwardness in
the outward; and in this regard she assumes a quasi-
sacramental and liberating function."[23]

This magnetic and deliquescent force of femininity has
the power to do even more, however, than, by melting sur-
faces, to draw our hearts inside of things. The feminine may
also function so as to elevate, to persuade the mind up the
ladder of being on to higher and higher levels. This elevat-

ing role is exercised in two distinct ways and at two specific levels of the ontological hierarchy, which we may call the spiritual and the Divine.

In order to understand the first, the spiritual operation or function, it is important to remember our earlier discussion of the masculine and feminine as powers within the Principle itself, whose manifestation requires that descending levels of cosmic radiation be polarized in turn. In its transcendence and absoluteness, we were told, the Principle is masculine, while its bounty, self-diffusiveness, or infinity disclose a feminine dimension. Now because it is allied to God's infinitude, which ensures that the Source be everywhere, the Divine feminine proves also to be, conversely, what enables beings not divine to participate in God. Femininity, in other words, is the capacity that the Principle has, having passed outside itself, to embrace what it is not, which is to say that which *is* not, so as to provide mere nothings with the dignity of being. The feminine is the connecting thread or bond between manifestation and its Source – a Source that would otherwise, as masculine and absolute, remain utterly apart and unapproachable. The feminine quality thus functions as cause, not only for the act of creation, but for its providential preservation, sustenance, and continuity. And in this sustaining and connecting role, it is able to lift man's awareness beyond the level of the material, and even subtle, orders all the way up to the Principle itself. As an expression of God's merciful condescension or benignity, the feminine "familiarizes" creatures with their Maker. Says Schuon, "It is not possible to go beyond Relativity... without the acquiescence and help of the Divine Relative,"[24] and this Relative is the feminine.

There is a second role, however, that is even more important if modern man would be freed from his prison. It is a role enacted at the level of the Divine Reality itself, where the opening and liberating actions of the feminine are intended to conduct man past both the subtle and the spiritual orders up and into the Principle *per se.* We have seen that femininity, as the infinite dimension of the Source, carries the power to lead the mind toward God. Perennialists teach even more strikingly, however, that creatures may be led past the frontiers as it were of God and into his own deepest recesses – into, in fact, the Source or Origin of God himself. For according to traditional doctrine, hierarchy applies in a sense even to the very Principle of hierarchy, and not simply to the planes of reality below it. It is possible to distinguish levels of divinity, even degrees (strange as it sounds to say) of absoluteness. Moreover, one may assign to the highest and most ultimate of these levels the quality of the feminine; it is possible to say, in other words, that femininity is the Source or Origin of the determinate personality, hence the masculinity, of God himself. I observed before that in most of its vertical applications, the perennial philosophy subordinates the feminine to the masculine, and an example of that rule has since been remarked. I had in mind, however, and wished to anticipate, the present most important exception. For even though, in Schuon's words, "virility refers to the Principle, and femininity to Manifestation,"[25] the Principle is not only virile. Instead, the masculinity of the Divine Person proves in the final analysis to be an echo or reflection of an even more ultimate Source.

This is the Source that I described earlier as being in some senses *so* real as to be better called, not being, but Beyond-Being. It is the *śunyata* or Void of Buddhist teaching and the Super-ontological Essence of Dionysius the Areopagite. "Beyond-Being – or Non-Being – is Reality absolutely unconditioned," according to Schuon, "while Being is Reality insofar as It determines Itself in the direction of manifestation and in so doing becomes personal God."[26] The point to attend to now, however, is the close association that the traditionalist authors draw between this supreme and unsurpassable dimension of the Divine and femininity. Coomaraswamy is perhaps the most succinct of all: the Supreme Reality, he says, "is of Essence and Nature, Being and Nonbeing, God and Godhead – that is, masculine and feminine."[27] This identification must be clearly understood. The perennialist teaching is not only that there exists a feminine aspect within the Divine. It is that the feminine takes a certain precedence in relation to God the creator, even as the masculinity of that God himself takes precedence with respect to creation. The impassibility, integrity, and sovereignty of the exoteric western Deity are seen here to be the veils or projections of something other and higher, which, utterly unlike all manifested qualities and insusceptible to every category, even that of being itself, remains in its very fluidity and indeterminacy rather more like the feminine than like anything else.[28] Schuon writes accordingly:

> Even though a priori femininity is subordinate to virility, it also comprises an aspect which makes it superior to a given aspect of the masculine pole; for the divine Principle has an aspect of unlimitedness, virginal mystery and maternal mercy which takes precedence over a certain more relative aspect of determination, logical precision and implacable justice.[29]

And he notes that "a Sufi, probably Ibn 'Arabī, has written that the Divine Name 'She' (Hiya), not in use but nevertheless possible, is greater than the Name 'He' (Huwa). This refers to the Indetermination or Infinitude, both virginal and maternal, of the Self or 'Essence' (Dhāt)."[30] The femininity of Non-being or Beyond-Being can thus be considered, at least in this context, as the Principle of the Principle, as constituting and deploying the very divinity of God himself, and as administering what must surely be the final alchemical shock to those who are content with what exists – the ultimate subversion of their complacency, because the ultimate implosion or intussusception of "that which is."[31]

But now for a word of caution as I bring this chapter to a close. None of my observations has been meant to suggest that the Divine is without masculine aspects that may be in certain cases more crucial or more decisive than the feminine, or that the perennialists are not prepared to emphasize these aspects when necessary. If these have not been stressed in the present context, it is simply because to do so would be to write another essay. Nor do I wish to leave the reader thinking that the Jewish, Christian, and Muslim traditions have somehow been "wrong" – *quod absit* – to place their emphasis on God as a "He." Quite the contrary, exoteric and dogmatic emphases, whether in the form of doctrines, symbols, or rituals, would seem – at least in the western context – to be peculiarly inappropriate and disproportionate to the quality or dimension or "energy" that we have been considering here. For as the traditionalists see it, the operative power and true efficacy of the feminine consist precisely in its hiddenness, indirection, and unspecifiable amplitude, which would only be compromised if placed in the foreground. Nevertheless, at the risk of seeming to define the indefinable or of appearing to promote a competing religion – and this manifestly is not their intention – they believe as well that the characteristic tendencies and preconceptions of the modern world have made it important for us to attend more closely than before to the importance of femininity as an expression of the Real.

For ours, they insist, is an era of density and hardness, of heaviness and eclipse: It is the *Kali Yuga* or "Dark Age". The doors of perception having *not* been cleansed, men and women have come not merely to doubt or disbelieve, but to deny the reality of higher worlds. Or if they do still believe, their faith is without the traditional complement of knowledge and reason, and it is directed toward a realm of shadows, seemingly no more real, and often less, than the plane of matter, whose phenomenal contingency and fragility they seldom glimpse, and then forget. "In this state," warns Schuon,

the soul is at the same time hard as stone and pulverised as sand, it lives in the dead rinds of things and not

in the Essence, which is Life and Love; it is at once
hardness and dissolution.[32]

What such a soul needs in part, what modern man needs,
is a means of melting – what Schuon calls "the spiritual lique-
faction of the *ego*."[33] And for this it needs the feminine.
Theophanic, maieutic, recollective, and freeing, the role of
the feminine must be to transport a mind grown too attached and masculine from exterior through interior to
superior, by exposing that mind – again in the words of
Schuon – to "the warm, soft quality of spring, or that of fire
melting ice and restoring life to frozen limbs."[34]

Two concluding observations. It is important to emphasize first, lest there be some confusion, that for the perennialists, the masculine is never exclusively the privilege or
possibility of the human male, nor the feminine of the female. As Schuon says, "Each sex, being equally human, shares
in the nature of the other."[35] Because they are contingencies
and accidents, creatures – including human creatures – are
by their very nature always other than themselves, impure
and mixed. Only in the Divine Reality are the polar qualities
distinctly "placed," with specific and persistent operations of
their own. In human beings, they inevitably overlap, with
yang and *yin* expressing their powers through males and
females both. It is rather a question of predominance. And
yet even so, as suggested before several times, men and
women do remain in some sense emblematic of their corresponding archetypes, and they are therefore, even at the
level of their physical bodies, hierarchically complementary
revelations of their ultimate Principle. This fact cannot be
without implications for how we live our lives.

My reference yet again to hierarchy brings in its train a
second and final comment. As readers should by now have
realized, relationships between the masculine and the feminine are for the perennialists anything but simple or static.
Sometimes "horizontal" and sometimes "vertical," they are
never, however, what one might call "democratically" re-

lated. For even though these twin qualities are equally revelatory, and though through them male and female equally
speak of God, they do not speak equally of God, for what
they have to say is not the same, nor in the traditionalist view
are men and women ever equivalent, that is, interchange-
able. While some of our contemporaries may find this fact
distasteful, I hope that it is clear from what has been said
that the distortions and abuses so often associated in our
time with hierarchy need not be feared by persons otherwise
attracted to these teachings – that there is in any case no
necessary connection between the doctrine and its historical
perversions. For in fact what one glimpses in the perennialist
vision is "a continual interchange of complementary minis-
trations," to borrow a phrase from C. S. Lewis [36] – not domination or usurpation of one gender by the other, but a
kaleidoscopically shifting though extremely lawful series of
transforming actions, where momentary position must always mean instant displacement. It is therefore perhaps only
this vision that has the capacity, not only to prevent the
abuse of power by despotic hierarchies, but to rescue the
people of our time from a purely quantitative egalitarianism,
itself only one of the leveling effects of modern thought,
which in the name of human "interest" would seem often to
rob us of our true humanity and of the differences and
special qualities that reflect our participation in the Source.

[1] I gratefully acknowledge the assistance of Mr. Alvin Moore, Jr.
and Professor Huston Smith, who read and commented upon an
earlier draft of the present chapter.

[2]Frithjof Schuon, *Esoterism as Principle and as Way* (Middlesex,
England: Perennial Books, 1981), 44.

[3]*Esoterism*, 51.

[4]C. S. Lewis, *Perelandra* (New York: Macmillan, 1944), 200.

[5]Seyyed Hossein Nasr, "The Male and Female in the Islamic Perspective," in his *Traditional Islam in the Modern World* (London KPI, 1987) 47-58.

[6]Frithjof Schuon, *The Essential Writings of Frithjof Schuon*, ed. Seyyed Hossein Nasr (Amity, New York: Amity House, 1986), 406.

[7]Ananda K. Coomaraswamy, *Hinduism and Buddhism* (Westport, Connecticut: Greenwood Press, 1971), 11.

[8]Frithjof Schuon, *From the Divine to the Human: Survey of Metaphysics and Epistemology* (Bloomington, Indiana: World Wisdom Books, 1981), 87.

[9]*Esoterism,* 50n.

[10]*Esoterism,* 49-50.

[11]*Divine to the Human,* 87.

[12]Frithjof Schuon, *Stations of Wisdom* (Middlesex, England: Perennial Books, 1961), 86.

[13]*Divine to the Human,* 95.

[14]*Hinduism and Buddhism,* 13.

[15]Frithjof Schuon, *Light on the Ancient Worlds* (Bloomington, Indiana: World Wisdom Books, 1984), 89.

[16]*Hinduism and Buddhism,* 3.

[17]René Guénon, *The Reign of Quantity and the Signs of the Times* (London: Luzac, 1953), 125.

[18]Frithjof Schuon, *Logic and Transcendence* (London: Perennial Books, 1984), 19-20. It is clearly impossible to do more than summarize the perennialist evaluation of modernism, specifically modern "ontology," in the context of this chapter. I must simply record the results of this assessment, in very general terms, leaving it to the skeptical, but interested, reader to examine elsewhere the particular arguments and observations that have led to these conclusions. I would especially recommend Guénon's *Reign of Quantity* and the chapter entitled "In the Wake of the Fall" in Schuon's *Light on the Ancient Worlds.*

[19]*Stations of Wisdom,* 87.

[20]*Esoterism.* 143.

[21]*Stations of Wisdom,* 86.

[22]Samuel Taylor Coleridge, *Aids to Reflection* (Port Washington, New York: Kennikat Press, 1971), 349.

[23]*Essential Writings*, 404.

[24]Frithjof Schuon, "Dimensions of Omnipotence," *Studies in Comparative Religion*, Vol. 16, Nos. 1-2, p. 11.

[25]*Divine to the Human*, 95.

[26]*Stations of Wisdom*, 24n.

[27]Ananda Coomaraswamy, *Coomaraswamy*, ed. Roger Lipsey, Vol. 2: *Selected Papers: Metaphysical* (Princeton: Princeton University Press, 1977), 231.

[28]The phrase "rather more like" is essential. However accurate the application of the concept of gender to certain dimensions of the Divine Reality, that application, especially with regard to the second of the feminine's elevating roles, must remain, like all positive descriptions of the Principle, strictly *ad extra* and *pro nobis*. For the ultimate Source is in itself beyond distinction.

[29]*Divine to the Human*, 94-95.

[30]*Logic and Transcendence*, 119n.

[31]One may note that this primacy or priority of the divine feminine over the divine masculine is very clearly reflected, to choose but one example, in the esoteric implications of the Christian anti-Nestorian dogma that the Blessed Virgin Mary is the Theotokos, the mother not only of Christ the man, but of God himself – that she is, in the words of St. Peter Damian, "the origin of the beginning." Of course, for the Christian perennialist, within the framework of the worship of Christ, the Virgin is the object of veneration not only here, but at all the levels of the feminine, and it is upon her that his contemplation rests as he participates in its various interiorizing and elevating operations.

[32]*Stations of Wisdom*, 151.

[33]*Stations of Wisdom*, 151.

[34]*Stations of Wisdom*, 151.

[35]*Essential Writings*. 406.

[36]C. S. Lewis, *The Weight of Glory and Other Addresses* (Grand Rapids, Michigan: Eerdmans, 1979), 36.

Présence et Vertu du Sacré

Roger Du Pasquier

Le fait s'impose avec une évidence lumineuse : le Maroc est un pays privilégié à maints égards. Tous ceux qui 1 'ont visité en conviennent et, dès avant l'avènement du tourisme, en ont abondamment célébré les beautés et l'enchantement. Et désormais, chaque année, de nouvelles publications en exaltent les "visions de rêve" les "horizons vierges", les "villes mirages", la "fascination exotique", et les inépuisables "sortilèges" qui, en plus des agréments d'un climat idéal, suscitent l'enthousiasme des visiteurs européens.

Assurément la prose louangeuse, dithyrambique à l'occasion, ne manque pas. Cependant, se demande Henri J. Hugot dans un récent ouvrage illustré, "par quel miracle ce pays unique reste-t-il toujours à dire?", Car, comme il le constate pertinemment, "aucun des centaines de livres qui lui furent consacrés n'a encore réussi à enfermer dans ses pages son âme profonde, ses visages multiples et ses beautés secrètes. Toujours quelque chose d'essentiel échappe à la plume attentive de l'écrivain..."

Bien d'autres ont eu quelque perception de cet essentiel qui transcende les agréments seulement terrestres du Maroc. Introduisant en 1954 une publication illustrée intitulée *Maroc, terre et ciel*, l'écrivain suisse Jacques Mercanton rappelait avoir ressenti, dès son débarquement à Tanger, une sorte de présence sacrée, "un calme mystérieux et surnaturel" qui saisit le voyageur, "avec, le long du môle, les femmes en voile blanc et les princes astrologues qui se meuvent lentement sur un ciel d'étoile irradiée". Il poursuivait : "A Casablanca même, le plus pauvre porteur, sa djellaba en loques et son turban défait, demeure un roi découronné. Il n'y a pas besoin d'approcher le seuil interdit des mosquées ni même prêter l'oreille à l'appel des muezzins, vibrante mesure du jour dans les petits bourgs solitaires. Tout est ici de l'ordre du sacré : les gestes, les saluts, la plainte et l'ardeur des visages, ces admirables vêtements surtout qui, dans les villes, le long des routes, au plus haut des cols de l'Atlas et jusqu'au bord des sables, font une des permanentes beautés du paysage marocain. S'il est vrai qu'un paysage ne peut exclure la figure de celui que, selon l'Islam, 'Allâh a fait roi de sa création'."

Plus objectifs et moins poétiques qu'on pourrait penser, pareils propos, à trente-trois ans de distance, correspondent encore à un aspect essentiel de la vie marocaine, laquelle, certes, a évolué, mais n'a pas changé fondamentalement. Au *Maghreb al-Aqsâ*, l'Extrême-Occident du domaine de l'Islam, le sacré demeure une présence concrète que tous les étreangers ne ressentent peut-être pas au même degré, la perception des réalités spirituelles étant une faculté inégalement répartie parmi les humains, mais à laquelle la plupart sont sans doute sensibles dans quelque mesure au moins.

Tel que l'a parfaitement défini F. Schuon, l'incomparable auteur de *Comprendre l'Islam,* le sacré est "l'interférence de l'incréé dans le créé, de l'éternel dans le temps, de l'infini dans l'espace, de l'informel dans la forme (...) Le sacré est l'incommensurable, le transcendant, caché dans une forme fragile de ce monde..." (*Principes et critères de l'art universel*). Il est donc rappel de Dieu, Absolu et Infini, dans sa création relative et finie, de l'Au-delà dans l'ici-bas. Cela revient à dire que l'Islam, c'est le sacré.

Qu'est-ce en effet que l'Islam, dans sa pratique individuelle et collective, dans les formes de vie des sociétés qui s'y rattachent, sinon rappel actif et constant de Dieu, Créateur de toutes choses, et invitation à l'adorer sans cesse ? Au contraire de la *ghaflah,* qui est oubli et dissipation dans le quantitatif et le contingent, il est *dhikr,* ou *tadhkīr,* "souvenir" ou "remémoration" de 1 'essentiel, de Dieu, et cela non seulement dans les actes spécifiquement religieux, mais dans le style qu'il imprime, en la sacralisant, à la vie des peuples constituant *l'ummah,* la communauté des croyants.

Telle était sans doute la civilisation musulmane de l'époque dite "classique" qui, dans le cadre de la tradition procédant de la Révélation, avait su aménager la vie de l'ici-bas de maniére à la doter de tous les agréments la rendant digne d'être vécue, mais sans en faire une fin en soi et toujours en vue de l'Au-delà. Empreinte de sacré, cette civilisation avait éclairé le monde d'une lumière venue d'En-haut et manifesté la grandeur terrestre de l'Islam, mais qu'en reste-t-il aujourd'hui ? La question est amère à poser, car il est trop évident que ce n'est pas le "réveil islamique" dont on parle tant qui est en passe de la restaurer. Au moins, entre Pacifique et Atlantique, ses vestiges et survivances permettent d'imaginer ce qu'elle dut être en ses siècles d'or.

Ayant visité depuis nombre d'années une assez grande partie du vaste domaine de l'lslam, je ne saurais assurément nier la réalité du "réveil", ou du "renouveau" si l'on préfère, qu'il connaît actuellement, en particulier en ce qui concerne la pratique quotidienne et la piété. Un peu partout se construisent de nouvelles mosquées et l'assiduité des foules à la prière impressionne les non-musulmans. L'lslam manifeste sa vigueur même dans des pays officiellement laïques comme la Turquie ou l'Inde, et ailleurs, en Afrique notamment, il paraît gagner constamment du terrain. Pareilles constatations rejoignent les informations qui filtrent de l'URSS et confirment qu'il résiste victorieusement à toutes les campagnes de l'athéisme au pouvoir menées depuis bientôt soixante-dix ans pour tenter de l'extirper. Quant à l'Afghanistan, la guerre qui s'y prolonge depuis tant d'années illustre quotidiennement l'héroïsme de son peuple et de ses *moudjahidine,* authentiques combattants de la foi.

Pourtant, malgré cette vitalité, cette foi combative et ce regain de piété dans certaines populations musulmanes, on doit bien reconnaître que le monde de l'Islam est entraîné dans un mouvement général de sécularisation et de désacralisation. Les idéologues de la déstabilisation à l'oeuvre dans maints pays de *l'ummah* ne manquent certes pas de se parer d'étiquettes et d'atours islamiques, mais, en réalité, travaillent le plus souvent à saper les valeurs traditionnelles de l'Islam et à éliminer ce qui reste de sa civilisation. Ainsi se trouve ouverte la voie à une modernisation qui, procédant d'une mentalité étrangère et fondamentalement profane, va dans le sens de l'uniformisation et de la perte d'identité.

A cet égard le Maroc est certainement moins menacé que la plupart des autres pays islamiques. On ne saurait pourtant à son propos parler d'inadaptation au monde moderne où, au contraire, il sait fort bien défendre sa place et affirmer sa personnalité. Or justement, pour l'en rendre capable, l'attachement aux valeurs et formes traditionnelles d'ordre sacré est sans doute d'une importance décisive.

Parmi les expressions de cette fidélité à l'héritage du passé, protection encore efficace contre l'uniformisation sécularisante subie par tant d'autres pays musulmans, on en signalera trois. Elles se situent à des niveaux différents, mais, chacune à sa maniére, sont caractéristiques de la personnalité marocaine.

La première, qui retient au premier regard l'attention du visiteur étranger, est la persistance du vêtement traditionnel jusque dans les grandes villes vivant au rythme de la modernité. Pour en saisir l'importance, il suffira de citer ces lignes de Titus Burckhardt, éminent islamisant et grand ami du Maroc : "En un certain sens, l'art vestimentaire est collectif et même populaire; il n'en est pas moins, indirectement, un art sacré, car le costume viril musulman est en quelque sorte un costume sacerdotal généralisé, de même que l'Islam généralisa le sacerdoce en abolissant la hiérarchie et en faisant de chaque croyant un prêtre (...) C'est le turban qui, d'après le

dire du Prophète, indique la dignité spirituelle, donc sacerdo-
tale..." Et le même auteur constate : "Partout où la civilisation
islamique commence à déchoir, c'est d'abord le turban qu'on
bannit, puis le port des vêtements larges et souples qui
facilitent les gestes de la prière rituelle." (*Principes et méthodes
de l'art sacré*). Les nombreux turbans apparaissant encore aux
yeux de qui parcourt le Maroc attestent ainsi que la civilisation
islamique y est toujours vivante.

Autre expression de fidélité à la tradition, l'artisanat continue à occuper une place plus qu'honorable dans l'économie
marocaine. Il importe à ce propos de rappeler que la civilisation islamique n'a jamais établi de véritable différence entre
art et artisanat, tous deux ayant ensemble pour fonction
essentielle de modeler les formes servant de cadre de vie à la
communauté des croyants et ainsi de créer l'ambiance propre
à sacraliser leur existence terrestre. Dès lors les objets d'usage
courant deviennent des oeuvres d'art répandant un air de
beauté et d'harmonie éminemment favorable à la pratique de
la religion et à la remémoration de Dieu, acte sacré par
excellence.

Fait significatif, les intérieurs bourgeois, au Maroc, sont,
beaucoup plus fréquemment que dans les classes sociales
correspondantes des autres pays arabes et musulmans, meublés
et décorés à la mode traditionnelle, avec des mosaïques, des
stucs et des bois sculptés ainsi que des céramiques et autres
objets, comme des plateaux de cuivre, produits de l'artisanat
local. En cela ils se conforment à deux exemples insignes : les
lieux de culte et les palais royaux. Car il est remarquable que,
sauf exceptions rarissimes, les mosquées, dont de nouvelles ne
cessent de s'élever de terre, demeurent fidèles, dans leur
conception architecturale comme dans leur ornementation,
au modèle traditionnel qui est une des marques de l'identité
marocaine et semble s'inspirer du célèbre *ḥadîth* (enseignement prophétique) : "Dieu est beau, il aime la beauté." Quant
aux palais, dont tous les visiteurs sortent éblouis, ils illustrent
merveilleusement ce qu'il y a de meilleur et de plus achevé

dans ces arts anciens auxquels la protection royale procure la première garantie de survie face aux agressions de la civilisation industrielle.

Enfin, couronnant au sens propre et figuré les deux expressions de fidélité traditionnelle qu'on vient de mentionner, il est indispensable de relever l'importance capitale de la monarchie pour la sauvegarde au Maroc d'une présence sacrée liée à l'Islam. En effet, ainsi que tout esprit libre de préjugés modernistes doit le reconnaître objectivement, la notion de république est étrangère à l'Islam et à sa tradition. Et telle qu'elle est entendue et appliquée aujourd'hui dans d'autres pays du domaine islamique, elle ne peut, jusqu'à l'instauration du régime kémaliste en Turquie, se réclamer d'aucun antécédent dans l'histoire des peuples musulmans, mais procède en droite ligne de la Révolution française, c'est-à-dire de l'événement qui a le plus puissamment contribué au mouvement de sécularisation dans le monde entier.

Le maintien du régime monarchique au Maroc est certainement un privilège providentiel en même temps qu'une garantie de fidélité à la tradition musulmane la plus authentique et la plus orthodoxe. Cela est d'autant plus important que la dynastie alaouite régnante est d'origine chérifienne, c'est-à-dire remontant à la famille du Prophète, instrument de la Révélation de l'Islam, et en tient un caractère sacré dont les bénédictions s'étendent à toute la nation marocaine. Le souverain lui-même est *amîr al-mu'minîn*, "Commandeur des croyants", ce qui lui confère une autorité et un prestige dépassant largement les limites de son royaume. En Afrique occidentale, en particulier, nombreux sont les musulmans qui en gardent conscience et ne parlent du souverain marocain qu'avec vénération.

Le sacré est assurément chose beaucoup plus réelle qu'on ne le pense ordinairement et, lié à une tradition comme celle de l'Islam, garde pour les peuples et pour la qualité de leur vie une importance échappant à la mentalité moderne qui ne juge de tout qu'en termes quantitatifs. Peut-être ne se révèle-

t-il pas également à tous, mais, au Maroc, il est assez rayonnant
pour que beaucoup d'étrangers en aient perçu la présence
comme un mystérieux enchantement.

La "Contemplatio Naturalis"

et son Rôle dans la Mystique chrétienne

Jean Hani

L'union à Dieu, quel que soit le degré de cette union que l'on considère, est le but de toute voie mystique. C'est, d'ailleurs, en principe, le but de toute existence humaine. Mais il est trop évident que, dans sa condition actuelle, l'homme est incapable d'atteindre d'emblée cette fin; il doit d'abord passer par des étapes intermédiaires destinées à le rendre apte à cette union avec le Principe divin, car, dans l'état où il se trouve, sa nature "déchue" ne peut entrer en contact direct avec Dieu.

Si l'on néglige les caractères secondaires qui les affectent, les étapes de la réalisation spirituelle sont fondamentalement les mêmes dans toutes les traditions et se ramènent à trois principales: la purification, l'intégration et l'union. Cette dernière exige, en effet, tout d'abord, que l'homme "déchu", qui est impur, se purifie de ses péchés et de ses passions pour être capable d'approcher la Pureté absolue. Mais, même purifié, l'homme n'a pas enore récupéré son état propre primordial; c'est un être "séparé", muré en son moi et en position conflictuelle aves le monde, les êtres et les choses, et cette situation doit faire place à un état d'harmonie: l'homme ne doit plus se considérer comme un "moi" face au monde et aux aux autres, séparé d'eux, mais comme en osmose et en symbiose avec eux. Il intègre alors sa personnalité véritable, provisoirement enfouie par la "chute", il réalise ce qu'il est véritablement: un microcosme, résumé de l'univers, en "sympathie" avec tous les êtres: il se dilate, pour ainsi dire, jusqu' à englober consciemment l'univers en lui. Alors, au terme de cette deuxième étape, celle de l'intégration, l'homme, ayant acquis du monde et de lui-même une vision analogue à celle que Dieu en a, est prêt pour parcourir la dernière étape, celle de l'union.

Cette étape de l'intégration a, dans la vie spirituelle, une, importance capitale, comme on peut le constater, par example, dans la doctrine et la pratique du yoga exposées par Patañjali [1]. Le yogi se désolidarise de la vie ordinaire, qui est dispersion et agitation, pour discipliner ses facultés et se concentrer. Il s' agit pour lui de s'unifier: d'unifier, d'abord, ses facultés et d'abolir le multiple et la fragmentation. Il s'agit de se retirer de la vie profane pour trouver une autre vie, plus vraie parce que plus "rythmée", la vie du cosmos. Les premières pratiques du yoga visent à une "cosmisation" de l'homme, afin de le mettre à l'unisson de l'harmonie universelle. Il ressort de l'enseignement de Patañjali que l'union – c'est le sens du mot *yoga* – ne peut être obtenue sans cette étape intermédiaire de cosmisation, parce qu'on ne peut passer du chaos de la vie profane à la liberté de la vie spirituelle. Il s'agit donc de réaliser, sur tous les plans de la vie, le rythme que nous révèle le spectacle de la structure de l'univers, le rôle "unifiant"joué, en particulier, par les astres, qui intègrent, par leur rythme, dans un même ensemble, nombre de réalités hétérogènes. De là cette physiologie subtile du *micranthropos* homologuée à celle du *macranthropos* et identifiant les "soleils" et les "lunes", c'est à dire leurs rythmes. C'est à partir d'un cosmos parfait que le yogi trancende la condition cosmique. Cette cosmisation s'opère surtout par la pratique du rythme respiratoire *(prāṇayama)*, qui empêche la pensée de se disperser et permet aux forces psycho-mentales de ne plus circular de façon anarchique; par la respiration, le yogi cosmise son corps et sa vie psychomentale, il s'unit au rythme du monde en homologuant les deux phases du rythme respiratoire, inspire et expire, au rythme du temps et des astres, aux cycles du temps, celui du jour et de la nuit, celui des saisons, etc... jusqu' aux grands cycles de la manifestation universelle, et, ainsi, il revit le processus de toute la manifestation et donc le surmonte. Par ailleurs, en unissant les deux canaux subtils, *iḍā et piṅgalā,* identifiés au soleil et à la lune, dans le canal central *suṣumṇā,* il abolit le temps et même le cosmos par une réintégration des contraires. Cette sortie hors du temps est capitale car, comme le dit Maître Eckhart," il n'existe pas de plus grand obstacle à l'union avec Dieu que le temps".

On trouvera un processus de réalisation analogue, bien que dans un contexte formel très différent, dans la spiritualité des Sioux, que Frithof Schuon a étudiée de façon si pertinente, en particulier dans le rite du calumet. La pipe sacrée, en effet, est un symbole macro-microcosmique: elle représente l'univers et l'homme total qui en est le résumé; en remplissant la pipe avec le tabac, on récite des prières qui sont offertes à toutes les puissances de l'univers et à toutes les formes créées. Le fourneau est assimilé au coeur de l'homme, qui est le centre de l'homme et le centre du monde. Ainsi tout le créé est rassemblé rituellement dans ce centre de l'homme; en fumant ensemble, les fumeurs retrouvent, chacun pour son compte, leur propre centre et prennnent conscience du fait que celui-ci est le même centre que celui de chaque homme et le centre du monde [2].

Dans la mystique chrétienne cette deuxième étape du processus de spiritualisation porte la plupart du temps le nom de "contemplation naturelle" (*theoria physiké,* en grec, *contemplatio naturalis* en latin), la première étape étant l'ascèse *(praxis),* et la troisième, la "déification" *(théosis).*

C'est à l'examen de la deuxième étape, celle de la *theoria physiké,* que nous voudrions nous attacher, étant donné son importance signalée plus haut et, d'autre part, du fait qu'elle est bien moins souvent envisagée que la première et la dernière; ce qui est dû, peut-être, tout d'abord, au fait que l'activité propre à cette étape, se trouve mêlée à celle des deux autres, comme il est normal, d'ailleurs, car il va sans dire qu'il n'existe pas de séparation rigoureuse entre chacune d'elles, que l'ascèse ne cesse jamais complètement au cours de la vie du spirituel, de même que la contemplation naturelle trouve son épanouissement dans l'état du spirituel "déifié". Mais la raison plus profonde de cette mise à l'écart relative de la contemplation naturelle doit certainement être cherchée dans l'ignorance plus ou moins grande que l'on constate, à l'époque moderne, dans le christianisme, – en Occident, tout au moins,– des rapports étroits unissant l'homme au monde, l'ignorance qui est une conséquence de l'individualisme forcené, lequel a radicalisé l'état de séparation. Or, oublier, ou même voiler, l'existence de ces rapports, c'est coublier du même coup le sens et la portée de la création de l'homme qui, dit la Genèse (1, 26), a été fait "à l'image de Dieu". Mais l'Image de Dieu, du "Père", c'est d'abord le Verbe éternel, le Logos, en qui, nous dit Saint Paul, tout a été créé: "Il est l'Image du Dieu invisible, le Premier-né de la Création, car c'est par Lui que toutes choses ont été créées, au Ciel et sur la terre, les choses visibles at les choses invisibles... Tout a été créé par Lui et en Lui... et tout subsiste en Lui" (Col. 1, 15-20). Ainsi l'homme terrestre est, pour reprendre l'expression de certains Pères, "une image de l'Image"; et, du même coup, un élément important de ce que constitue cette image, c'est son état de microcosme par quoi l'homme terrestre est, tout à la fois, image de la création qu'il résume, et image du Verbe divin, en tant qu'il possède un esprit, reflet de l'Intellect divin, capable de concevoir les "Idées" des choses et des êtres, activité analogue, sur un plan inférieur, à celle de l'Intellect divin du Verbe qui les fait exister. C'est en vertu de cette "parenté" entre l'homme et le Verbe divin que celui-ci est appelé aussi "Homme" : il est l' "Homme universel", l'*Adam qadmon* de la tradition hébraïque, Archétype direct de l'homme terrestre, l'*adam ha-rishon*. Et c'est encore en vertu de cette parenté que l'homme terrestre est destiné à être le roi de la création visible (Genèse 1, 26-27). Mais, par là il n'est pas seulement *microcosmos,* mais aussi *microthéos,* destiné à participer à la vie de la Divinité, en passant, selon l'interprétation des Pères concernant ce texte de l'Ecriture, de l' "image" à la "ressemblance" de Dieu (Genèse 1, 26), cette "ressemblance" constituant un état infiniment supérieur à celui de l'état édénique, celui de l' "image", ce qui implique le dépassement du cosmos.

Mais ce dépassement ne peut s'opérer, c'est bien évident, et nous l'avons déjà laissé entendre, qu'à partir du moment où l'homme est en possession de l'intégralité de l'état humain, c'est à dire rétabli dans l'état édénique, lequel comprend la réalisation de sa nature de microcosme et de maître de la nature visible. L'homme "déchu" doit donc refaire en sens inverse le parcours de la "chute" pour récupérer cet état. L'incarnation du Verbe divin a permis de le retrouver et, en particulier, de rassembler le monde visible autour de l'homme: le baptême opère le retour à l'état édénique, mais, comme toute initiation, de façon virtuelle; l'individu doit, à l'aide des moyens de grâce qui lui sont offerts, rendre ce retour effectif. C'est le rôle de sa voie mystique, et, plus particulièrement, de cette "contemplation naturelle" dont le but ultime n'est autre que la "cosmisation" de l'individu selon une modalité différente de celles que nous avons rapportées plus haut, mais fondamentalement identique.

La théologie mystique considère le monde naturel, surtout depuis Maxime le Confesseur qui en montre l'importance à travers toute son œuvre, comme un complément ajouté à l'autorité de l'Ecriture et de valeur égale. Pour lui, "la contemplation de la nature *(theoria physiké),* avec toutes les ressources de sens cachés inhérentes à chaque être, devient la voie unique et nécessaire qui mène à la connaissance (effective) de Dieu"[3]. Le fondement de la contemplation naturelle est d'ordre métaphysique: il repose sur l'analogie et l'identité finale des essences particulières avec l'Essence universelle, analogie et identité dont la perception et l'expérience intérieure vécue est le chemin tout tracé, c'est évident, vers l'Unité et l'union. En effet, comme le dit Nicolas de Cusa, "l'Essence parfaitement simple et infinie... est, en soi, l'Essence absolument simple de toutes essences... Toutes les essences particulières, présentes, passées, futures, sont en acte, de façon permanente et éternelle, cette Essence même, et toutes les essences sont, en quelque sorte, l'Essence universelle elle-même... Cette Essence universelle est elle-même toute essence, en ceci du moins qu'elle est à la fois toutes les essences, sans être individuellement aucune d'elles, et que, comme la ligne infinie est la mesure parfaitement adéquate de toutes les lignes, cette Essence maxima est également, de toutes les essences, la mesure parfaitement adéquate". Ainsi "toute créature est en quelque sorte l'aspect fini de l'Infini, ou l'aspect créé du Dieu créateur"[4].

La source chrétienne de cette vue métaphysique est dans Denys l'Aréopagite, initiateur de toute la théologie mystique: "Par la connaissance analogique, dit-il, nous devons nous élever autant que nous le pouvons jusqu'à la Cause universelle. C'est à cette Cause qu'il nous faut référer tous les êtres selon un mode d'union unique et transcedant, car c'est à partir de l'Etre que, par un mouvement processif et producteur d'essences, elle illumine toutes choses de Sa Bonté... Dans la Nature, qui embrasse la totalité de l'univers... les raisons de chaque nature sont rassemblées dans une seule unité sans confusion. Et dans l'âme aussi, de façon unitaire, les puissances providentiellles correspondent à chaque partie du corps entier..." On peut donc "remonter jusqu'à la Cause universelle et contempler avec des yeux qui ne sont pas de ce monde la totalité des choses, y compris celles qui s'opposent entre elles, dans la Cause universelle sous la forme de l'unité et de l'union"[5].

Cette conception de monde débouche sur une vision magnifiquement décrite par un spirituel, Calliste Cataphygiotès, dont les écrits figurent à la fin du recueil de la *Philocalie;* voici ce qu'il dit: "Il n'est pas une chose dans l'univers qui ne témoigne du rayonnement (de la Gloire) et ne porte comme un parfum de l'Un créateur... Donc, dès lors que l'Un est appelé par toute chose, que toute chose tend vers l'Un et que l'Un plus haut que le monde se révèle à l'intelligence à travers tous les êtres, il est nécessaire que l'intelligence soit conduite, guidée et menée vers l'Un plus haut que le monde. Elle y est forcée par la persuasion de tant d'êtres... De la recherche vient la vision et la vision vient la vie, afin que l'intelligence exulte, s'illumine et se réjouisse, comme l'a dit David: "En Toi est la demeure de tous ceux qui se réjouissent", et: "Dans Ta lumière nous voyons la lumière. Sinon... comment aurait-il semé dans tous les êtres ce qui est à Lui et par quoi, comme à travers des fenêtres, se révélant à l'intelligence, Il l'appelle à aller vers Lui, comblée de lumière?" [6]

D'une façon plus précise, c'est dans le Verbe divin, le Logos, qu'il convient de situer cette vision, conformément au texte de Saint Paul cité plus haut; c'est dans le *Logos* que se rencontrent les "idées" particulières, les *logoi*, des créatures, comme le dit fort bien Maxime le Confesseur, évoquant du même coup le dynamisme spirituel qui anime tout l'univers: "L'unique *Logos* est la multitude des *logoi* et tous les *logoi* sont l'unique *Logos*. Selon la "procession" créatrice et conservatrice pleine de bonté de l'Unique, l'Unique est multiple; selon l' "ascension" *(anaphora)* du retour et la providence conductrice remenant au Principe omnipotent et au centre des lignes droites qui émanent de Lui, les multiples sont l'Unique" [7]. A quoi fait écho Maître Eckhart exprimant la même idée par une image hardie, selon son habitude: "Le Fils est modèle de toutes les créatures et Image du Père, un Archétype où l'essence de toutes les créature est en suspension" [8].

Maxime le Confesseur parle d'une incarnation du Verbe dans les choses: "Il Se cache, dit-il, mystérieusement dans les raisons intérieures *(logoi)* des êtres créés... présent en chacun totalement et avec toute Sa plénitude... En tout le divers est

caché Celui qui est Un et éternellement identique" [9]. Et cette
vérité métaphysique a été réactivée, si l'on peut dire, pour
l'homme déchu, par l'incarnation humaine du Logos divin
en Jésus-Christ. La consommation du monde en Dieu, ex-
plique-t-il dans les *Centuries gnostiques,* se parfait par l'Incarnation du Logos et l'union hypostatique de la nature créée
et de la nature incréée: l'Incarnation et la Croix, la mort et
la résurrection ne sont pas seulement le centre de l'histoire
du monde, mais encore l'idée fondamentale du monde" [10].
Tout le mystère de l'univers est concentré, comme les rayons
au foyer d'une lentille, dans le rapport entre les deux natures du Christ: " Le Christ, ayant achevé pour nous Son
action salvatrice et étant monté au avec le corps qu'il avait
adopté, opère en Lui l'union du ciel et de la terre, des êtres
sensibles et des êtres spirituels, et démontre ainsi l'unité de
la Création dans la polarité de ses parties" [11]. La Création
ainsi unifiée, Il la présente au Père en sa totalité; "résumant
l'univers en Lui-même, Il montre l'unité du tout en celle
d'un seul homme, l'Adam cosmique. Car, en Lui, Dieu,
possède un corps et une âme et des sens comme nous par
lesquels, en tant que parties, Il réunit toutes les parties en
unités qu'Il peut unir elles-mêmes en une totalité suprême"[12].
Le Christ, homme total, "unit la nature créée à la nature
incréée dans l'amour... et montre que, par la grâce, les deux
ne sont plus qu'une seule chose identique. Le monde total
entre totalement dans le Dieu total et, devenant tout ce
qu'est Dieu, excepté l'identité de nature, il reçoit, à la place
de soi, le Dieu total" [13].

On a rarement, à notre avis, su exprimer d'une façon
aussi perfaite et vigoureuse ce que Saint Paul appelle le
"mystère du Christ" et que la tradition patristique
nomme l' "économie du salut". Le "mystère du Christ", c'est
donc la réintégration de l'homme et de toute la création,
réintégration déjà totalement accomplie dans l'Homme-Dieu,
mais qui doit s'accomplir ensuite dans l'homme individuel,
par une participation et, finalement, une identification à la

Personne du Fils. C'est là le but de la voie mystique. Celle-ci, pour y atteindre, dispose de deux moyens de grâce, la Divine Liturgie et l'oraison. La première est la source de toute la vie spirituelle, en tant qu'actualisation du "mystère du Christ" dans la vie de l'homme, et elle joue un grand rôle au cours de l'étape de la voie mystique que nous étudions, celle de la *contemplatio naturalis*. Car la Divine Liturgie, la messe, possède une dimension cosmique indéniable, les Saints Dons, le Pain et le Vin, constituant, selon toute la tradition patristique, les prémices du monde restauré et transfiguré, en même temps que l'homme, dans la lumière du Ressuscité. [14]

Et c'est évidemment à cette source que, mue par l'Esprit Saint, la *contemplatio naturalis* puise toute l'énergie qui se déploie au cours de l'oraison [15]. Nous employons à dessein ce mot, qui est d'un usage traditionnel en Occident, pour désigner la méditation et la contemplation. Il ne signifie par lui-même rien d'autre que la "prière", mais l'usage l'a réservé à la prière méditative et contemplative, dont la forme la plus élaborée est la "Prière du Coeur" ou "Prière de Jésus", de l'Eglise byzantine, particulièrement pratiquée dans la tradition hésychaste.

La méthode, on le sait, consiste en une invocation répétitive, et qui doit finalement devenir continuelle, du Nom de Jésus, soit de la formule "Seigneur Jésus Christ, Fils de Dieu, aie pitié de moi", soit du Nom de "Jésus" seul. Nous n'avons pas à exposer en détail la technique utilisée pour cette prière; nous rappellerons simplement quelques points fondamentaux qui éclairent la façon dont elle opère au niveau de l'étape mystique que nous étudions.

Il s'agit, en invoquant le Nom, de concentrer l'attention sur le coeur, qui est le centre de l'être, et, à la limite, de l'y fixer; le résultant recherché est, selon la formule connue, de "rassembler ce qui est épars", de faire descendre le mental dans le coeur, parce que le mental est dispersion dans le domaine des apparences, du phénoménal, du multiple et de la successivité, auxquels il faut échapper pour réactualiser la grâce baptismale, récupérer l'état édénique, reconstituer l'unité du "coeur conscient" ou, si l'on préfère, l'intelligence du "coeur spirituel". Parce que le coeur est le centre immobile, coeur physique et spirituel à la fois où l'Amour et la Connaissance *(eros-agapé* et *gnosis)* sont indissolublement liés, lieu où se joignent transcendance et immanence, où réside l'image divine en l'homme. Le coeur est, en particulier, le centre du corps humain, microcosme et résumé de l'univers; ce n'est pas une réalité purement individuelle, mais écclésiale et cosmique, miroir du Centre total, image de Dieu qui est, selon le mot de Saint Clément d'Alexandrie, le "Coeur du monde", où toutes choses se joignent comme les rayons sont tous présents au centre du cercle. En se fixant dans le coeur, l'homme s'établit en ce point d'où sa vision s'unifie au lieu de se disperser, et s'universalise: il cesse de faire tourner le monde autour de son moi et se met à le faire tourner, au contraire, autour de Dieu, dont il prononce sans cesse le Nom. Cette invocation réactive en lui l'image divine originelle; il redevient peu à peu le "roi de la création" qui fait rayonner sur le créé la lumière divine à partir de son coeur transfiguré.

Car, alors, il contemple la nature en Dieu. Il voit, petit à petit et de plus en plus, Dieu dans les êtres et les choses; dépassant le voile des apparences, il perçoit peu à peu les essences, les *logoi*; il les voit dans l'unique *Logos* où ils sont "en suspension", comme dit Eckhart.

La réalisation de cet état se fait, conformément à la spécificité du christianisme, en mode bhaktique, par la dévotion dans l'invocation du Nom et par l'offrande dévotionnelle de tous les êtres à la Divinité. Nous sommes ici en face d'une conception liturgique de l'existence fondée sur la beauté, la beauté du monde; car, "la beauté, est un Nom divin devenu, ou plutôt redevenu en Christ un nom divino-humain et divino-cosmique, un Nom, c'est à dire une modalité de la Présence divine" [16]. Par l'invocation de ce Nom, le spirituel actualise la présence divine en lui et, en même temps, hors de lui, sur le monde, parce que, écrit un moine, "le Nom de Jésus contient le monde, comme, dans le rayon de lumière, se fondent les couleurs du prisme. C'est dans Son Verbe que le Père a tout créé. L'invocation du Nom de Jésus sur tout ce qui existe permet de transfigurer, de 'christifier' l'univers et de lui rendre son vrai sens... Non seulement c'est dans Son Verbe que Dieu a créé l'univers, mais le Dieu incarné attire à Lui tous les mondes. Comme le dit Saint Paul, la création entière 'soumise à la vanité' (au mal physique, aux catastrophes, à la rigueur des lois naturelles), 'gémit et souffre les douleurs de l'enfantement' et 'attend avec un ardent désir la révélétion du Fils de Dieu'"[17]. Le même auteur écrit encore: "Le Nom de Jésus nous aide à transfigurer le monde entier en Jésus-Christ. Cela est vrai de la nature inanimée elle-même. L'univers matériel, qui n'est pas seulement le symbole visible de l'invisible Beauté divine, mais qui s'efforce en gémissant vers le Christ et dont un mouvement mystérieux élève tout le devenir vers le Pain et le Vin du salut, cet univers murmure secrètement le Nom de Jésus... et il appartient au ministère sacerdotal de chaque chrétien d'exprimer cette aspiration, de prononcer le Nom de Jésus sur les éléments de la nature, les pierres et les arbres, les fleurs et les fruits, la montagne et la mer, de donner san accomplissement au secret des choses... Nous pouvons aussi transfigurer le monde animal... Comme Adam dans le paradis, nous avons à 'donner un nom' à tous les animaux... Nous invoquerons sur eux le Nom de Jésus, leur rendant ainsi leur dignité primitive... Mais c'est surtout par rapport aux hommes que le Nom de Jésus nous aide à exercer un ministère de transfiguration... C'est sur les traits des hommes et des femmes que nous pouvons, par les yeux de la foi et de l'amour, voir le Face du Seigneur... Or, le Nom de Jésus est un moyen concret et puissant de transfigurer les hommes en leur plus profonde et divine réalité" [18].

C'est, en effet, d'abord sur les hommes que l'amour doit se répandre au moment où le coeur spirituel comprend que l'ensemble des humains ne constitue, selon l'étonnante expression de Saint Grégoire de Naziance, qu' "un miroir brisé où l'unique et parfaite image du Fils se reflète". En prononçant le Nom du Sauveur sur les autres, le spirituel prend peu à peu conscience de la consubstantialité de tous les hommes dans le Christ, selon la parole de Saint Paul: "Vous êtes tous un seul être dans le Christ *(heis este en Christo)*" (Gal. 3, 26 ss.), parce que tous les hommes sont destinés a se rencontrer tous dans le Corps du Christ "de manière à former un seul Homme parfait *(eis andra teleion)* parvenu à la mesure de la stature et de la plénitude du Christ" (Eph. 4, 12-13).

Le "souvenir de Dieu" que constitue l'invocation du Nom est aussi, comme le dit la *Philocalie,* "réminiscence de notre identité avec la lumière céleste de notre propre image incorruptible" et, ainsi, de notre coincidence intemporelle avec notre origine adamique; dans cette origine l'humanité est inhérente à chaque homme et le prochain n'est pas "un autre" [19].

Mais, encore une fois, l'amour des hommes ne peut être séparé de celui de tous les êtres pour que soit récupéré intégralement la condition édénique, car tout doit être ramené à l'Un. Or, les êtres et les choses du monde participent à la vie divine dans le Verbe divin. Et cette vision du monde chez le spirituel qui invoque le Nom de Jésus est une source de joie indicible: "La lumière du Nom de Jésus, dit l'un d'eux, illumine, à travers le coeur, tout l'univers. Cet état ne peut être décrit par la parole, mais c'est déjà le prototype de 'Dieu sera tout en tous'" [20]. De même, c'est un spectacle de paradis retrouvé que nous décrit le "pélerin russe": "Quand je priais au fond du coeur, tout ce qui m'entourait m'apparaissait sous un aspect ravissant: les arbres, les herbes, les oiseaux, la terre, l'air, la lumière, tous semblaient me dire qu'ils existent pour l'homme, qu'ils témoignent de l'amour de Dieu pour l'homme; tout priait, tout chantait gloire à Dieu! Je comprenais ainsi ce que la *Philocalie* appelle 'la connaissance du langage de la création', et je voyais comment il est possible de converser avec les créatures de Dieu". Et encore: "Le monde extérieur m'apparaissait sous un aspect ravissant, tout m'appelait à aimer et à louer Dieu: les hommes, les arbres, les plantes, les bêtes, tout m'était comme familier et partout je trouvais l'image du Nom de Jésus" [21].

Dans cette perspective, êtres et choses célèbrent à leur manière une sorte de liturgie cosmique: "Il me semblait que chaque herbe, chaque fleur, chaque épi de seigle me chuchotait de mystérieuses paroles sur une *essence divine toute proche* (c'est nous qui soulignons), toute proche de l'homme, de chaque animal, de toute chose; herbes, fleurs, arbres, terre, soleil, étoiles, et de tout l'univers" [22]. Nous avons ici le récit de l'expérience vécue de la réalité métaphysique décrite en mode théorique dans les textes, cités plus haut, de Nicolas de Cusa et de Calliste Cataphygiotès. Cette liturgie cosmique de la nature visible est relayée par l'homme. Car si la vie universelle est en état de prière, cette prière est muette et a besoin de la bouche humaine et du coeur humain pour s'exprimer et retentir. C'est là, justement, qu'intervient la *contemplatio naturalis* au cours de la "Prière du coeur", où la posture du corps et le rythme respiratoire jouent un rôle auquel fait allusion un auteur de la *Philocalie* "Par cette rétention mesurée de la respiration, écrit-il, toutes les autres puissances de l'âme s'unissent et reviennent à l'esprit et, par l'esprit, à Dieu, ce qui est admirable à dire. Ainsi l'homme offre à Dieu toute la nature sensible et intellectuelle, dont il est le lien et la synthèse suivant Grégoire de Thessalonique, *Vie de Pierre l'Athonite*" [23]. La suite des idées peut n'apparaître pas tout de suite clairement à cause du raccourci de l'expression: l'auteur veut dire l'unification intérieure de l'homme (microcosme) entraîne un ressemblement de tout le visible (macrocosme) prélude à l'offrande à Dieu.

Cette offrande consiste, selon Maxime le Confesseur, en une contemplation qui immole le phénoménal pour dégager le spirituel: "Nous apportons, "des dons à Dieu losque nous

offrons au Seigneur les idées *(logoi)* sprituelles des créatures...
L'esprit gnostique offre les idées spirituelles qui lui sont
tendues par la création, comme des dons de Dieu" [24]. Dans
cette offrande, dit-il encore, "l'homme entre avec le logos et,
avec Lui et sous Sa conduite, il offre l'univers à Dieu dans
son intelligence, comme sur un autel" [25].

Quand elle atteint sa perfection, la *contemplatio naturalis*
débouche sur ce que l'on a appelé la "charité cosmique". Le
spirituel est devenu un "coeur qui brûle d'amour pour la
création tout entière, pour les hommes, les oiseaux, les bêtes,
pour les démons, pour toutes les créatures... mû par la pitié
infinie qui s'éveille dans le coeur de ceux qui s'unissent à
Dieu". C'est une amplification cosmique de l'être "constamment absorbé dans l'avènement de la régénération de toutes
choses"[26]. Le spirituel réalise intérieurement la mort et la
résurrection du cosmos entier dans la plénitude métacos-
mique du Logos "en qui tout a été créé" (Eph. 1, 10; 4, 13).
Mais c'est qu'alors il a déjà pénétré au delà de l'état édénique
sur la voie de la "déification": "Celui qui aura rendu pur son
coeur ne connaîtra pas seulement les raisons *(logoi)* des êtres
inférieurs: il fixera aussi dans une certaine mesure Dieu Lui-
même, lorsque, ayant franchi la succession de tous les êtres,
il atteindra au faîte suprême de la félicité" [27]. Il est celui
"pour qui, selon l'*Imitation*, toutes choses sont l'Un et qui
voit toutes choses dans l'Un". Et celui qui "voit dans l'Un, il
voit tout et, étant dans le tout, du tout il ne voit rien. Voyant
dans l'Un, par Lui il se voit lui-même, les autres et tout le
reste; et, caché en Lui, il ne voit (distinctement) aucune
chose"[28].

[1] Mircea Eliade, *Patañjali et le yoga*, Paris, 1962, et *Yoga et immortalité*, Paris, 1954.

[2] Hehaka Sapa, *Les Rites secrets des Indiens Sioux*, intr. de F. Schuon, Paris, 1953.

[3] Hans Urs von Baltasar, *Liturgie cosmique, Maxime le Confesseur*, trad. fr., Paris, 1947, p.18.

[4] Nicolas de Cusa, *De la Docte ignorance*, I, ch. 16; II, ch. 2.

[5] *Noms divins* 5, 9 et 5, 7.

[6] Cité dans J. Serr et O. Clément, *La Prière du coeur*, Ed. Abbaye de Bellefontaine, Paris, 1977, p. 115.

[7] Maxime le Confesseur, *Ambigua* (PG 91-1081 C)

[8] Eckhart, *Sermon* 56 (Pfeiffer) dans *Traités et sermons* (éd. Aubier), p. 248.

[9] *Ambigua* (PG 91-1285 C et 1288 A).

[10] *Centuries gnostiques* 1, 66-67 (PG 90-1108 AB). Cf. Urs v. Balt., op. cit. p. 210 ss.

[11] Maxime le Confesseur, *Diss. sur l'oraison dominicale* (PG 90-877 AB).

[12] *Ambigua* (PG 91-1308 A (1309 BC, 1312 A).

[13] *Ibid.* 1308 C.

[14] Voir, poir exemple, Saint Irénée, *Adv. haer.* 4, 18, 5. On remarquera aussi que le "lieu de la Divine liturgie", le temple, est la traduction plastique du mystère: image géométrique de l'univers et image du Corps de l'Homme-Dieu, il figure le cosmos transfiguré et, par là, il s'assimile à la Jérusalem céleste. Nous avons développé ces idées relatives au temple et à la liturgie dans deux ouvrages: *Le symbolisme du temple chrétien* (Paris, Ed. Trédaniel, 1978) et *La Divine Liturgie* (Paris, Trédaniel, 1981).

[15] "L'âme, écrit Maxime le Confesseur, se réfugie, comme dans une église et un asile de paix, dans la contemplation spirituelle de l'univers" (*Mystagogie*, 23 (PG-91-697 D).

[16] O. Clément, *op.cit.*, p. 53.

[17] *Jésus*, par un moine de l'Eglise d'Orient, Ed. de Chévetogne, Paris, 1960, p. 81-82.

[18] *Sur l'usage de la Prière de Jésus*, par un moine de l'Eglise d'Orient, Ed. de Chévetogne, Paris, 1952, p. 8-9.

[19] D'après les *Centuries* de Calliste et Ignace (XIVème s.), dans H. de B., *La Prière du coeur,* Ed. Orthodoxes, Paris , 1953, p. 12-13.

[20] S. Boulgakof, *L'Orthodoxie,* Paris, 1932, p. 205.

[21] *Récits d'un pélerin russe,* trad. J. Gauvain, Paris, 1948, p. 56-57 et 149.

[22] Archimandrite Spiridon, *Mes Missions en Sibérie,* Paris, 1950 et 1964, p. 19.

[23] Nicodème l'Hagiorite, *Enchiridion,* ch.dans *La Petite Philocalie de la prière du coeur,* trad. J. Gouillard, Paris, 1953, p. 315. On rapprochera ce rôle de la respiration dans l'hésychasme de celui qu'il joue dans le yoga indien et dont nous avons parlé plus haut.

[24] Maxime le Confesseur, *Quaest. ad. Thalass.,* 51 (PG 98-481 C).

[25] Id., *Mystag.,* 4 (PG 91 - 672 C)

[26] Isaac le Syrien, *Centuries: la Prière,* dans la *Petite Philocalie,* p. 82 et H. de B., *op, cit.,* p. 14-15.

[27] Maxime le Confesseur, *Centuries théologiques* 2, 79 ss. (PG 90-1161 ss.) (= *Petite Philocalie,* p. 159).

[28] Grégoire le Sinaïte, dans H. de B., *op cit.,* p. 9. La même pensée est développée par Eckhart dans un sermon (éd. Aubier, p. 244):" Toutes les créatures se rassemblent dans ma raison afin que je les prépare toutes à retourner à Dieu".

Notes on the Light of the Eastern Religions

with Special Reference to the Writings of Ananda Coomaraswamy, René Guénon, and Frithjof Schuon

Bernard Kelly

In Gredt's *Elementa Philosophiae Aristotelico-Thomisticae,* "Brahmanism" is listed under pantheism as *monismus emanationis.* Before attempting any closer approach to Hindu traditional teaching it is well to give some account to the relative truth of such a judgement. Gredt's brief summary of the pantheistic doctrine is *absolutum a se emittit et dividit partes suae substantiae.* The absurdity of an "absolute" which is a substance susceptible of division into parts is, of course, patent. What at first arouses our incredulity is that anyone with knowledge of "Brahmanism" should impute so crass an error to an intellectual tradition which is nothing if not subtle.

Yet, if a certain assumption is made, there is plenty of evidence for such a judgement. And the assumption in question is naturally and inevitably made by every intellectually hopeful purchaser of potted "Hindu Scriptures" – unless he deliberately unmakes it – the assumption that he is going to understand something of what he reads without having it explained to him by one who knows and lives by the tradition in which it is written.

Teachers so qualified are not found every day, even when

they are sought, and, in effect, what the Western reader of
Hindu texts generally does is to struggle to make sense of
verbal passages against a background of thought which,
whether instructed or not, is purely Western and of the
twentieth century. What, in that case, is he to make of the
images with which Hindu teaching abounds: the river returning to the sea (Muṇḍaka 3,28; *Praśna*, 6,5); the earthen-
ware pot of which the abiding reality is the clay (Chandogya,
6,1,4); the evolution and involution of the universe from the
Imperishable as a spider emits and draws in its thread
(Muṇḍaka, 1,7), but pantheism of the type named by Gredt?

The history of the infiltration of Hindu "thought" into
Western milieus is not one of unmixed intellectual light.
From the middle to the end of last century the interest of
professional scholars in Sanskrit texts was predominantly
linguistic. It was not long before professors of Sanskrit
literature had made statistical counts of all the vowels and
consonants in the Ṛig Veda. At the end of the period we
find Lanman complaining of the jejune puerilities of the
Brāhmaṇas. It did not seem to occur to these good men that
such criticism might reflect upon their own approach to
their subject matter. Meanwhile translations were appearing
in several European languages but it is impossible really to
trust one of them without a Sanskrit text beside it. All the
same, no one could translate the Upanishads so badly [1] as to
offer no suggestion to the literary and philosophical imagination of the contemporary Western world. This suggestibil-
ity has been exploited by Blavatsky and the Theosophists.
There is no need to underline the words "confusion of
thought" in speaking of all this. Confusion of thought is not
a good thing.

Neither the nineteenth century nor our own possesses a
philosophical language able to render metaphysical truth
with precision. The attempt to find words for exact metaphysical terms has baffled the translators of St. Thomas no
less than of the Upanishads. There is however a difference,

for while the translators of St. Thomas may be presumed to have one traditional intellectual discipline at their fingertips, the translators of the Upanishads, who needed to have two, generally had neither. It has been said, with some justice, that they appear to have taken their philosophical language from the newspapers. The Hindu texts are not the cause of confusion, but the occasion for its display [2]. Although it is absolutely false to equate Hindu metaphysics with pantheism, in a relative and practical sense there is a great deal of truth in the judgement that "Brahmanism" is to be shunned as pantheistic. For "Brahmanism" in that sense is the child of Western sensationalism and a mirror of our own intellectual chaos.

Something of the same kind of confusion is inevitable whenever cultures based on profoundly different spiritual traditions intermingle without rigid safeguards to preserve their purity. The crusader with the cross emblazoned on his breast, the loincloth and spindle of Mahatma Gandhi when he visited Europe, are images of the kind of precaution that is reasonable when traveling in a spiritually alien territory. The modern traveler in his bowler hat and pin-stripes is safeguarded by that costume against any lack of seriousness in discussing finance. Of more important safeguards, he knows nothing. The complete secularism of the modern Western world, and wherever its influence has spread, has opened the flood-gates to a confusion which sweeps away the contours of the spirit. Where there is no vision, the people perish. And "vision" is not just the personal endowment of this or that exceptional person. It is the luminous eye of a tradition turned towards the source of its light.

The recall to tradition was sounded, above all, by Ananda Coomaraswamy. He it was who scattered the pedantries of the orientalists by the sufficiently self-evident proposition that it is idle to attempt to understand a metaphysical tradition if all one knows about metaphysics is some silly flippancy about looking for a black hat in a dark room. The

Western mind unversed in the disciplines of truth inherent
in its own tradition – the discipline, for example, of Plato
and Aristotle, Boethius, Augustine, Bonaventure and Aquinas – has no medium in which to understand Hindu doctrines or the raison d'être of Hindu art. Coomaraswamy
proceeded to teach the principles of mediaeval aesthetics to
those who came to see the Indian collection in the Boston
Museum. Never, perhaps, until the publication of *The Transformation of Nature in Art* (Harvard University Press, 1934)
had it been possible for the student to hold together parallel
passages from the East and West and to see clearly that they
were both teaching, with differences of style, the self-same
truths that the modern world had forgotten. The recall to
tradition was not addressed only to the West.
Coomaraswamy's exegetic work on Vedic texts qualified him
as a teacher of Hindu tradition to Hindus, as well as its most
brilliant exponent to the scholars of America and Europe.
His method was essentially collation, the bringing together
of parallel texts to enable them to interpret each other. He
did not formulate a technical vocabulary to facilitate this
work, for such an undertaking would have been a perversion
of the work itself, an intrusion of his own individuality between light and light, but his extraordinary semantic power
in the use of words gave to his metaphysical writings a purity
and pregnancy of which it is hard to find the equal in
English. He was nothing if not a challenging writer, challenging to intelligence, able to put egoism, prejudice and
impure intentions in their place without the crude resort of
contempt, but above all, challenging to sanctity. Under his
influence the task of effecting mutual understanding between East and West from a hopeless dream became an
intellectual vocation; a vocation addressed not primarily to
scholars in the secular sense, for Hindu tradition knows no
distinction between sacred and secular, least of all in the
realm of knowledge, but primarily to theologians: to those
versed in sacred doctrine. One thing is abundantly clear

from the work of Coomaraswamy, that any *a priori* assumption limiting the scope of the Hindu doctrines for example, to the sphere of "natural mysticism", if there is such a thing, can only obscure the evidence provided by the doctrines themselves, as well as deluding the student by highly dubious conceptions.

The technical vocabulary followed in the works of René Guénon. If common discourse were to be facilitated, a common metaphysical language was at least a practical necessity. If common discourse were actually taking place at the level of purely metaphysical ideas in spite of the wide difference of Eastern and Western points of view, then something at least was susceptible of formulation in terms intelligible to each.

In the works of Guénon the recall to tradition has the utmost urgency. His polemical works attack, without quarter asked or given, the complacent individualism of the twentieth-century world, its obliviousness to its own lack of anything approaching genuine spirituality, its rationalism, its materialism, its literary philosophizings, its humanism, its persuasion of its own progressive superiority, its blindness to traditional truth. With very good reason he disclaims any pretension to put forward a "system of ideas" to compete with the systems of modern philosophers. The ideas he puts forward are not indeed his own. He recalls Westerners to their own Catholic tradition, the Moslem world to Islam, India to Hinduism, each to the tradition from which they may draw life, and to a truth which transcends the opinions of men. In all the work of Guénon it is tradition as such which possesses authority as passing on the light of primordial revelation and making possible the knowledge of divine Truth; traditional wisdom which alone merits the name of science; traditional norms which provide the criteria of culture and civilization. Traditional orthodoxy is thus the prerequisite of any discourse at all between the traditions themselves.

The Guénonian position is thus situated far above the syncretism of an Aldous Huxley or a Gerald Heard, which retains the literary individualism of the 1920s. It is not a syncretism at all. In principle his point of view is situated in the transcendent unity of traditional doctrines: not in the theory of their unity, but in that unity itself.

The inevitable and indeed necessary objection to such a position is: "Whom does such a man make himself?" In principle, he makes of himself nothing at all, but of the doctrines everything. The luminous penetration of his expositions is his testimony.

Inevitably, too, from the exalted nature of the task undertaken in his writings, the human limitations of the writer obtrude and rankle to the extent of inhibiting the reader's confidence in their otherwise patent truth. By far the most important of these limitations – not indeed a limitation of intellectual capacity but an inhibition of another kind – is his inability to grasp the spirit of the theological tradition which stems from St. Thomas. Here, where light might indeed have been expected we have a restricted and external accuracy which, on that very account, is less than accurate, as may be seen in the limited scope he concedes to the sacraments in post-Nicaean Christianity.

For the rest his expositions show a remarkable facility at a certain logical or quasi-mathematical level which may too easily obscure the depth of the metaphysical ideas they render explicit. His writing is not eirenic. Its tone is withering, intransigent, unbending; he scolds.

Nevertheless, in a world of philosophical opinions, Guénon writes from, and in the name of, a knowledge which far transcends his own failings as a writer. It is supremely difficult to oppose him in any essential matter without finding oneself in opposition to truth [3].

A further important consequence of his own position in relation to his work, is to preclude the possibility of a "Guénonism". To follow Guénon is not to follow Guénon the man, but to follow the light of traditional truth in that tradition in which its authority compels. If the legacy of Guénon is not a "philosophy", he has indeed handed on the technical terminology which facilitated his expositions. This terminology has been the metaphysical language of a group of writers associated with him until his death in 1951. Its precision and comprehension renders it *de rigueur* for an Occidental working in the field of Eastern metaphysics whether of the Far East, of Hinduism or of Islam. Precisely as terminology it has considerable difficulty for anyone brought up in the Thomist tradition, more so, perhaps than for one who has not been brought up in any tradition at all, because the ultimately indefinable terms have a sense oblique, if not sometimes contrary to the Thomist sense of the same words. But its difficulty is precisely inherent in the metaphysical ideas it expresses, a difficulty we can test by the simple question: "How many Thomist writers of today are capable of sustaining a metaphysical insight and of those who can, how many do?"

Metaphysics with Guénon or with Frithjof Schuon, whose work has the intrinsic authority of a contemplative intelligence, is something very different from a secular prelude to theology excluded from the holies by the limitations of the natural reason. It is not limited to "natural theology", but is susceptible to the analogies of traditional formulations of Truth far beyond the limits of that rather artificial science – artificial, that is, so far as it understands itself to be autonomous.

In the writings of Frithjof Schuon and Titus Burckhardt the interior understanding of the Christian spiritual life is certainly as profound as in Coomaraswamy. In three books published up to the time of writing (1954), Schuon has put his work before a wider public [4]. These works not only show an understanding of Christian truth precisely as truth, which recalls the early Fathers of the Eastern Church, but also exhibit an interior dimension in that understanding which no mere scholarship could produce. If in The *Transcendent Unity* Schuon speaks of the way of Grace as one who understands that Divine economy in relation to the exoteric and esoteric paths of Islam, and to the ways of *bhakti* and *jñāna* in Hindu tradition, in *Spiritual Perspectives* he speaks of Grace as one in whom it is operative and as it were in virtue of that operation. The book has a fullness of light which we have no right to find in the twentieth century, or perhaps in any other century.

There are, of course, difficulties. There will be no attempt in the present essay to deal as such with the major thesis expressed in the title: "the transcendent unity of the religions". What is of quite vital importance is to seek a position which will not falsify evidence when we see it. This task belongs fundamentally to the kingdom of heaven where the final answers reside. But the kingdom of heaven is always now, and there is unhappily no escape from the labour imposed by it on the plea that a century of preparation would be needed. As Schuon says: "He who does not know how to discern the truth in every mental form that contains truth runs the risk of losing, with some particular form, all truth." (*Spiritual Perspectives,* p. 74). And this is true because the ability to discern truth at the level at which Schuon is speaking depends, not primarily on mental qualifications, but on purity of heart.

Obviously then, there can be no question at this stage of finding an adaptable position of Thomist teaching to accommodate some fragment of Oriental doctrine already mediated by Westernizing swamis. That is to trifle. At a certain level of incomprehension the attitude of Gredt is the only tenable one. But to keep that attitude in the face of increasing light would be a monstrous perversion of intelligence.

All language of the intelligence depends on the light of principles which are pre-conceptual and, in the Guénonian term, "formless". "Being" is ultimately ineffable, not simply

because it is logically presupposed in every attempted definition of it, but because it is one of the names of God. If
metaphysical exposition were only a matter of correct logical
procedure on grounds accessible to anyone so far as he has a
thinking apparatus at all, then the more able logician might
stiffen his neck to win the day. But in doing so he would
render the concept of Being opaque to its pre-conceptual
light. On the contrary, metaphysical knowledge is essentially
contemplative: intellectual rather than rational, real rather
than notional. Its exposition involves concepts and the discourse which uses them. But the "concept of Being" is
always and necessarily a contraction of pre-conceptual light
and is true so far as it is open to that light. As soon as the
concept is closed to that light and is substituted for it, it is
false.

The Eastern doctrines have the source of their light beyond the explicit scope of Thomistic concepts. The concept
of Being in St. Thomas, taken from below, is open and
illimitable upwards in the direction, that is, of *Esse.* And this
is so because it is taken from below and vehicles the approach of the created intelligence to the Uncreated. Being,
in the Eastern perspectives is seen from above. It is the
primordial affirmation of what is itself beyond affirmation
and beyond Being. The manifested world is related to Being
as to its principle, but Being is related to what is beyond
Being as to its principle.

For a Thomist, a principle beyond Being is an impossibility. But when he has recovered from the verbal shock of
such a statement, it is surely possible for him to understand
something in his own terms of what is meant by the "Beyond-
Being" (*Sur-Etre*) of Guénon, the "Non-Being" of the Tao,
the transcendent implication in the *sadasat* of the Upanishads.

Being (*Esse*), so far as it is expressed in a concept taken
from below, is not merely a notion more generalized than
the categories, for if so it would transcend them only in

point of vagueness. It is a principle and a meaning diversely
expressed in all the categories; for each of the Aristotelian
categories, and not merely that which is called "relation", is a
diverse relation to *Esse*, and is meaningless save as a relation
to *Esse*. Any thing in the created world is related to *Esse* in a
twofold way. The first is the relation to *Esse* as its transcendent principle, and that relationship is vertical. The second
is the relation to its participated being so far as this is its own,
and this relation is horizontal.

In this second sense, the participated being of the creature is an *actus compositi* and its determinate import, as the
being of this or that, derives from the limitation of the
particular created essence which determines "this" as "not-
that". In the first and vertical sense, the created essence is a
pure potentiality to *Esse*, and apart from *Esse* it is nothing. As
potentiality it is wholly and really related to *Esse*, but it is only
in the horizontal sense and not in the vertical that being is
really related to the particular *essentia* which participates it.
Esse as such and *per se* is illimitable and absolute; it is uncreated and uncreatable. There is no real distinction in God
of *essentia* and *Esse*. God's *Esse* is His *Essentia*. Or, in a more
strict sense, God is illimitable *Esse* and has no *essentia* apart
from *Esse*. For God is *omnino simplex*.

The vertical relationship implies that all creatable perfection ("quality", in the Guénonian terminology) is in God;
but what is in God is God. As Anselm says: *Creatura in creatore
est creatrix essentia*. So far as the "qualities" or perfections of
creatures are in God, they are there in the illimitable and
impartible simplicity of *Esse*. God supereminently is everything. It *is* only in participated being that every thing is
distinct from every other thing, and being a thing implies a
limitation.

> *Creatio active significata*, says St. Thomas, *significat actio-
> nem divinam quae est eius essentia, cum relatione ad creatu-
> ram: sed relatio in Deo ad creaturam non est realis, sed secun-
> dum rationem tantum. Relatio vero creaturae ad Deum est
> relatio realis.* (S. Th. *Prima Pars XLV*, Art 3 ad 1).

The relation of God to creatures which is *secundum ra-tionem tantum* is an aspect of Divinity which necessarily arises so far as the real relation of creatures terminates in Him. So far as the word "God" means the Lord of all creatures, it denotes a relation which is *secundum rationem tantum,* and in that sense it is necessary, as Eckhart said, to go beyond "God". But it is a shocking thing to say because the word "God" in Christian use always means everything that is comprised in the Uncreated.

Precisely because we are creatures, we can predicate perfection of God only by affirming in Him those distinct perfections of creatures which imply no intrinsic imperfection, and then denying that in Him they are really distinct. They are virtually distinct in God in the sense that what in Him is absolute simplicity is diversely imitable in participated being. They are distinct in reason insofar as the meaning of Truth is distinct from that of Love or of Necessity, and to confuse them is falsehood. They are identified and not confused in the simplicity of the divine *Esse* in which they are simply one, without any distinction.

The above considerations are necessary in order to approach such a passage as this from Schuon:

"There are three great divine mysteries: the world, Being, and Non-Being.

"In the world, no quality is another quality, and no quality is God. In Being, no quality is another quality, but each of them is God. In Non-Being – Beyond-Being – there are no qualities; but since Non-Being is transcendence and not privation, in the sense that it is devoid of qualities because it transcends all diversity, it can be said that in it every quality is the other qualities and their indistinction or their transcendence is God.

"What reason cannot understand is how it is that the world is metaphysically reducible to God and how God is Non-Being, or better, Beyond-Being. The world exists, but it 'is' not. And God, inasmuch as the whole

Divine Reality is envisaged, 'is' not, but 'possesses Being'.
God envisaged as Being is in reality only the Being of
God. But it is not false to say, in relation to the world,
that God 'is'. Humanly speaking, it can even be said,
though the expression is improper, that God 'exists', in
order to specify that he is not 'inexistent', that is, that
he is 'real', 'positive', 'concrete'." (*Spiritual Perspectives*
page 166.)

   In an earlier footnote (page 78), he says: "God is
infinite. If certain theologians identify God with Being,
this is not because they deny the infinity of God, far
from it, but because they identify Being with the Infinite, which is quite another matter. To see only the
ontological aspect of the Infinite is not to deny the
Infinite as such. To accept the Infinity of God is thus
implicitly to accept 'Beyond-Being', of which Being is as
it were the 'determinative affirmation'."

Schuon himself has made it plain enough that Non-Being
does not mean mere nothingness, for he says that Non-
Being (or better, Beyond-Being) is transcendence and not
privation. Neither does the non-distinction of qualities mean
their confusion, for confusion belongs to what is beneath
Being, not to what is above it. In a manner complementary
to his own footnote, we may say that the doctrine he expounds appears to limit Being to an aspect of Itself and to
reserve another term for what is beyond that aspect. In
Thomist terms, the distinction of "qualities" or transcenden-
tal perfections in the divine *Esse* is in the creature's knowledge of God, and necessarily so, not in God's knowledge of
Himself. God's knowledge of Himself is simply God, illimitable *Esse*. But the creature, so far as it *is* not but participates
in Being and so exists, has distinction (limit) in itself implicit
in the distinction of *essentia* and *esse*. How far it is true that
what is an aspect from below is an "affirmation" from above
is a question on which Mr. Schuon's guidance would be
helpful. But we may note that St. Thomas (in *Boethium de*

Trinitate, QIV, Art. 1) places the principle of plurality not in otherness (*diversitas*), but in *divisio: quia divisio non requirit utrumque condivisorum esse, cum divisio sit per affirmationem et negationem.* It follows that God in a perfectly strict sense denies Himself in the creature, and this self-denial in God is the possibility of the creature's existence, without which God's affirmation of Himself in the creature would be nothing but God. What, in terms of Being, is denial, in terms of Non-Being is affirmation.

If it were a question of ideas and terms equally derived from the same traditional understanding of Being, it would no doubt be possible to dismiss the Eastern doctrines as deviations from the truth. What, however, is implicit in the contrast of the metaphysical language of Schuon and indeed of the perspective common to many of the Eastern traditions with that of St. Thomas is a certain obliqueness in the use of the word "Being". In the Hindu tradition, which is central in respect to the other Oriental traditions, the metaphysical language is couched in terms of "manifestation" equivalent in many respects to the language of "creation", but having certain aspects which Westerners tend to overlook.

The first consequence of the point of view is that the subject of manifestation is the Self. That is to say, it is the Principle It-Self which discloses its aspects in manifestation through the primordial affirmation of Itself as Being. Thus:

> "The things of nature are the indirect objectivations of the Self.... The cosmic objectivation of the Self presupposes the divine Objectivation, Being, *Ishwara,* or *Apara-Brahma.* Sufism expresses it by this formula: 'I was a hidden treasure, and I willed to be known'." (*Spiritual Perspectives,* page 103.)

The well-founded horror which Catholics have at subjectivist and solipsist philosophies has made of that one word "Self" an almost insuperable obstacle to the understanding of truth in the form in which Vedantic or Sufi tradition expounds it. Accustomed to the rigour of analogical trans-

positions when Knowledge and Love are used as names of
God, they are held back by psychological associations from
seeing that the same rigour is required to understand the
"Self". As if the Self were not transcendent! And if the Self
were not transcendent, what a tangle of subjectivist and
psychological monstrosity must be the Upanishads. Just
what the nineteenth century made of them !

A second consequence is that the word "Being" in these
perspectives lies closer to the sense of "meaning" than it
does in our own use. Essence is meaning as principle of
Being [5].

> "The essence of the world, which is diversity, is
> *Brahma*. It might be objected that *Brahma* cannot be
> the essence of a diversity seeing that It is non-duality.
> To be sure, *Brahma* is not the essence of the world, for,
> from the standpoint of the Absolute, the world is not;
> but one can say that the world, insofar as it exists, has
> *Brahma* for its essence; failing this it would possess no
> reality whatsoever." (*Spiritual Perspectives*, pages 102-103.)

> "Everything," Schuon writes elsewhere, "is true
> through its qualitative content and false through its
> existential limitations." (*Spiritual Perspectives*, page 89.)

What appears to be said is that God is the *esse formale
omnium* in the precise sense in which this is denied in *St.
Thom. C. Gent.*, 1, 26. But this is not the case. The *esse formale
rerum* is on the horizontal plane of participated being. But it
is clear from the first sentences in the quotation from Schuon
that he is speaking of the world in its direct relation to God
according to its vertical axis and of *Brahma* as the transcendent principle of its being.

The following very approximate transposition of terms
may assist adjustment to the point of view:

The world *means* God. Or, as Father Hopkins said: "... the
bluebell I have been looking at ... I know the beauty of our
Lord by it."

God is the meaning of the world. For the word "meaning", insofar as it conveys the conformity of the creature with its exemplary being in the Word, provides a key to the transcendent sense of the word "essence" in the passage quoted.

Or there is this superb statement from St. Thomas (C. Gent., 1, 66):

> *Et tamen omne esse cuiuscumque rei Deus cognoscit per essentiam suam; nam sua essentia est repraesentabilis secundum multa quae non sunt, nec erunt, nec fuerunt. Ipsa etiam est similitudo virtutis cuiuslibet causae, secundum quam praeexistunt effectus in causis; esse etiam cuiuslibet rei, quod habet in seipsa, est ab ea exemplariter deductum.*

From the point of view of existence, the direct consequence of creation is that the creature should *be*; and it is immediately implied that its being imitates the divine *Esse*. Because the creature stands in its own existential being, its approach to God is to a Principle outside itself – possible in virtue of the likeness within itself. It is implicit in existence that God should be the "Other".

From the point of view of the manifested, the direct consequence of its manifestation is the presence in itself of a divine meaning which is the principle in manifestation; but it is immediately implied that the manifested ex-sists from its principle. Its approach to its Principle is therefore by reversing an ex-sistence into an in-sistence: but this reversal is necessary only because the manifested state is removed from the Principle. Thus it is implicit in manifestation that the Principle should be the "Self".

"According to the Vedanta, the contemplative must become absolutely 'Himself'; according to other perspectives, such as that of the Semitic religions, man must become absolutely 'Other' than himself – or than the 'I' – and from the point of view of pure truth, this is exactly the same thing." (Schuon, *Spiritual Perspectives,* page 96.)

The word "meaning", as a connecting link between the two perspectives, is unsatisfactory because its associations tend to be dissipated at modern literary levels and it does not evoke the authority of traditional light. The vertical axis of the Eastern doctrines is in the line of intellect rather than of existential dependence. In view of the sharply defined position taken by St. Thomas in the *De Unitate Intellectus contra Averrhoistas* when Eastern perspectives were again in question, but in Aristotelian terms which distorted them, it is necessary to consider certain points in the Thomist position before it will be possible to understand any other perspective save as a contradiction of the truth as we know it.

If we are to interpret the *De Unitate Intellectus* as being a sort of Johnsonian "Sir, our knowledge is our own, and there is an end of the matter", we shall be in danger of eliminating the dimension of Intellect from Thomism.

Knowledge – *intellectus* – in St. Thomas is not primarily something that happens, but something that *is*. Knowledge happens or comes about in us as an elicited act because we, as receptive subjects of intelligible light, are ourselves subject to becoming. It is more true to say that we are subject to becoming in knowledge than that knowledge itself comes to be; though at the level of contingent and mutable fact the (merely empirical) knowledge that such a thing is so must wait upon its being so.

Knowledge is implicit in being and shines from being. God's knowledge of Himself is His act of being God. The participated being, by its very being, participates light for light is being's radiance. Material existence, because of the incommunicability inherent in matter, cannot interiorize light and is impenetrable to it as opaque bodies are impenetrable to the light of the sun and reflect its rays only on their surface.

The light participated by immaterial creatures, because it is proportioned to their participation of being, is not only the luminous principle of the natural knowledge of the created intellect, but also sets a limit to the comprehension of that natural knowledge according to the hierarchy of angelic natures. In the hierarchy of forms – and the spiritual creature is *forma subsistens* – the higher includes the lower in a more perfect mode of being and thus comprehends it in its own self-knowledge. But the lower cannot comprehend the higher, though it may understand it by analogies made evident in its own light. The human is the lowest in the hierarchy of intellect. Its natural light makes intelligible the forms inherent in material things and provides its proximate analogy for the understanding of intellect as such – which can be absolutely identified of none but the divine Intellect.

But in all this there is no knowledge and no truth save insofar as the sun of the divine Intellect, the *Prima Veritas*, illumines all by Its exemplary light. Thus:

> *Id quod facit in nobis intelligibilia actu per modum luminis participati, est aliquid animae, et multiplicatur secundum multitudinem animarum et hominum. Illud vero quod facit intelligibilia per modum solis illuminantis, est unum separatum, quod est Deus. (De Spiritualibus Creaturis, Art. 10. C.)*

From the truth of the divine Intellect, as from its exemplar, proceeds in our own intellect the truth of the first principles according to which it judges. (*De Ver.*, 1, Art. 4 ad 5.) This is the "horizontal" participation of light. But in the following, St. Thomas approaches the vertical axis, which is the *sol illuminans:*

> *Cum posuerimus intellectus agentem esse quamdam virtutem participatam in animabus nostris, velut lumen quoddam: necesse est ponere aliam causam exteriorem a qua illud lumen participetur: et hanc dicimus Deum, qui interius docet, in quantum huiusmodi animae infundit; et supra huiusmodi lumen naturale, addit pro suo beneplacito copiosus lumen ad cognoscendum ea quae naturalis ratio attingere non potest. (Q. Disp. de Anima, Art. 5 ad 6.)*

This truth, the apparent paradox of a *causa exterior qui interius docet*, mediates the very possibility of the creature's being taught by the Holy Spirit.

Reason is to intellect as circumference is to centre and as time is to eternity. Intellect is the principle of reason and the reasonable being is so in virtue of participated intellectual light. But Intellect *as such*, and absolutely, is God. It is, as Eckhart said, uncreated and uncreatable. What was shocking in this statement of Eckhart's was that he seemed to say that Intellect in this sense is something in man as if it were a part of man's nature. God is not part of any nature. But man's intellectual nature, which is rational and peripheral, has as its centre the point (the *heart*, in the language of the Bible) at which it is open to the direct ray of the *Prima Veritas*. That is why hardness of heart is equivalent to spiritual blindness. Schuon comments:

> "Intellectual qualification lies far less in the always relative and often illusory capacity to understand certain metaphysical conceptions than in the purely contemplative quality of the intelligence. This quality implies the absence of passionate elements, not in the man but in his spirit. Purity of intelligence is infinitely more important than its actual capacity. 'Blessed are the pure in heart,' said Christ, not 'Blessed are the intelligent.'
>
> "The 'heart' means the intellect and, by extension, the individual essence, the fundamental tendency of man. In both senses it is the centre of the human being." (*Spiritual Perspectives*, page 76.)

The difference between the Schuonian and Thomist perspectives is that it would be more natural for Thomists to say that the "heart" means the individual essence and by extension the intellect.

In effect the direct axis of the creature's relationship to God, whether this relation is in the path of existence or in that of intellect, is supernatural. And this is so whether or not *what* the creature knows *about* God in this direct relation is expressed in terms that would be inaccessible to us if not verbally implicit in revelation. All such terms, whether or not they are verbally distinct from the terms naturally available to us, are implicit in a mode of knowing and a mode of being which situates us in direct relation with God's reality *as He is* rather than with the aspects of Him which may be traced from creatures. That is why creation is a divine mystery, although it can be proved from creatures that they need to be created in order to be. That is why "pure creature" in terms of this direct relationship, is perfectly expressed in the supernatural role of the Blessed Virgin (of which Islam, incidentally, knows a very great deal), but is much less perfectly expressed by the Aristotelian term *materia prima* (which is likewise less than perfect as a translation of the Vedantic principle *prakriti*). The role of the Blessed Virgin is the obedience of the "nothing" and is therefore the principle of every obedience. It is the receptivity of the "nothing" which alone is receptive to the Infinite. *Materia prima*, in the Aristotelian sense, is the obedience of the would-be-something and therefore of distinct and incommunicable existence at the horizontal level.

The path of pure intellect is a path in God or it is not the path of pure intellect. That is to say, it is a possibility born in the obedience of Mary and lit by the Holy Spirit. That is the essential consideration. "Pure intellect" means contemplation rather than rational discourse. In the following quotation from Schuon's *L'Oeil du coeur* (page 28), it is precisely at the level of rational discourse that we find difficulty, and consequently may fail to grasp that the words are those of a contemplative who fully understands the difficulties.

"When Supreme Reality is affirmed distinctively, and consequently outside of its Aseity, the distinctive nature of Its affirmation must be expressed by duality or by the complementarism of knower and known; thus man may know, on the one hand, Pure Reality, and, on the other hand, the world and in it the ego – Metacosm, macrocosm, and microcosm – without man, in so far as he knows, being anything other than Knowledge, and without the external world and the ego, in so far as they are capable of being known (that is to say, in so far as they are real), being anything other than Reality. To say that we know ourselves amounts to saying that we know Reality in so far as It is ourselves; for there is no object of knowledge, neither around us nor in us, which is not essentially – not existentially – the One Reality, and there is no person who knows, except it be Knowledge which knows within him and which is infinite."

There are certain consequences of the "point of view" of pure intellect which it will be sufficient to indicate here without any suggestion of schematic solution. Until the point of view is understood, there will be points of contradiction with our own which will not be resoluble in any terms available to us. Schuon suggests a path of resolution when he insists on the complementariness of the unitive way of Divine Love and that of Pure Intellect, in the sense that each must imply what the other renders explicit. It is when they overlap that difficulties may arise – and, to a greater or lesser degree, that is always. Again, speaking this time of Islam, Schuon says in *Spiritual Perspectives* (pages 83-84):

"In Islam there is, so to speak, no sanctity apart from esoterism; and in Christianity there is no esoterism apart from sanctity."

This formulation is not intended as an absolute antithesis, but as an indication of how Eastern and Western perspectives differ and how they meet.

In the metaphysical perspectives of the East, there is a certain priority of truth (= reality) over being (= affirmation), which is antithetic to the ontology of St. Thomas. It is possible to manipulate concepts in order to see that what is being said in those terms is not by any means necessarily untrue. But that is a different matter from seeing the truth in those terms. Until we can do that we can neither receive in any full measure the light of the Eastern religions nor communicate with them in the fullness of the light of Christ. The task involved cannot possibly be achieved merely at the rational level, but is necessarily contemplative *because* contemplation is only indirectly concerned with it. No truth is alien to the depth of the reality of God: only there indeed is it perfectly true.

[1]It should not be taken for granted that translations done by Indians themselves are any more trustworthy. In general, Indian translations and explanatory matter fall under three heads: the naïve, which render a real understanding into a smattering of Western philosophical language; the efforts of Indian minds uprooted by Western education from the living flow of their own tradition; and the deliberate adaptations of Westernizing Hindus under the impulse of Swami Vivekananda. From the first something genuine may be learned, especially when the language is least philosophical; the second are a sheer waste of time; from the third source, translations are amongst the best to be had, but explanations are not to be trusted.

[2]Not only, we should note, by Westerners. The Vaishnavite, His Holiness Jagadguru Shankaracharya in an exuberant English foreword to a collection of Vedantic commentaries, is capable not only of the following, but of pages more like it: "... *it is not the maker but the material of which it is made which pervades and permeates a thing!* God's omnipresence in the Universe therefore indisputably proves that God is the material of which the world has been created! Q.E.D." The italics are his.

[3]From the Guénonian point of view the exception made above with regard to the Christian sacraments would be regarded as belonging to the judgement of fact without any principial bearing. This judgement, though it colours his writing in its reference to modern Christianity, is not essential to his position, still less to the principial Knowledge in the name of which he speaks.

[4] *The Transcendent Unity of Religions* (first French edition, Gallimard 1948; latest reprint of the English translation by P. N. Townsend, TPH Quest Books, Wheaton, Illinois, 1984); *L' Oeil du coeur* (Gallimard, Paris, 1950; second edition, Seuil, Paris, 1979); and *Spiritual Perspectives* (first French edition, Cahiers du Sud, Paris, 1953; latest reprint of the English translation by Macleod Matheson and P. N. Townsend, Perennial Books, London 1987).

[5] "God is a meaning" was a saying of Coomaraswamy.

Hinweis auf Frithjof Schuon

Hans Küry

"Wer den Dichter will verstehen, muß in Dichters Lande gehen." Den Rat Goethes kann man abwandeln: Um einen Denker zu verstehen, muß man sich vorerst einmal auf den Boden begeben, auf dem er sich selber bewegt. Das ist nicht immer leicht, bildet aber die Voraussetzung jeden Verständnisses. Eine noch so knapp gehaltene Einführung in das Werk von Frithjof Schuon z. B. muß von der Tatsache ausgehen, daß sich dieser Verfasser ausdrücklich außer die abendländisch neuzeitliche wissenschaftliche oder philosophische Betrachtungsweise stellt, und zwar, wenn man es kurz sagen will, weil er die menschliche Ratio wohl als Werkzeug bei der Darlegung von Erkenntnissen, niemals aber als deren Quelle anerkennt: Gewißheit kann vielmehr nur eine unmittelbare Schau geben, Frucht einer überrationalen geistigen Eingebung, in der die Zweiheit von Subjekt und Objekt, als Ursache aller Unsicherheiten, überschritten ist.

Man wird sagen: Neuplatonismus, Gnosis. Einverstanden; wenn jedoch diese Feststellung bloß geschichtliche Einordnung und Abfertigung bleibt[1], vermag sie nicht aus dem geschlossenen Kreise neuzeitlichen Denkens hinauszuführen, und keineswegs enthebt sie der Aufgabe, die zunächst vielleicht befremdende Berufung auf den Logos (den "Geist", im alten Sinne dieses arg mißbrauchten Wortes) nach Voraussetzung und Ergebnis vorurteilslos zu prüfen[2].

Der Leser von Büchern Frithjof Schuons[3] gewinnt bald
den Eindruck, daß dieser Verfasser "ex cathedra" redet;
nicht etwa, als ob er sich je auf irgendein Amt beriefe: Das
kann er schon aus dem einfachen Grunde nicht tun, da er
nicht nur eine, sondern sozusagen alle orthodoxen Religionen in seine Betrachtung einbezieht, wozu ja keinerlei
äußere Stellung innerhalb einer einzelnen Religion die
Befugnis zu verleihen vermöchte. Vielmehr leitet sich das
Empfinden, die Aussagen eines Bevollmächtigten vor sich
zu haben, her von der Verbindung größter, heute durchaus
ungewohnter Entschiedenheit des Stiles mit peinlich gere-
chter Berücksichtigung der verschiedenen jeweils in Betra-
cht kommenden, oft sich widerstreitenden Gesichtspunkte
und deren salomonischen Scheidung durch Zuweisung auf
die jedem von ihnen gemäße Ebene, welche "Hierarchisi-
erung" viele Rätsel gleichsam von innen heraus löst; es erscheinen alle behandelten Fragen als auf eine feste Mitte
ausgerichtet: Unverrückbar und unwandelbar aber ist dieser
Beziehungspunkt, da er frei gehalten wird von einschränkenden Festlegungen, die notwendigerweise an ihren eigenen
Grenzen zerbrechen und damit eine Veränderung hervor-
rufen müßten; es ist diese Mitte nichts anderes als das "Un-
endliche" im Sinne der hinduischen "advaita"
(Nichtzweiheit), des chinesischen "tao", des buddhistischen
"nirvâna", des kabbalistischen "ain", des "Ungrundes" von
Jacob Böhme, der "nox profunda" der Mystiker, kurz jener
letzten göttlichen Wirklichkeit, die nur über die "via negativa", d.h. durch das Verfahren der schrittweisen Aufhebung
aller einschränkenden Bestimmungen einem zu seinen
höchsten Möglichkeiten sich aufschwingenden Erk-
enntnisvermögen nahegebracht, in seiner Überförmlichkeit
niemals aber beschrieben werden kann.

   Diese innerste und freieste Möglichkeit ist auch der
"Punkt"[4], in dem allein sich die verschiedenen orthodoxen
Religionen treffen, wie Strahlen, die von Punkten auf dem
Umfange eines Kreises ausgehen, um gemeinsam in dessen
Mittelpunkt zu münden[5]. Das Sich-Aufschwingen, das Sich-

Öffnen dem Unbeschränkten gegenüber könnte man auch einem Horchen nach innen vergleichen – "drum höre, wer da Ohren hat, zu hören" – und die folgerichtig sich aus diesem Lauschen auf den Logos (auf das "Wort" im johanneischen Sinne) ergebende Haltung wäre der Ge"hor"sam der geistigen Gewißheit gegenüber.

Halten wir diesem inneren Gehorsam die äußere Gesetzes- und Dogmentreue entgegen, so sind wir bei der – für Schuons Werk wichtigen – Unterscheidung zwischen Esoterik und Exoterik angelangt. Esoterik hat bei Schuon nichts mit irgendeiner gewollten Geheimhaltung bestimmter Erkenntnisse zu tun, sie bezeichnet vielmehr eine andere Sicht, unter der dieselben Gegebenheiten von Religion und Tradition ins Auge gefaßt werden, von denen auch die Exoterik ausgeht.

Die Esoterik ist nur für jene Menschen geheim, deren Fassungsvermögen sie übersteigt.

Die Exoterik aber ist, wohlbemerkt, nicht etwa eine Entartung der Esoterik, sondern ein Gnadenmittel, das Gott aus Barmherzigkeit für jene offenbart hat, die dafür geschaffen sind[6]. Dennoch ist die Esoterik, wenn sie sich innerhalb einer Religion kundgeben will, darauf angewiesen, deren exoterische Aussagen aus allzuenger Begrenzung herauszulösen; dadurch wirkt sie in geistigen Blütezeiten immer wieder verjüngend und auftauend, sie erzieht die Menschen vom bloßen "Hören" zum "Horchen", von der "Hör"igkeit des Sklaven zum Ge"hor"sam des geistig Freien, wobei sie allerdings jederzeit Gefahr läuft, zum "Skandalon" der Exoteriker zu werden.

Ein Hauptdogma der Religionen betrifft den Glauben an die Alleingültigkeit oder mindestens an die Überlegenheit ihres jeweiligen Weges. Der wahre Kern dieses Dogmas ist darin zu finden, daß eine orthodoxe Religion auch für die höchsten Ziele, die ihre Anhänger anstreben mögen, unbedingt ausreicht; sie bedarf – in der Regel[7] – keiner Anleihen anderwärts, ja, solche müßten, wenn sie eine "Relativisierung"

der eigenen Heilsmöglichkeiten in sich schlössen, sogar als
hinderlich für die Erreichung geistiger Ziele bezeichnet
werden. Andererseits aber steht Gott über den von lhm
ausgehenden Offenbarungen; Gott ist weder Hindu, noch
Jude oder Christ und Moslem, und zweifellos ist es überzeu-
gender, im Vorhandensein vieler, nach Blickwinkel und
Formensprache voneinander abweichenden Religionen
einen Ausdruck der Unabhängigkeit Gottes von Seinen
eigenen Kundgebungen zu sehen, als alle fremden Überlieferungen des Irr- oder Aberglaubens zu zeihen; das ist, wie
wenn man unter den Sprachen der Völker nur gerade die,
die man selber mit der Muttermilch eingesogen hat, gelten
ließe und die anderen als bloßes Gestotter oder Gelalle
ansähe. Die Vielheit der Religionen kann als Zeichen der
göttlichen Barmherzigkeit ausgelegt werden, insofern jedem
Teil der Menschheit der ihm besonders gemäße Weg zum
geistigen Heil offenbart worden ist; andererseits ist diese
Vielheit ein Fingerzeig dafür, eine bestimmte äußere Form
nicht mit Gott Selber zu verwechseln. Wenn sich Paulus in
Athen zum Zeugnis für die Wahrheit seiner Botschaft auf
griechische Dichter berief, was bei weitem nicht nur "Diplo-
matie" war, wenn die Kirchenväter und die Mystiker (z.B.
Meister Eckehart) gerne "heidnische Meister" herbeizogen,
wenn Jacob Böhme gar schrieb: "Wahrlich es ist nur ein
Gott: wenn aber die Decke von deinen Augen gethan wird,
daß du lhn siehest und erkennest, so wirst du auch alle deine
Brüder sehen und erkennen; es seyen gleich Christen, Ju-
den, Türken oder Heiden. Oder meinst du, daß Gott nur
der Christen Gott sey? leben doch die Heiden auch in Gott:
Wer recht thut, ist ihm angenehm" (Aurora, Kapitel II, 34),
so hebt sich diese Freiheit und Unmittelbarkeit, die den
Geist überall aufnimmt, wo er weht, merklich ab von der
Eifersucht und dem absichtlichen Nichtverstehenwollen, mit
dem Verfechter der Ausschließlichkeit andere Religionen
zu entwerten versuchen. Schuon weist darauf hin, daß sich
mit solcher beflissener Verleumdung fremder Heiliger Offenbarungen und Formen im Grunde weltliches, ungeistiges

Denken dafür rächen will, daß es im Rahmen der eigenen
Religion schweigen muß. Umso giftiger äußert es sich
fremden, schutzlosen Offenbarungen gegenüber. Folge-
richtigerweise kehrten sich denn auch im Laufe der
"Säkularisierung" und "Verweltlichung" die ursprünglich nur
an die "Naturreligionen" gerichteten Vorwürfe plötzlich
ebenso heftig gegen das Christentum selbst, das früher als
Ausnahme behandelt worden war. Die Religionsvergleichung
und die Religionspsychologie relativierten die Offenbarung
völlig, indem sie zu zeigen versuchten, daß im "Kindes"alter
der Völker aus denselben überall vorhandenen seelischen
Bedürfnissen notwendigerweise als Wunsch- und Angstvor-
stellungen immer wieder ähnliche Mythen
(Weltdeutungssagen) entstanden seien. Was können die
"Exoteriker" diesem Gedankengang entgegensetzen, es sei
denn die unbeweisbaren Inhalte ihres Glaubens? Nur "esot-
erisch" ist eine Widerlegung möglich, und sie wurde denn
auch, in unserem Jahrhundert, in großem Maßstabe unter-
nommen, wenn auch – entsprechend ihrem "esoterischen"
Gehalt – abseits vom lauten Tagesgespräch, vor allem durch
René Guénon und durch Frithjof Schuon, von verschiedenen, keineswegs jedoch sich widersprechenden
Standpunkten aus: Sich auf die morgenländische Metaphysik
stützend, wie sie besonders rein im "Vedânta", der Krone
des Vedas, dargelegt wird, wies Guénon in den Symbolspra-
chen der verschiedenen orthodoxen "Traditionen" (Religionen) ein ihnen allen gemeinsames Urwissen nach; dessen
Vergessen verschuldet die Verfinsterung und den Zerfall der
"modernen", vom Abendland geprägten Welt. In der Sicht
Guénons erscheinen die Unterschiede und scheinbaren
Widersprüche zwischen den Traditionen gleichsam als zu
vernachlässigende Nebensache[8].

Ganz anders bei Schuon: Das Antlitz der einzelnen orthodoxen Religionen löst sich hier nicht einfach in demjenigen
der Urtradition der Menschheit auf, sondern erscheint in
seiner einmaligen Bedeutung als durch nichts zu ersetzen-

der Anblick der Göttlichen Wirklichkeit; wir wüβten keinen
anderen derartig unbestechlichen und tiefblickenden "Physi-
ognomiker" der verschiedenen Religionen zu nennen. Auf
einer ersten Ebene der Betrachtung treten die Widersprüche
zwischen den einzelnen Wegen zu Gott in schärfster Klar-
heit hervor. Eines desto gröβeren Aufschwunges bedarf es
dann aber auch, um auf einer zweiten, hohen Ebene den
Streit der Gesichtspunkte im Frieden einer unmittelbaren
Gottesschau zu überwinden.

Schon der Titel von Schuons erstem französischen Buch[9]
"De l'unité transcendante des Religions", ist bezeichnend:
Es geht um die Gesichter der verschiedenen Religionen,
hier besonders derjenigen von Christentum, Judentum und
Islam, darüber hinaus aber um deren innere Einheit, die
aber nur im Letzten, im Transzendentalen zu finden ist; ja,
der Vergleich verschiedener Überlieferungen und die Suche
nach ihrer gemeinsamen geistigen Quelle erweist sich sch-
lieβlich als ein Mittel der oben erwähnten "via negativa", der
Selbstaufhebung der Welt der Formen zugunsten des über
jeder Form liegenden göttlichen Ungrundes; der Leser fühlt
sich, wenn man so sagen darf, auf einmal selber in eine Art
von Pilger, von Reisendem nach der höchsten Schau verwandelt; er spürt, daβ der Verfasser keineswegs nur seine
Wiβbegierde anspricht, sondern ihm seine Gottesebenbildli-
chkeit, seine Verwurzelung im göttlichen "Ungrunde" in
Erinnerung ruft; diese Wirkung ergibt sich jedoch nicht aus
irgendeiner Absicht, zu überzeugen, sondern von selbst, aus
der Anziehung, die mit dem Standpunkte des Verfassers
und der Art seiner Darstellungsweise gegeben ist, die keinen
Zweifel darüber aufkommen lassen, daβ es sich nicht bloβ
um eine gedachte, sondern um eine weit über den Ged-
anken hinaus den ganzen Menschen erfassende Lehre handelt. Dieser Anruf unterscheidet Schuons Werk abermals
sehr deutlich von jeder sich bloβ an den Verstand richten-
den oder gar unverbindlich mutmaβenden wissenschaftli-
chen Abhandlung.

Die Umfassendheit dieses Standpunktes erweist sich auch an einer bezeichnenden Einzelheit, nämlich daran, daß schon in diesem ersten Buche Schuons keimhaft alle Leitgedanken seines Gesamtwerkes enthalten sind; es kann hier, wo es um Eingebung des Logos geht, keine "Entwicklung" geben, die ja voraussetzt, daß das menschliche Gehirn immer wieder neue Weltbilder gebärt, die, da nichts ihre Wahrheit verbürgt, jederzeit durch andere, einem neuen Lebensbedürfnis – oder oft sogar nur einer neuen Mode – entsprechende ersetzt werden können. Demgegenüber mußte Schuons Schau unverändert bleiben, auch durch Jahrzehnte hindurch; der fast unübersehbare Reichtum der Gesichtspunkte ergibt sich nicht aus einer Wandlung, sondern aus der Fülle von Sichten, die von Anfang an im göttlichen "Ungrunde" enthalten sind; es ist wie ein Sprühregen, dessen tausende von Tropfen die Sonne und gleichzeitig einander widerspiegeln, wobei aber auch noch die so entstehenden Spiegelbilder in unendlicher Vielfalt weiter spiegeln und weiter gespiegelt werden.

Ein Angelpunkt schon im ersten Buche ist z.B. das Wissen um die "Verzahnung" des Unbedingten mit dem Bedingten (des Absoluten mit dem Relativen); dieses Ineinandergreifen versinnbildlicht unter anderem das chinesische Yin Yang, das Stehen einer weißen Kreisfläche im schwarzen und dasjenige einer schwarzen im weißen Felde; jede Verbindung von Gott und Welt beruht letztlich auf dieser Verflechtung. Schuon zieht sie immer wieder heran, in meisterlicher Weise z. B., um den geheimnisvollen Mythos des Bodhisattwa Dharmakara zu deuten, der ein Gelübde ablegte, nicht ins Nirvâna einzugehen, es sei denn zusammen mit den nach Gott Strebenden, die reinen Herzens seinen höchsten Namen, Amitâbha, angerufen hätten[10], wobei die rätselhafte Wechselbeziehung von Gottesliebe im Menschen und Menschenliebe in Gott sehr tief erörtert wird.

Nicht weniger ergiebig erweist sich die Besinnung auf die im Hinduismus, aber in irgendeiner Form auch in jeder anderen orthodoxen Religion anzutreffende Dreiheit der Wege zu Gott, nämlich Überwindung des Ichs, sei es – erster Weg – durch die Opfertat (hinduisch karma yoga), oder – zweiter Weg – durch die Liebe zu Gott und zum Du (hinduisch bhakti yoga) sei es, endlich – dritter Weg – durch die Erkenntnis, als Mittel zur Einung von Subjekt und Objekt (hinduisch jnâna yoga), wobei jeder dieser Wege zwei Pole aufweist, Entsagung und überwindende Tat stellen sich auf der ersten, Ergebung in Geduld und Vertrauen auf Erlösung auf der zweiten, scheidende Weisheit zwischen Absolutem und Relativem (Ge"scheit"heit, Intellekt) und Bewuβtsein des "Selbst", der Einheit unseres innersten Wesens mit Gott, auf der dritten Stufe gegenüber.

Versuchte man, die Wirkung von Schuons Büchern selber an diesen Möglichkeiten menschlicher Haltung zu messen, so könnte man sagen: Die ausstrahlende Mitte dieser Wirkung liegt zweifellos in der geistigen Erkenntnis; um ein anderer zu werden, bedarf es keiner "Predigt"; die Erkenntnis verwandelt von selbst denjenigen, dem sie zuteil wird, im Maβe allerdings, als er sie sich einverleibt. Diese Einverleibung der geistigen Erkenntnis, ihre Verankerung in unserem Wesen aber wird erleichtert, einmal durch die Einbeziehung aller Schichten des menschlichen Wesens in die Betrachtung, ferner durch den seelischen Duft und den Rhythmus des dichten und gleichzeitig klaren Stiles, dessen sich Schuon bedient: Es handelt sich bei diesen Eigenschaften "summa summarum" um die von der geistigen Erkenntnis ausgelöste Schwingung, die sich übrigens auch noch über den seelischen Bereich hinaus bis auf die Stufe der Tat fortpflanzt, nicht im Sinne der heute so beliebten, meistens sehr kurzsichtigen Anleitungen zur Weltverbesserung allerdings; derartiges wird man bei Schuon nirgends finden, sondern durch die Ausrichtung des Tuns auf den göttlichen und allein wirklichen Ursprung. Nichts könnte mehr zur Heilung un-

seres kranken Zeitalters beitragen, als wenn diese Ausrichtung
von denen, die ihrer fähig sind, auch tatsächlich vollzogen
würde.

[1] Über den Unterschied zwischen ketzerischem Gnostizismus
und wahrer Gnosis vgl. Einleitung zu "Logique et transcendance"
(s. Angabe in Note [3]).

[2] Kaum wird jemand bestreiten, daß wir uns heute in einer
tiefgreifenden Zeitwende befinden. Ganz unabhängig davon, wie
wir sie deuten, ist es in dieser Lage gegeben, frühere entscheidende
Gabelungen im Wege des abendländischen Denkens zu überprüfen
und sich zu fragen, ob nicht besser eine andere Richtung
eingeschlagen worden wäre.

[3] Es kann hier nicht unsere Sache sein, von der Persönlichkeit
und vom Leben Frithjof Schuons, die in seinem gedruckten Werke
völlig zurücktreten, mehr als ein paar Andeutungen zu geben,
besonders, da äußere Tatsachen wenig über einen Menschen sagen,
dessen Leben nicht Sternen des Erfolges und der gesellschaftlichen
Stellung, sondern solchen der inneren Berufung und der geistigen
Sendung gefolgt ist. Mehr als das Geburtsjahr 1907 und die
Geburtsstadt Basel und eine in der Schweiz und im Elsaß auf der
Grenze zwischen germanischer und romanischer Kultur verbrachte
Jugend, mehr auch als die von einer patriarchalischen Privatschule
und von einem altberühmten Gymnasium vermittelte Bildung,
wirkten der Sinn des Kindes für Heiligkeit und seine langen
einsamen Zwiesprachen mit Gott nach. Die geistvolle Führung
eines heißgeliebten Vaters, Musiker und Dichter seines Zeichens,
brach wegen dessen frühen Tod bald ab. Der vom Jüngling
ergriffene Beruf eines künstlerischen Entwerfers war gewiß nicht
die Quelle von Schuons tiefem und vielseitigem Kunstverständnis,
sondern umgekehrt ließ ihn dieses letztere eine Arbeit wählen, die
nicht ganz ohne Zusammenhang, wenn auch sehr entfernt, damit
zu sein schien. Die Begegnung des Jünglings in Paris mit dem
Islam ließ ihn zu Scheich Achmed Al-'Alawi (vgl. Martin Lings, *A*

Moslem Saint of theTwentieth Century, Shaikh Ahmad Al-'Alawi, Georg
Allen & Unwin Ltd. London 1961) in Mostaghanem pilgern, die
erste vielversprechende in einer langen Kette von Reisen nach den
verschiedensten geistigen Mittelpunkten. Aus der nachfolgenden
Aufzählung von Schuons Werken läßt sich sein Aufstieg zum
anerkannten Deuter der Religionen ablesen; Hand in Hand damit
bildete sich ein Netz von Beziehungen zu Vertretern aller
orthodoxen Traditionen (hervorgehoben sei Schuons Freundschaft
zu hervorragenden Wortführern des Indianertums). Liste der
Werke: *Leitgedanken zur Urbesinnung.* Orell Füssli Verlag Zürich
1935. Vergriffen. Leopold Ziegler: "Zum ersten Male, soweit unser
geschichtliches Erinnern reicht, lernt man sich der Symbolik einer
überlieferten Religionsform bedienen, nicht mehr um diese
Religionsform gegen andere abzudichten; sondern im Gegenteil,
um hinter ihr den gemeingultigen Inhalt aufleuchten zu lassen." -
De l'Unité transcendante des religions, Gallimard, Paris, 1948.
Übersetzungen ins Englische, Italienische, Spanische,
Portugiesische. Der englische Dichter und Nobelpreisträger T.S.
Eliot: "Ich bin keinem eindrucklicheren Werke auf dem Gebiete
der vergleichenden Forschung von morgen- und abendländischen
Religionen begegnet". – *L'Oeil du coeur,* Gallimard, Paris, 1950 -
Perspectives spirituelles et faits humains, Les Cahiers du Sud, Paris,
1953. Übersetzung ins Englische – *Sentiers de Gnose,* La Colombe,
Paris, 1957. Übersetzung ins Englische – *Castes et races,* suivi de:
Principes et critères de l'art universel, Derain Lyon, 1957 – *Les Stations de
la sagesse,* La Barque du Soleil, 1958 – *Language of the Self,* Ganesh &
Co., Madras, 1959 – *Images de l'esprit,* (*Shinto, Buddhismus, Yoga*),
Flammarion, Paris, 1961 – *Comprendre l'Islam,* Gallimard, Paris, 1961.
Übersetzung ins Englische – *Dimensions of Islam,* Geoge Allen &
Unwin Ltd., London, 1968 – *Regards sur les mondes anciens,* Editions
traditionnelles, Paris, 1968. Übersetzung ins Englische. Deutsche
Übersetzung: *Das Ewige im Vergänglichen. Von der Einen Wahrheit in
den Alten Kulturen.* O.W. Barth, Weilheim, Oberbayern, 1970 –
Logique et transcendance, Editions Traditionnelles, Paris, 1970.

[4] Die Gegebenheit "Punkt" als ausdehnungsloser Grundsatz des
Raumes ist ein treffendes Bild für dieses ungreifbare Letzte.

[5] Nicht orthodoxe Religionen oder "Sekten" - das Wort ist sehr
bezeichnend - könnte man ebenfalls Geraden vergleichen, die sich
über die Kreislinie erheben (kraft dieses Ansteigens ziehen sie

Anhänger mit): aber der Winkel, unter dem sie verlaufen, ist falsch, so daß sie den Mittelpunkt verfehlen. Für den einzelnen Anhänger muß allerdings, falls seine Absicht rein ist, die Möglichkeit eines berichtigenden Eingreifens der göttlichen Gnade offen gelassen werden.

[6] "L'exotérisme ne vient pas de l'ésoterisme, mais directement de Dieu. Cette vérité nous fait penser à la thèse de Dante, selon laquelle l'empire vient de Dieu, et non de la papauté! Donner à César ce qui est à César et à Dieu ce qui est à Dieu". Frithjof Schuon, *Perspectives spirituelles et faits humains*. S. 102. (Angabe vgl. Note 3).

[7] "In der Regel" fügen wir bei im Hinblick auf besondere Fälle des Niederganges einer Religion, wo es möglich wäre, daß das Vorbild einer noch heilen Tradition einwirkte, nicht im Sinne der Hervorrufung einer Anlehnung, sondern im Gegenteil im Sinne einer Anregung zur Besinnung auf sich selber.

[8] Von René Guénon (1886-1951) erwähnen wir als scharfsinnige Analyse unseres Zeitalters: *Le Règne de la quantité et les signes du temps* (1945, 2.Auflage 1951), als *Einführung in die Lehre der Vedântâ: L'homme et son devenir selon le Vedântâ*. 4. Auflage 1952. Reichhaltig ist das nach Guénons Tod aus Aufsätzen zusammengestellte Werk: *Symboles fondamentaux de la Science sacrée*, Paris, 1962. Über Guénon unterrichtet Paul Chacornac: *La Vie simple de René Guénon*, Paris, 1958 – Überlieferungstreuen Geist atmen auch die tiefsinnigen Werke des englischen, von Hindus abstammenden Kunstgeschichtlers Ananda Kentish Coomaraswamy (1877-1947). Wir nennen: *Hinduism and Buddhism*, New York, 1943 – Aufgrund eigener Anschauung und eigenen geistigen Erlebens führt Titus Burckhardt (geboren 1908) mitten in die Welt der Überlieferung hinein, so in: *Vom Sufitum. Einführung in die Mystik des Islams*, Otto Wilhelm Barth Verlag, 1953. Ferner: *Vom Wesen der Heiligen Kunst in den Weltreligionen* Origo-Verlag, Zürich, 1955 – *Alchemie. Sinn und Weltbild*, Walter-Verlag Olten und Freiburg i.Br., 1960.

[9] Der Weltöffentlichkeit ist die innere geistige "Aktualität" (man möchte lieber gut deutsch sagen: die "Notwendigkeit", nämlich im Sinne des Herbeiführens einer "Wende" in der "Not" unserer Zeit) dieses Buches nicht entgangen. Man vergleiche in Note 3 die

Angaben der Übersetzungen des Buches und die Worte von T.S.
Eliot.

[10] *Logique et transcendance.* S. 275. (Vergl. genaue Angabe in Note
3)

Lucifer

Tage Lindbom

The Biblical narrative of the fall of man has an important double aspect. The fruits that the serpent offers to the first human beings are succulent and attractive, and the serpent's offer is an appeal to the delights of the sensual world, to the vegetative and animal, to materialism. But the fall of man has a deeper meaning. The serpent issues a still greater promise than the experience of sensual delights: the Tree of Knowledge gives man an insight; his eyes will be opened; he will leave his state of confident innocence; he will be given an intellectual capacity; and he will "be like God".

The serpent's seduction has therefore a double meaning. He will show man a way to vegetative and animal lust, to a sensualism, whereby man will be a slave to materialism. To that, however, is added something much more dangerous: to break the promise to the Lord, to give oneself up to the greatest of all sins, *superbia*, or spiritual pride, and try to elevate oneself to be equal to the Creator, "to be like God". This is Luciferism, the idolization of man. To sensual lust is added the haughty, narcissistic self-deception, whereby man falsifies, distorts and manipulates the constituent ground of our being, which is the truth that the world comes from the Creator, that man never can be "like God", but is given the position of trustee under the law of God.

Because of progressive secularization – and therefore confusion – the West has been ensnared in a Luciferism that has had disastrous consequences, not least for Western theol-

189

ogy. In varying, variable, and often seductive forms, we meet Luciferism, not least in the "beautiful" shape we call idealism. Idealism represents itself as an elevated, ennobled form of the human itself, and thereby idealism can easily be interpreted as a polemic negation of materialism and sensualism. The incense on the altar of idealism has as its function to conceal the fundamental fact that idealism, which exposes itself in its anthropomorphic form as humanism, is a form of Luciferism, and therefore not at all in contradiction to materialism and sensualism but, on the contrary, one of the double aspects of the fall of man. Idealism is complementary to materialism.

The sensual temptation towards the beautiful but forbidden fruits in the garden of Eden leads to a seduction less dangerous than the Luciferian promise that man will be "like God". To yield to all attractive things in the sensual world is not unpardonable – we live in a world of material things – and if the disobedience of the first human beings had been limited to the consumating of the delicious fruits, correction would have been possible. But to revolt against the Creator, to try to dethrone Him by idolizating oneself – that is a catastrophe. Here we meet the deeper aspect of the fall of man. The Luciferian is much more dangerous than capitulation before the attractions of the material world; moral decay is never so disastrous as the properly Luciferian message. The former is breaking a norm; it is a degradation, a degeneration, that God can encounter with His grace and His pardon. The latter is a denial, a negation of the divine order itself, a falsification of the intellectually given Truth.

Draped in the shining garment of idealism and humanism, the West has accomplished a manipulation, whereby the deepest meaning of the fall of man is concealed. In the name of idealism and humanism, secularization is given a legitimation. More and more, Western man is entering a world in which he listens only to his own voice, the voice of rationalism; and listening to this voice, he is able to refer continuously to the "legitimation" that he thinks the idealistic and humanistic pseudo-spirituality gives him. In this world, secularization makes its progress, because man can be represented as a higher being, carrying in his breast "the eternal", conquering all creation and, at last, proclaiming himself as the universal sovereign.

What we call "Western" has its source in Greek thought. And Greek thought, in its "classic" form is rationalist. In Greek thought, we meet a Luciferian element. The Greek reality in its rationalistic dimension excludes transcendence, and therefore the "perfect" is reached through the limited. Being is the highest category, and the infinite and the eternal are excluded. Some Greeks, according to a tale, were sailing at sea, and when one of them maintained that beyond the formal and closed world there must be something we are not capable of grasping with our rational capacity, he was thrown overboard.

In the Renaissance, the Luciferian is brought further on a wave of "liberation". We are less and less conscious that it is a road – even if it is a winding road – leading back to the fall of man. So much stronger is the consciousness of idealism and humanism, regarded as bearers of the spiritual light in a secularized world. To this we must add, as a psychological fact, that progressing secularization must have the support of narcissism, giving the promise of a "self-realization" under the lodestar of eternal progress.

The nineteenth century is the culmination of Luciferism, and it is in that century that we encounter three camps of Luciferian conquest. The first is the cultivating, opening and exploiting of a mighty landscape, where all forms of human non-material cultivation have to be brought together, form- ing a homage, not to the Creator, but constituting rather a celebration of the human spirit. Culturalism indeed is like a tremendous mirror, in which man has to regard himself and in which, in the name of idealism and humanism, the image in this mirror will always be pure and immaculate.

The second camp of Luciferian conquest is theology. Pietism, with its sentimentalism and intimacy, undergoes in the eighteenth century a shifting of its center of gravity from the theocentric to the Christocentric, and it is rather easy for the theologians of the nineteenth century, with the German Protestant Schleiermacher as the leading figure, to transform the Son of Man into an ideal and human model for humanity, thereby placing physical or sensual experiences at the centre of religion. Nineteenth century theology deals less and less with God and more and more with man; the transcendent is progressively replaced by the earthly and the horizontal. Religion becomes more and more religiosity: intimacy, brotherhood, welfare, consolation, mental and social therapy. Theology regards as its first duty collaboration with the secular institutions to form prescriptions – first of all moral – favoring strength and viability, liberty and loftiness. No longer a *sacra scientia*, theology, in its striving to achieve its Luciferian goal, regards itself as a lateral, collaborating element among other social forces. As the Spanish philosopher Juan Donoso Cortés severely remarks: they offer God worship, but they do not obey Him.

The third camp of Luciferian conquest is science, *le fils de l'orgeuil* ("son of pride"), as Joseph de Maistre formulated it. Even here we meet the nineteenth century as the epoch of triumphal progress. Now knowledge in its Luciferian dreamworld has given itself a double mission: knowledge has to reveal the governing forces by scientific research and, in reaching a conformity with law, it gives to man a position of omnipotence in the world. It was only a question of time for this position to be reached, and it is significant that the definitive literary formulation of it was published in 1899, when the German zoologist Ernst Haeckel published his famous work *Das Welträtsel* ("The Enigma of the World"). Very soon, Professor Haeckel assures us, the last white spots on the map of knowledge will be effaced and the great Luciferian day of triumph will arrive.

It is in the last trembling minute of the nineteenth century that Luciferianism can present itself as a victor. The liberalization of the Western world and belief in rational thinking were regarded as guarantees against any possible reversion to old barbarian times. Therefore the Western secularized man was not at all prepared for the bitter Luciferian crisis he had to face thereafter.

We must admit that non-material creations, rich emanations of phantasy, of artistic shape and configuration, gave the nineteenth century great riches – and we must not be surprised if people in that epoch were filled with self-esteem. But we must understand that here we encounter the last emanation from the spiritual source of higher, divine wisdom, such as has been given to man throughout the centuries. We can already, in the early nineteenth century, observe warning signs: for instance, by penetration in the nervous system, foreboding a coming mental crisis. Ambiguous romanticism made inroads into the human nervous system, and the music of Wagner manifested a morbidity in its peristaltic, vegetative upheavals. The great promise of culturalism had given a promise to bring the human spirit to a higher level, mobilizing "the eternal" in man's breast, but now we see signs indicating that the spiritual journey is in fact going in the opposite direction.

The *aggiornamento*, the accomodation of theology to a more and more secularized world, does not mean that the City of God is vanquishing Lucifer. It means on the contrary that the troops of doubters and deniers are increasing. It does not help when the theological confusers preach – in the name of brotherly love – that they will realize the City of Well-being. The Western forces for God have to face the bitter situation of loosing a social class, namely the industrial proletariat: in vain did the Pope Leo XIII issue his encyclical *Rerum novarum*: the working class chose the road of socialism.

One of the fundamental postulates in Luciferian rationalism says that the world is a solid, continuous, law-bound unity, and that this unity is the object of human knowledge. It is a mathematical and causal conception, formulated by Newton. But already in the last years of the nineteenth century, the physicists began to call in question this picture of the physical world, and during the first decades of the new century, the "classical" Newtonian interpretation was no longer considered valid. Modern atomic physics and morphological investigations give us a description more like Heraclitus' idea of being as a flow: *panta rhei*. And as this flow does not give solid local and causal connections, we cannot reach conclusive answers by structural analysis. So it is not in a "downward" direction that we have to seek the eternal truth, and even among the scientists this is sometimes realized: perhaps we have to look upwards. More than one of the great physicists of our time has openly declared that we have to reckon with the possibility of a higher, divine order. Lucifer's power begins to waver.

Man can live long as consumer of the fruits the Creator has given him, and he can consume these fruits even when he has forgotten from whence they come – he even begins to praise himself, as if he himself were the creator of these values. But it is with the beginning of our century that we are confronted with the bitter harvest of Luciferism. Let us look at art where the first signs are distinct at the turn of the century. We encounter, for instance, Cubism. Art is no longer pictorial; portraits and landscapes are no longer objects for the artist. The creative esthetic process is now purely subjective; it has to be "purified" of all outside objects or models. The artist now really is a "creator", as everything comes from an inner process, from which all outward sense is eliminated – first and foremost – beauty. In his famous letter to Emile Bernard in the year 1904, Cézanne writes: "We must interpret nature with cylinders, cones and spheres". Beyond time and space and beyond all esthetic rules, the artist is now creating "his" reality as a model or as models, among other things geometric figures. Man as artist puts himself in the place of God, for he declares that he creates his art *ex nihilo* without outside models.

Beauty is now an extinct star. Art becomes esthetic autism, delivered from every rule or norm. The artist and his product are a subjective unity; art is a process of creation, going on only inside the artist. Nothing is accepted before the artistic product; there is no model, no legislation, no esthetic views or attitudes. What the artist tells us he is creating is the fruit of a creation in its deeper meaning and therefore his product is declared in itself real; the reality in itself is the esthetic dimension. The artist as personality is, as Guillaume Apollinaire says, divinized. In this sense, the esthetic product is said to be "pure", that is, untainted by any outside influence. Art is real because it is identical with the artist himself; art is true, it is declared, because it springs from the artist's personality.

This esthetic revolution – for it is a revolution – broke out at the beginning of the present century. If we accept literally what the leading theorist of this revolution, Guillaume Apollinaire, says in his little program book *Les Peintres Cubistes,* the essential is that Luciferism is developed to its utmost consequences. But just as Haeckel's work *Das Welträtsel* receives an epitaph over a destroyed natural scientific philosophy, the same is true in the case of the esthetic revolution. In the apparent moment of triumph, the revolution opens the door to Luciferian destruction. When every rule, every norm, every model, every well-rooted establishment in time and space is denied and, first and foremost, when beauty is not perceived as an emanation from its divine, archetypal model – in this situation everything is transferred to the sensual world of man, and this world of fantasy and speculation very soon becomes empty of all content and meaning.

This process of destruction, whereby the beautiful and the ugly, the good and the bad, have lost their distinction and meaning, is going on at an accelerated tempo and expanding over vast areas. James Joyce's *Ulysses* contains eight hundred pages of senseless monologues and dialogues, senseless in content and in esthetics. The essential as regards this novel is that it destroys everything built up in the preceding century in respect of what has to be called literary form. In that formal destruction, the shadow figures that we meet in James Joyce's novel are able to continue their equilibrist nonsense.

Let us turn to another domain of art, namely, music. Here we meet a form of art acoustically turning towards the heart and the senses; nevertheless, music is, in spite of being free from every plastic model, deeply connected with the formal. Music is bound to time by rhythm; but music is also bound to space, as it always has an architectonic structure, the linear and vertical tone sequences, melody and harmony. In its wandering through Europe's cultural life, music formed its major and minor tonality. The musical revolution, however, also occurring at the beginning of our century and having Arnold Schönberg as its first protagonist, means not at all a break with every form. Nevertheless, atonalism opens the door to the liquidation of what we traditionally call Western music. In the continuing revolutionary process of music, a leap into a world without norms leads to electronic or industrially produced music, one which lacks an essential element of traditional music, namely the overtones.

Another leap is the multifarious "popular" forms, where we have to listen to the industrial rattle, combined with a rythmic intensification to the limit of sleepy monotony, and acoustically elevated to the insupportable. Music in this "popular" and "industrial" form possesses the important function of both stimulating and anesthetizing modern man's nerves.

What man as a sensual, biological being has to offer in art, is soon exposed. The impoverishment of secularization is more and more evident, and it is necessary to find quickly new forms for sensual stimulation. The ugly, the distorted, the morbid, and the malicious are mobilized; art becomes anti-art; the novel becomes anti-novel; musical consonance is replaced by dissonance. Art's divine source, beauty as the heavenly model for all that is beautiful on earth, is denied, forgotten. The beautiful in creation, all that we look at as in a heavenly mirror, has no place in the "creative process", as is promised by the Luciferian artists.

When the divine is totally denied, there is as a logical consequence nothing else than negation and the satanic. And that is what we now confront. Anti-art, anti-novel, and so on, have sensual stimulation as their aim, the double purpose being to further weaken vitality and to still inward anxiety. In these stimuli, in these meetings with the ugly, the distorted, the morbid, the satanic is lurking. The cult of sexuality can easily be presented as a hymn to life, but we ought to know that the biological sex function is an act of aggression and therefore deeply connected with violence. Moralists the world over lament over sex and violence, but that is more than a moral problem: these two are linked together, and can easily be engaged as servants to the satanic. "Rock" music has the double function of evoking and stilling anxiety, and at the same time it can lead to worship of the devil.

The Luciferian is on the road to the satanic. Secularized man proclaims himself to be the bearer of Light; instead he is the prisoner of the Lord of Darkness. It is here that the Luciferian "progress" looses its sign of victory. Science stands before its positivistic crisis; it cannot offer the point of Archimedes where we are told to put our foot and move the world. In its final stage, culturalism mobilizes hosts of functionaries, cultural administrators, and advisers, and under the umbrella of UNESCO we are given legitimation as cultural beings. But reality talks another language. The inward light, the spiritual light, is denied, and no longer leads man to the vision of God's revealed beauty as reflected in creation and constituting the source of all cultural creation.

The Luciferian process has an inner logic. Power is not sought in an upward direction; on the contrary the road goes downhill, and on this road we meet many signs. One is mental disharmonies. The Luciferian promise was to produce a free, happy, strong and harmonious man. Instead we encounter neurosis as a mass phenomenon, and how could it be otherwise? The Luciferian road goes downwards. No one has expressed it better than the father of psychoanalysis, choosing as motto for his book on dream interpretation: *Flectere si nequeo superos, acheronta movebo* ("if I cannot conquer Heaven, I will let loose the underworld.")

But theology? Has not Western theology seen the falsehood of the promises of eternal progress and all human dreams in this connection? Let us answer this briefly. Theocracy, proclaiming God's omnipotence over His own creation, was slowly changed in a Christocentric direction, and in our century has taken the next step of proclaiming the anthropocentric. It is said less and less that the Creator one day will take back His creation; it is said more and more that the world is existentially eternal, where man has to concentrate his power on a terrestrial and social paradise. What Platonism taught us, namely that creation is flowing from and a reflux to the Soverign Good, is now forgotten. Two pagan thinkers, Karl Marx and Martin Heidegger, promise that this world will never stand responsible before the Lord. Theology, more and more defenseless before those philosophers, is a prisoner in a hardened Luciferian grasp.

It is fundamental in understanding our situation to be conscious of the fact that existentialism, as formulated especially by the German philosopher Martin Heidegger, is the definitive philosophical foundation of Luciferism. A higher, transcendent reality is denied, the highest reality is Being, the "Ontic" itself, and on this eternal, immovable Being reposes our existence. This excludes every idea of a creation, and in the existential world man lives completely deprived of norms. His life has no deeper meaning; he has only to keep himself fleeting in the existential flow and this by a continuous activity. Man is, as Heidegger says, *entworfen* (dispossessed). What is good and bad, true and false, is nothing else than what comes out of restless – and meaningless – human activity. That means that man believes he creates his own spiritual world.

Marxism belongs to the nineteenth century, to the epoch of closed ideological systems. With its Hegelian system and its materialistic interpretation of history, Marxism is an "orthodoxy" which is now beginning to be old-fashioned: the Luciferian man of today is more and more heterodox and therefore existentialism has been established as the adequate philosophy, the philosophy for the City of Man. For the theological *aggiornamento,* existentialism is a sort of "laughing gas", as it offers endless possibilities of dissolving orthodox systems and interpreting them in a "new" way – and, first and last, existential philosophy delivers the theologians from the "burden" of transcendence. Heaven is a charming story for little children, but "the man who has come of age" has a "deeper" insight; God is "down there", included in our worldly being, God's act is manifested only in human activity. The contention between rationalism and faith over many generations will now be ended.

Marxism is always involved in a conflict with Western scientific positivism, and even here the existentialistic philosophy dissolves all of these conflicts. Culturalism, too, can enjoy unlimited freedom and posibilities. Surely, existentialism is the perfect philosophy for the Luciferian man of the twentieth century. But is Lucifer a victor? The world can be laid in darkness, cathedrals can be put in ruins, people can be confused and led astray, the light of spirit can be obscured, but the false bringer of light, Lucifer, cannot destroy the Spirit. And the Luciferian man in our time is confronted with a sign of the inner Truth. This sign is guilt.

The great secular promise was always the same, that man, free, strong, happy, would deliver himself from the burden of guilt. But always, from the Garden of Eden up to our time, man has striven in vain, as if he could run away from his own shadow. That is what Franz Kafka, in his novel *The Trial,* tells us. The leading character in the story, Josef K., meets the pastor of the prison in the cathedral. The pastor reminds Josef K. of the fact that the law has not only an outward, imperative

order, but also an inward order. All people have not understood that, even if they daily obey the law. We always meet
different opinions about law; they can be contradictory, but
they do not exclude each other, even if people become
desperate because it is so contradictory. Who is free and who
is bound in this world? The pastor gives an answer: to be in
one's service bound to the law, even if it is only as a porter, is
infinitely more precious than to live "free in the world".

This episode has a profound message as well as a pedagogi-
cally plain and clear meaning. Reality has a double
dimension, the outward and the inward. As a consequence
man lives in this doublesided reality. As creation is an order,
God has given us a law, having also an inward, invisible force.
Even the ordinary servant under the law is superior to the
Luciferian hero of liberty in the world – even if this ordinary
servant has no deeper insight into the Spirit as an inward
reality. That is what the pastor of the prison tells poor Josef K.,
persecuted by a guilt, whose meaning and basis he does not
understand.

Secularized Western man, as incarnated as Joseph K. in
Kafka's novel *The Trial*, is ignorant of the fact that man has two
sources of knowledge, *ratio* and *intellectus*, that man has within
him a fragment of God's immortal Spirit, and therefore an
immortal soul, that in his heart is spiritual light, and that he
has intellectual knowledge, an intuitive awareness of divine
Reality. Joseph K. cannot understand that his Luciferian
liberty and freedom from guilt can be denied. When therefore the servant from the court of justice informs him that he
has to stand before the tribunal, he declares that he does not
know the law which is the basis of the case against him, and he
insists that he is innocent. But the servant from the court
points out that if he says he is innocent, there must be a law,
confirming this innocence. And when Joseph K. insists that he
is a free man, the servant says that there must therefore also
exist a lack of freedom.

The Luciferian man believes that he has delivered himself from all guilt and judgement, that he is capable of living free and strong in his "gay heathendom". But the guilty man has feeling towards his Creator; he cannot escape. He does not understand that creation has a double meaning. Firstly, all creation is a flow of God's love, and all we are given of this love we cannot pay back, no matter how many sacrifices we perform. God's love exceeds the sum of all human striving, and therefore we are always in a debt to our Creator. Secondly, the creation is an order, a divine law, and if this law is denied, it does not help us: we are in a position of guilt towards our Creator. This guilt is therefore twofold – it denies God's love and it denies the order of God's creation.

Guilt is an existential fact, and we have to accept. We know that we cannot pay back, but in our inward light, we see that God lays His infinite grace on our side of the scale, brought out of balance by our guilt. Through His grace our scale is brought back into balance; and we reach a state of gratitude, which gives us inward peace. Secularized man, however, believing that he can get rid of his guilt – as if he could run away from his own shadow – has to meet, not God's grace, but guilt as a heavy burden. One of the witnesses in our time of a growing feeling of guilt is the growth of neurotic disorders. That is what Kafka's novel tells us, under the symbol of a trial.

A growing feeling of guilt is one of the many signs of the inward crisis in the City of Man. The helplessness of Western theology is often expressed in essays which seek to establish it as a psychotherapeutic institution, instead of telling the truth about God and His work. But God's Spirit lives in the world, even if it is denied, concealed, forgotten. In the Luciferian confusion, in the growing burdern of guilt, beyond the Western theological ruins, man can every day meet God.

Man's meeting with God is a meeting with the holy. We meet God in inward and outward meaning, and this meeting is like a point of crystallization of the holy in the earthly life, a manifestation of the uncreated Absolute in the created relative. But we meet the holy only when, in inward meaning, we are quiet. The meeting place is the heart, and the heart's quietness gives our soul the form of a mirror, in which, with "the eye of the heart", we see the rays of the divine Sun. The restless activities in the world leads us away from the holy, but in the quietness of the heart the door that leads to the holy opens.

Our terrestrial existence is a continuous wandering between dream and reality. The play of contradictions in life tempts us to seek refuge in dreams, illusions, utopias, ideological castles in the air. Secularized man thinks in his self-deception, that what he receives with his mental organ is the real and the objective but at the same time he hopes that, by means of his dreams, utopias, ideologies *et cetera*, he can change the world and make it better. His self-deception is twofold: what he calls real or objective, is only the outward layers of creation, accessible to sensory observation; and what he will do with the world is founded on subjectivism: subjective impressions, dreams, and speculations.

Man reaches objectivity only when he goes beyond the limit, in which he lives as a sensual ego. In the inner light of our heart we can escape from the labyrinth of existence and become aware of divine Reality. Through objectivity, we can encounter the holy in the world; we can conceive of creation as a gigantic symbol of God's Omnipotence; we can separate the real from the illusory. In this objectivity man is conscious of his own position and limitations, but also of his possibilities, by means of which he is capable of receiving God's ineffable grace.

We encounter the world with the holy and with objectivity; and also, as a third element, with love, God's love. As Creator, He is generous, and this generosity is love. As the Absolute, He has given to man spirituality, a part of His eternal Spirit. We were created by our Father, and in our soul we are immortal and in this twofold meaning we are bound to God. All we have, we have from Him, and all we have, we have received as an emanation of His love. Therefore, we say that God is love and that the world exists as a manifestation of His love. Therefore, the world, and man in the world, have to witness God's love.

The holy is presence, but the holy is also attraction. We seek the holy, because the holy means purity and perfection. Objectivity is presence, but objectivity is also attraction. We seek objectivity, because we desire Reality and Truth, not illusion and lies. Love is presence, but love is also attraction. We seek love, because we will not be isolated or abandoned; we seek God, the very source of our being.

The Symbolism of the Triad of Primary Colours

Martin Lings

*For this **Festschrift** I had promised to review the new and long-awaited anthology **The Essential Writings of Frithjof Schuon**. But in his masterly introduction to that book, Seyyed Hossein Nasr has said in advance much of what I would have liked to say. So I have decided to offer this article in its place on the grounds that it is, implicitly if not explicitly, a testimony to the great debt which my writings owe to those of Frithjof Schuon. Let readers take note of all the crucial quotations from his works, here in particular but also throughout my books, and they will see how immensely I am indebted to this greatest writer of our age.*

There are certain ternaries in the world which may be called true triads in that they are irreducible to any other number except the unity from which all multiplicity proceeds. The three terms, all of the same kind and at the same level of existence, form together a harmonious totality, and each is needed by the other two in the sense that its absence would leave a gap and disrupt the equilibrium. The primary colours are an outstanding example of veritable threeness which cannot be reduced to two.[1] Take away red, and the perfect balance would be broken in the direction of too much cold; the absence of blue would make for excessive heat; without yellow, the residue would be too ponderous.

This triad of colours may be said to affirm the truth of all the true triads which transcend it, in the way that a symbol is a "proof" of its archetype. One of these archetypes *in divinis* is the Christian Trinity. Another, at the same degree of relative Absoluteness[2] is the Hindu ternary of the three aspects of Īsvara, the Divine Personality. These aspects are *Sat - Chit-Ānanda*, Being-Consciousness-Beatitude. Hinduism is particularly explicit with regard to the inevitable effect of this unmanifested triplicity upon all that lies beneath it. According to the doctrine, everything in the manifested universe – in monotheistic terms, every created thing – partakes in varying degrees of three *gunas,* that is, qualities or tendencies, and these are *sattva, rajas* and *tamas. Sattva* denotes a luminous quality and an upward tendency; *rajas* is the *guna* of expansive horizontal growth; and it is the dark and heavy *tamas* which induces ignorance and inertia and which, in a more positive sense, enables night to succeed day and guarantees, on the material plane, the operation of the law of gravity.

Sattva is said to be white, *rajas* red, *tamas* black, and this description is instructive. White and black, which are not strictly speaking colours, symbolize the extreme contrast between *sattva* and *tamas*[3]; colour, which lies between these two poles, thus symbolizes *rajas,* the intermediary *guna;* and red may be taken to stand for colour in general because it is, of all colours, the most vivid, that is, it produces the maximum of vibrations in the eye. We cannot help noticing however that unlike the *gunas* themselves, white, red and black do not constitute a true triad. The point of view which assigns them to the *gunas* would seem to be above all methodic, which means that the approach is subjective or anthropocentric rather than objective, mystical rather than cosmological. We are in the domain of practical theology rather than that of universal symbolism. The symbolic element is there, as we have seen. But we are not being told that white, red and black owe their existence to the same transcendent threefold archetype as that which is the source of

the *guṇas;* we are being given the imperative injunction:
Count *sattva* as white and *tamas* as black – imperative because for one who is seeking to escape from the chain of
saṃsāric births and deaths, *sattva* is precisely the means of
escape, and must therefore be considered as a pure positive,
whereas for opposite reasons black is needed to bring home
to us the negativity of *tamas.* In a somewhat parallel way, the
Koran addresses men and jinn as "ye heavy ones"[4] in the
sense that they are psychic rather than spiritual; and in
respect of this limitation the human being does not stand in
any such need of weight as might give *tamas* a positive significance from his point of view, that is, from the point of view
of a fallen soul that is cut off from direct contact with the
Spirit.

In order to consider the question of colour more objectively, let us revert once more to the level of the Principles
themselves, without confining ourselves to Hinduism and
Christianity. In the ancient Persian, Egyptian and Greco-
Roman religions gold, therefore yellow, was unanimously
held to be sacred to Mithras, Horus and Apollo respectively.
We may note also in this connection that Ovid speaks of
flava[5] *Minerva*; and she, in Greek Pallas Athene, born fully
armed from the head of Zeus, is in a sense parallel to Apollo
as a personification of the Divine Consciousness or Intelligence[6]. By analogy, albeit at a more transcendent level,[7] the
luminous colour must therefore be assigned to the Second
Person of the Christian Trinity, as also to *Chit* in the corresponding Hindu ternary.

As to red, its symbolism partly coincides with that of fire,
and fire has over light a certain priority[8] which is suggestive
of the priority of the First Person of the Trinity over the Second, the more so in that light is "of one substance" with fire.
It is significant that for Moses the first sign of the presence of
Jehovah was the burning bush; and at Mount Sinai "the Lord
descended upon it in fire"[9]. For the Romans, red was associated with Jupiter, and in Greek the name Zeus is closely

related to words which have the sense of life, heat, fire. According to St. Clement, Zeus was considered the supreme God "on account of his igneous nature".[10]

The colour blue was sacred to Juno, whose Greek name Hera is etymologically related to "air", an element which may be said to have the colour of the sky. Her bird, the peacock, makes an overall impression of blue. In Christian iconography blue is especially associated with the Blessed Virgin, one of whose titles is *Regina Caeli*, Queen of Heaven, and who "incarnates" as it were the Holy Ghost[11] whence, according to certain Gnostics, the "femininity" of the Third Person of the Trinity[12]. Moreover, the Virgin is not only *Regina Caeli* but also *Stella Maris*, Star of the Sea; and there is a partial symbolic coincidence between blue and water as between red and fire. According to the Persians, the Word was created by the union of the primal Fire and the primal Water[13], and there is analogy, if not identity, between this and the Hindu ternary *Puruṣa, Prakṛti* and *Buddhi*, and also that of the opening of Genesis: "And the Spirit of God moved upon the face of the waters. And God said, Let there be light." As one of a triad, the Spirit here has its archetype in the First Person of the Trinity, the Waters in the Third and the Light in the Second.

As to the Trinity as such, it would be impossible to speak of its Three Persons if they were not prefigured in the Divine Essence Itself. As Frithjof Schuon has remarked: "Infinitude and Perfection (or the Sovereign Good) are the intrinsic dimensions of the Absolute." He also says: "The Absolute is Infinite; therefore He radiates and in radiating He projects Himself, the content of this projection being the Good. The Absolute could neither radiate nor produce thereby the image of the Good if He were not in Himself, in His Immutability, both the Good and Radiation, or in other words if He did not possess these intrinsic dimensions."[14] This means that the Supreme Archetype of the Trinity lies in the Absolute Infinite Perfection of the Essence. The First Person is rooted in the Absolute, the Second in the Sovereign Good, and the Third in the Infinite; and all true triads throughout the universe, beyond their other symbolisms, exist above all to affirm and "prove" – or, as the Psalms and the Koran would say, to praise – the three intrinsic dimensions of Essential Reality. The triad which is our theme is particularly eloquent in this respect. As we have said elsewhere[15] in a somewhat different context, it is the right of the Absolute that we should know which is Its colour before we have time to think, while the Infinite has the parallel right that our thoughts should unfold in the direction of Its two great symbols, the sky and the ocean. Nor is it difficult to see that gold is a manifestation of the Sovereign Good or Perfection.[16]

It will now be clear, as regard the three *guṇas,* that although according to practical theology they are white, red and black, the ultimate source from which these qualities or tendencies derive is symbolized in its intrinsic dimensions by the three primary colours. As reflections of Absolute-Infinite-Perfection, *sattva, rajas* and *tamas* must therefore be considered as yellow, red and blue respectively.[17] This means, at first sight somewhat paradoxically, that *sattva* results directly from *Chit* rather than from *Sat;* but the essentially *"sattvic"* nature of *Chit* becomes evident if we bear in mind that It is, precisely, *Sat's* Self-Consciousness of Perfection. In Christian terms the same truth could be expressed by saying that the whole message of the Logos, the Divine Word[18], is summed up in the precept: "Be ye perfect, even as your Father in Heaven is Perfect".

Sat, which corresponds to the Trinity's First Person, is reflected at every level of the manifested universe by *rajas* which is, as we have seen, of the "colour" of the Absolute. Whereas the Infinite is mirrored in time and space and other more transcendent modes of duration and extent, and whereas Perfection is the source of the qualitative aspects of things, the Absolute is responsible for a thing's existence, as opposed to its non-existence, and existence may be said to include growth.[19] This is precisely the domain of *rajas* which ensures expansive development at a given level and which is not concerned with either upward or downward movement.

Just as *Sat* is the first determination of the Absolute, so *Ānanda*, Beatitude, which corresponds to the Third Person of the Trinity, is the first determination of the Infinite. The doctrine of Divine Manifestation is summed up in the Islamic Tradition : "I was a Hidden Treasure and I loved to be known and so I created the world," and we have already seen that it is the Infinite which prefigures the means of this outward radiation. Blue, its colour, is therefore also the colour of extent and of distance, which in itself is a blessed liberation.[20] It is to this aspect of distance that the vault of heaven bears witness. But when outward manifestation reaches a certain stage, its aspect of freedom inevitably changes to limitation and danger, at any rate in respect of fallen man. Distance, for him, takes on the negative aspect of remoteness from God, and the movement away from the Principle is a current of degeneration that must be resisted. From this standpoint it would be inopportune and misleading to describe *tamas*[21] as blue. It has to be thought of as black, with a saving opposite of white.

To revert once more to distance in its positive sense, far-sightedness or breadth of vision may be counted as a subjective aspect of it. Moreover, blue is the cold colour and therefore the colour of impartiality and objectivity. All these qualities make it clear why blue is universally one of the great symbols of Truth and of Wisdom. It is also a symbol of Eternity, which is one with Truth in as much as that which is True or Real is that which can never pass away. This aspect of Truth is reflected in the static quality of blue as compared with the more volatile red and yellow; and by extension from Eternity, as the colour of immortality, blue plays a large part in many different traditions in connection with the dead in varying ways – amulets placed in the tomb, hearse-cloths, shrouds *et cetera*.[22] Another projection of Eternal Truth is the virtue of constancy or fidelity, whence the mediaeval and still current phase "true blue"; and as the colour of depth, blue has not only an adamantine firmness but also an aspect of unfathomability in virtue of which it is a symbol of the Divine Mystery, the Secret *(al-Sirr)* as it is termed in Sufism. For the Taoists in particular, blue symbolizes the inscrutable nature of Tao.[23]

Nothing that is below the Divine Essence can fail to reflect, in some degree or other, Its Absolute Infinite Perfection, and we have already seen how this ternary appears at the level of the Personal God as *Sat-Chit-Ānanda*. At the next level in the hierarchy, which marks the outset of manifestation, Buddhi, who corresponds to the created Logos, has a triple manifestation, *Trimūrti*[24], whose persons are Brahmā,[25] Viṣṇu and Śiva. The same triplicity is expressed in Christianity in the formulation "I am the Way, the Truth and the Life". As the exteriorization of Īśvara in his aspect of *Sat*, Brahmā is the productive principle of manifested beings. He therefore corresponds to "the Life", with *rajas* as his *guṇa* and red as his colour. Viṣṇu exteriorizes *Chit* and fulfils the function of Logos in the strict sense. He corresponds to "the Way" with *sattva* as his *guṇa* and yellow[26] as his colour. Śiva, who exteriorizes *Ānanda* and thereby the Infinite, is the transforming principle, which means that he is *a priori* the power that terminates existences[27] on lower planes with a view to their regeneration. He corresponds to "the Truth"[28], with *tamas* as his *guṇa* and blue as his colour – or black according to the standpoint.

Since the religions are manifestations of the Divine Word, let us consider in this same context the triad of monotheistic religions which have been said to correspond, in the order of their revelation, to the Three Persons of the Trinity. They are also said, in Sufism, to correspond to the three great principles of spirituality, namely to fear, love and knowledge[29]; and there is an analogy between these principles and the Hindu ways of action, love and knowledge.[30] Judaism may be termed a path of action because its very substance consists of a multitude of ritual acts accomplished in obedience to a strict and complex law which covers every aspect of life. It goes without saying that each of the monotheisms is a self-sufficient, totally independent whole, and that it is therefore representative of each of the three terms of all the triads we are considering here. But there are none the less questions of stress, apart from a certain continuity and development between the three faiths; and it is to Judaism, the first, that we owe the formulation "Fear of the Lord is the beginning of wisdom", an axiom with which the religion of Moses is deeply penetrated. Now red, the colour of the Divine majesty, is by extension expressive of justice and of danger. It may thereby be considered the colour of fear; and as the essentially dynamic colour, it is likewise the colour of action.

We have seen, with reference to the Old Testament, the connection between fire, therefore red, and Jehovah. But it might be objected that the religion that is named after the Second Person of the Trinity has also a powerful claim on red which, in addition to its other significations[31], is a symbol of love. This is true, and it has already been admitted that each religion has necessarily a claim on all the colours. But apart from the fact that yellow is also the symbol of love, in particular of Divine love[32], what distinguishes Christianity above all from the other two religions in question is the manifestation of the Divinity, the living presence of God, and manifestation is of the colour of light. Thus in Hinduism the guarantors of the maintenance of religion throughout the cycle of four ages, namely the ten Avataras (Divine descents), are incarnations, not of Brahmā or Śiva, but of the yellow-robed Viṣṇu; and the followers of the *bhakti-marga*, the way of love, are generally known as *Vaiṣṇava* (Vishnuites). It is moreover in the nature of things that the Divine Presence should be the source of a perspective of love.

By contrast, Christ predicted for Islam a perspective dependent upon "the Spirit of Truth which proceedeth from the Father"[33]. The difference between it and the Christian outlook is also implicit in the words: "I have yet many things to say unto you but ye cannot bear them now. Howbeit when he, the Spirit of Truth is come, he will guide you unto all truth[34]". The Gospels are as it were wrapped round the person of Jesus. The perspective of love does not tolerate too much looking to the right or the left, but the Koran demands on the contrary that one should look well in all directions for "wheresoever ye turn, there is the Face of God"[35] This change from "yellow" to "blue" was in the nature of things, for there is an obvious connection between Truth and old age, the time of life that is normally characterized by serene objectivity, and Islam is the religion of the old age of the cycle, the threshold of the meeting of extremes, death and regeneration, of which Śiva is the Lord. Nor could Sufism, Islamic mysticism, be other than a way of knowledge; and it may be noted in this respect that the Divine Essence is often addressed by the Sufis as Laylā, a woman's name which has the meaning of night. In this highest sense, night is the symbol of Absolute Reality in its "feminine" aspect of Infinitude. The blue-black night sky with its stars reflects the "womb" of Infinite Totality in which the supreme archetypes of all existing things are mysteriously contained in undifferentiated Oneness.

The Koran is called the Book of Truth, and it can also be called the Book of Mercy in as much as all its chapters but one begin with the words "In the Name of God, the Infinitely Compassionate, the Boundlessly Merciful." The identity of Infinitude and Mercy is affirmed in the verse "My Mercy embraceth all things".[36] The first of these two Names of Mercy, al-Rahmān, is related to the Name al-Muhīt, the All-Embracing; and this word has by extension the meaning of ocean. Like the blue sky and the blue cloak of the Virgin, the seas (maria in Latin) in as much as they surround the land are a symbol of Infinite Mercy. The Name al-Rahmān could almost be translated the Infinitely Comprehending, which would serve to indicate the profound cognitive connection, not obvious at first sight, between Mercy and Truth, both of which are symbolized by the same colour.

The second Name of Mercy, *al-Rahīm*, the Boundlessly Merciful, is also by extension a name of the Prophet. Whereas the first Name denotes the Divine Source of Mercy, this second Name is expressive of all manifested Mercy; and here lies the explanation why green is generally considered to be the colour of Islam. Yellow is the colour of manifestation, and if it be brought to bear upon blue the result is green. The Koran speaks of the green garments worn by blessed souls in Paradise, and Paradise itself, symbolized by the oases in the desert, and named in Arabic "the Garden", is always thought of as verdant. But if this compound colour[37] stands for the religion as such, there is no doubt that by a typically Islamic ellipsis – for Islam loves to dwell on the roots of things – blue rather than green is the dominant colour of Islamic art. More than one famous mosque is known as the Blue Mosque, while there are very many others to which this name might well be given; and in Koran manuscripts, apart from the illuminators' evident love of blue, there seems to be an unwritten law that wherever sections of text or ornamentation are framed within borders, the outermost border shall be blue, as if in illustration of the above quoted verse "My Mercy embraceth all things."

Needless to say, these general considerations lay themselves open to many apparent inconsistencies which can however be explained away if we bear in mind that everything is bound to partake of all the three intrinsic dimensions of the Supreme Reality, even though it be eminently representative of one of them in particular. We have seen for example that red is traditionally associated with Jupiter and blue with Juno. But if she is Queen of Heaven, he, for his part, is King of Heaven, and as such he also has a claim on the colour of the firmament. Astrologically speaking, blue

corresponds to his planet, the greater benefic, whereas green
corresponds to Venus, the lesser benefic; and the parts played
in Virgil's *Aeneid* by the two deities who give their names to
these planets are analogous, though at a lower level, to the
functions of the two Names of Mercy in Arabic which we
have just been considering and of which the same two colours
are symbols.

To take another example, Kṛṣṇa is the eighth Avatara of
Viṣṇu; but he is invariably depicted as being of the colour of
Śiva, and this is indicated in his name. The explanation is no
doubt that the ninth Avatara was the founder of Buddhism,
whereas the tenth will have a universal function that concerns all religions. Kṛṣṇa is thus, for this cycle of time, the
last Divine descent on behalf of Hinduism; and it is in perfect accordance with his finality that within the framework of
Viṣṇu he should be eminently representative of Śiva. This is
borne out by the Bhagavad-Gita, the Song of the Lord,
namely of Kṛṣṇa, for its perspective is Shivaite rather than
Vishnuite.

Leaving the reader to resolve other apparent contradictions along similar lines, let us, in conclusion, dwell briefly
once more on the supreme symbolic significance of the triad
which is our theme. Very relevant to this is a note by Frithjof
Schuon, in his previously quoted *From the Divine to the Human,* on Beyond-Being which, as we have seen, he defines as
Absolute, Infinite, Perfection. The note is partly necessitated
by the unwillingness of Christian theologians in general to
raise their intelligences above the level of the Trinity. "Concerning the transcendence of Beyond-Being, it is necessary
to emphasize that in reality this transcendence is absolute
plenitude, so that it could not possibly have a privative meaning: to say that the Trinity is surpassed therein means, not
that the Trinity is abolished in its essentials, but that it is
comprised – and prefigured in respect of its ontological or
hypostatic projection – in Beyond-Being in a way which,
while being undifferentiated , is eminently positive; in the

same way as the Vedantic *Sat-Chit-Ānanda* which, though it corresponds to an already relative vision, is nonetheless ineffably and supereminently comprised in the pure absoluteness of *Atmā*".[38]

What is said here of the Christian Trinity and its Hindu equivalent can and must be said of the primary colours. To suppose that their ultimate undifferentiated Oneness simply means that they are as it were absorbed into white would be a most misleading simplification. Such a reduction to unity would be an abolition of the essentials of colour, and it would therefore be a privation altogether out of keeping with the plenitude of Beyond-Being. The colours are given us in this world to bear witness to the wealth of the "Hidden Treasure" and to affirm precisely that it is not "monotonous" in any negative sense. Among the essentials of red, yellow and blue is their harmonious contrast. The word "ineffable" in the above quotation is altogether to the point, for we are here beyond the limits of what the mind can conceive and what the tongue can express. It is a contradiction in terms that there should be any room for contrasts in undifferentiated Oneness. But it is well known in more than one mysticism that the perplexity[39] caused by certain apparent contradictions can be a basis for intellection. In other words, it can serve as a stepping stone from the mind to the heart, for the heart can intuit what the brain cannot think. The Koran tells us: "And whatsoever He hath created for you on earth of diverse hues, verily therein is a sign for people bent on remembrance".[40] The reference here is clearly to the "Platonic" remembrance of a Divine Archetype, the remembrance which a sign or symbol of that Archetype has power to awaken in the higher reaches of the intelligence.

It is said in Sufism that knowledge of the Truth entails the grasping of "the union of opposites"[41]. Adapted to our immediate context, this means the certitude that the piercing distinctnesses which delight us in colour are not obliterated in the Oneness, but that on the contrary they are to be seen there, and there only, in all the fullness of their divergence. This doctrine is moreover latent in the symbol itself, for to see a colour at its purest and best, as one does sometimes in a flower, is to see an imprint of the Absolute which guarantees that the beatific vision in the highest sense will not fail to reveal the Eternal Origin of that particular aesthetic experience. When the Koran says "There is nothing that doth not praise Him,"[42] it authorizes us to say when we see a colour, singly or with others: "If this be merely the shadow, Glory to the Substance!" The colours are bearers, from their Supreme Source, of this message: "Beware of estimating My Infinite Beauty according to the poverty of mental conceptions of My Oneness."

[1]It might be objected that one has none the less seen a self-sufficient complementarity of red and blue which leaves nothing to be desired. But the triplicity is still there, for the orange red and turquoise blue in question can only be produced, in both cases, by the addition of yellow.

[2]This term, which has been borrowed from the writings of Frithjof Schuon, is necessary to safeguard the rights of the Absolute in the full sense.

[3]This contrast is itself symbolic of the opposition between the Absolute and the relative, *Ātmā* and *māyā*.

[4]LV, 31.

[5]Golden yellow.

[6]She differs from Phoebus Apollo in as much as she is the archetype of discursive or mental knowledge, whereas the solar deity is the source of direct heart-knowledge.

[7]Allowance must however be made for considerable fluctuation as regard the level at which Apollo and his equivalents were worshipped. In this respect, everything would depend on the intention of the worshipper.

[8]In itself, the sun is a globe of fire which produces both heat and light, and this relationship is irreversible. It is not heat and light

that produce the fire of the sun.

[9]Exodus, 20, 18.

[10]Frédéric Portal, *Des Couleurs symboliques*, p.90.

[11]Frithjof Schuon, *From the Divine to the Human*, p.41.

[12]Schuon, *ibid.*, p.40.

[13]Portal, *ibid.*, p.42.

[14]*ibid.* p.37.

[15]*The Eleventh Hour*, p. 75, note 17.

[16]"The ancients would liken what they deemed to be particularly faultless and beautiful to gold; by 'the Golden Age' they meant the age of the virtues and of happiness, and by 'the golden verses' they meant, according to Hierocles, those verses which contained the doctrine at its purest. This same tradition is to be found in 'the golden legends' of the saints." (Portal, p.52.)

[17]The two different correspondences of colours to the *gunas* result, as we have now seen, from the fact that on the one hand *sattva*, *rajas* and *tamas* manifest, all equally, the vibrations of the Absolute in the relative, of *Ātmā* in *Māyā*, and on the other hand *sattva* and *tamas* manifest the opposition between *Ātmā* and *Māyā*.

[18]"The Divine word, which is the 'knowledge' that God has of Himself, cannot but be the Good, God Being able to know Himself as Good only." (Schuon, *ibid*, p. 39).

[19]*Sat* is both Being and Power, and these two complementary aspects are ultimately reflected on the physical plane by matter and energy. (See Schuon, *ibid.*, p.39)

[20]As the "colour" of the air, blue is thereby the colour of the wind, which is one of the great symbols of the Trinity's Third Person.

[21]The very term *tamas* seems to have been chosen expressly in view of the predicament of fallen men. The root *tam* denotes exhaustion both in the sense of faintness and of finality. This last word is however a key to the *guna's* positive aspects.

[22]See Portal, *ibid.*, p.99.

[23]*ibid.*, p.88.

[24]The three *gunas* have their summit in the *Trimūrti*.

[25]So named because he reflects the Absolute Itself, also named Brahmā or Para-Brahmā (Supreme Brahmā), a name that is neuter

in gender as distinct from the masculine Apara-Brahmā (non-supreme Brahmā) of the *Trimūrti*.

[26]Viṣṇu is sometimes described as *pītavasas*, dressed in yellow (see Portal, p.44, note 4).

[27]In view of his initially destructive aspect, the connection between Śiva and *Ānanda* may seem at first surprising. But it must be remembered that his alchemy prefigures the supreme transformation – in Christian terms the Apocatastasis – when the Infinite brings all finite things to an end and reabsorbs them into Itself.

[28]A glance from the third eye in the forehead of Śiva reduces all illusion to nothing.

[29]In Arabic *makhāfah, maḥabbah, maʿrifah.*

[30]*Karma-marga, bhakti-marga, jñāña-marga.*

[31]We must bear in mind throughout that each colour is a vast synthesis of meaning.

[32]See Portal, *ibid.*, pp. 41-2.

[33]St. John, 15, 26.

[34]*ibid.*, 16, 13. As Frithjof Schuon has remarked, the Christian identification of these promises with the miracle of Pentecost does not mean that they cannot refer also and above all to the Revelation of Islam, for sacred utterances can generally be taken in more ways than one, and "if Muhammad is a true Prophet, the passages referring to the Paraclete must inevitably concern him – not exclusively but eminently – for it is inconceivable that Christ, when speaking of the future, should have passed over in silence a manifestation of such magnitude," (*The Transcendent Unity of Religions*, p. 116).

[35]II, 115

[36]VII, 156.

[37]For the reasons why green excels beyond measure the other compound colours, and also for many other profound considerations with regard to colour, see Frithjof Schuon, *Spiritual Perspectives and Human Facts*, ch. II

[38]p.28, note 11.

[39]See *Letters of a Sufi Master* (Perennial Books), p.11, note 3.

[40]XVI, 13.

[41]*Jamʿ al-ḍiddayn.*

[42]XVII, 44

From the Koranic Revelation to Islamic Art

Jean-Louis Michon

Part One: The Message of Islamic Art

اقرا باسم ربك الذى خلق
خلق الانسان من علق
اقرا وربك الاكرم
الذى علم بالقلم
علم الانسان مالم يعلم

"Read: In the Name of thy Lord Who createth,
Createth man from a clot,
Read: And it is thy Lord the Most Bountiful
Who teacheth by the pen,
Teacheth man that which he knew not..." (XCVI: 1-4)

It was with this summons, this command given to the Prophet Muḥammad by the Archangel Gabriel that the Koranic Revelation opened 14 centuries ago in 612 AD, ten years before the start of the Hijrah. And this same summons which exhorted Muḥammad to read aloud, to proclaim the Divine Message is, it seems to me, well suited to introduce an exposition the subject of which is the art of Islam.

This is so not only because these verses of the Koran were the first to be revealed, thus marking the beginning of the great adventure of Islam, but equally for more precise reasons, because with these first words of the Sacred Book, with what they say and with the form in which they say it, the art of Islam is already present.

219

These words as said in Arabic have a very precise resonance, an intrinsic force which is linked to, among other things, the principial meanings of the following triliteral roots and the alliterations and permutations of letters which they give rise to:

KHLQ– to create and 'LQ – the clot

QR'   – to read and QLM – the pen or calamus

'LM   – to know, recognize and again QLM, the calamus.

In short the Koran which as its name suggests is the "reading", the "recitation" par excellence, given to be heard, memorized and repeated in full, carries within itself the roots of the first art of Islam which is *psalmody*. And since the words of the Revelation are assembled in a Book and are composed of letters we have already in embryo, the second major art of Islam which is *calligraphy*, an art which man carries within himself, in a certain manner, from the beginning of the Revelation since "God teacheth man with the pen," that is to say with the reed which, having been plunged in ink, traces the sacred signs which grant the human being access to knowledge.

Psalmody, the art which manifests the sound and modulations of the verses of the Koran in time; calligraphy, the art which transcribes visually the vocables and fixes them in space, ... with these two modes of expression we find ourselves at the very source of the art of the Muslim, the source from which the artists of Islam have never ceased over the centuries to draw their inspiration.

Specialists on Islamic art usually approach their subject from an angle that is both chronological and geographical; they describe its evolution in time, analyse the borrowings and original contributions, point out the individuality of works created at different periods, in the various parts of the Islamic world and in the various spheres of application; architecture, music, the industrial and decorative arts. Such an approach is evidently impossible within the framework of a single essay where it would only lead to a tedious enumeration of facts, of necessity very incomplete. Besides, the analytical character of this approach does not always allow it to set it in relief the permanent values of Islamic art which enable the latter, everywhere and at all times, to be true to itself and confer on it an incontestable originality.

That is why I deemed it important to consider Islamic art from another point of view that is neither historic nor descriptive but which is based on what one could call the "spiritual universe" of Islam. Without doubt this universe is not the property of artists alone. Being that of the Revealed Message, it belongs to every Muslim. But as soon as the artist intervenes, the ideas which he entertains are transferred to the material objects which become the common property of the community. Hence the necessity of knowing the meaning of these ideas if one wishes to be able the better to read and understand the language into which they are transcribed.

The undertaking to approach Islamic art through its interpreters has been made easier for me by the recollection of my numerous meetings with traditional artisans, from the far east to the far west of Islam. Everywhere, I have found them similar; humble and honest, intelligent and pious, conscious of the values of which they are the trustees and which they strive to keep alive, often in unfavourable circumstances. It is therefore first their aspirations, then the means of expression which they have used and finally some of the works which they have created that we are going to review hereafter.

(1) Art – An Integral Part of Muslim Life

In the Koran, God says, in speaking of man, "I created him only that he might worship Me." (LI: 56) Further, it is said, "Nothing is greater than the remembrance of God!" (XXIX: 45)

It follows then that the real *raison d'être* of man is to worship God, which implies that the whole of his existence should be an act of devotion and remembrance vis-à-vis his Maker.

The idea of remembrance, of recollection – *dhikr, tadhkīr* –

is fundamental to Islam. The Koran is called *dhikr Allāh*, Remembrance of God, and *dhikr Allāh* is also one of the names given to the Prophet Muḥammad, not only because he was the trustee and transmitter of the Koran, but also because his behaviour, his words and his teachings – in short all that makes up the *Sunnah*, the Prophetic Tradition – show to what extent he remembered his Lord, and as a result of this constant remembrance, was near to Him.

This preoccupation, this obsession one might even say, with the recollection, the remembrance of God is not only a factor in individual perfection. It is also a stimulating ferment to social life and artistic development. In order to remember God often, such as is insisted upon by the Koran, it is necessary in effect that the members of the Muslim community should contrive to surround themselves at every moment of their lives – and not only during the ritual prayer – with an ambience favourable to this remembrance. Such an ambience would need to be beautiful and serene so that the human beings one met as well as all the things, natural or artificial one encountered could become the occasion for and the support of the *dhikr*. With regard to the human and social milieu, such an ambience is realized through the practice of the *Sharīʿah*, the revealed Religious Law which contains the rules to which all are obliged to conform. In this Law one distinguishes five essential pillars: testimony of faith, prayer (five times per day), fasting, almsgiving, pilgrimage. Thanks to these, a network of sacralized behaviour patterns, as much individual as collective, is woven into the heart of the collectivity, the *ummah*.

As to the imprint given to the material environment so that it too might become a mirror of the spiritual world, it is here, precisely, that one enters the domain of art, of sacred art which, according to the words of the contemporary *Maître à penser* Frithjof Schuon, "is first of all the visible and audible form of Revelation and then also its indispensable liturgical vesture."[1]

The function of artists consists in translating the principles of Islam into aesthetic language, in other words, transposing them into forms and motifs which will be incorporated into the structures and used in the decoration of all things from sanctuaries and palaces to the most humble domestic utensil. "God is beautiful; He loves beauty," says a *hadīth (Allāhᵘ jamīlᵘⁿ, yuḥibbᵘ al-jamāl)* ², which could be regarded as the doctrinal foundation of Muslim aesthetics.

According to the Islamic perspective, which underlines the absolute supremacy of the rights of the Creator over those of the creature, artistic creativity is nothing other than a pre-disposition *(istiʿdād)* which God has placed in man to help him follow the path which leads to Him. The artist is therefore only one among others of the servants of God; he does not belong to any exceptional category. He should himself, the better to fulfil his role in the collectivity, become, by means of effacement and disinterested service, an as transparent as possible interpreter of the Tradition to which he subscribes. Whence the relationship that has always existed with Muslim artists between the practice of the virtues and the excellence of professional work. The Prophet said, "God desires that if you do something, you do it thoroughly." And one can confirm that this advice has been followed to the letter, in particular by the artisans of the guilds and brotherhoods of the entire classical period for whom the artisanal pact was a unanimously respected professional code of honour.

Another characteristic of artistic creativity in Islam is that it is never exercised "gratuitously", by which we are to understand that it always answers to well-defined ends. Unlike the art of the modern West, Islamic art has never known the distinction between an art supposedly 'pure', or 'art for art's sake', and a utilitarian or applied art, the first aiming solely at provoking an aesthetic emotion and the second supposedly responding to some need. In fact, Islamic art is always 'functional', that is to say useful, whether the utility is directly of the spiritual order – like the Koranic verses engraved on the pediment of a mausoleum or embroidered on the veil which covers the Ka'bah at Mecca, – or whether it pertains to many levels at the same time, as with a chandelier or a bronze basin inlaid with arabesques.

It will perhaps be noticed that I use the terms 'artist' and 'artisan' without distinction to designate those who are responsible for the artistic expression of Islam. This is because in classical Arabic there is only one word to indicate the man who works with his hands; it is *ṣāni'*, a worker, and artisan, someone who practises a craft or trade, *ṣinā'ah*, he who is obliged to do an apprenticeship in a technique or an 'art' in the sense the Middle Ages gave this word and which, in Arabic is called *fann*, with the same Mediaeval connotation. This meaning is found expressed, notably, in the adage *ars sine scientia nihil*, "technique/skill without knowledge," that is to say wisdom, "is nothing" – an adage Muslim artisans could have made their own and of which, it may be said in passing, our modern technocrats would do well to take note. Therefore, the artist, as we know him today, with his search after individual expression and his rather marginal position in society does not exist in the world of traditional Islam which is what we are now concerned with and that is why, I think, the use of either term, 'artist' or 'artisan' should not lend itself in this context to any misunderstanding.

There are, no doubt, some crafts which by their nature do not give rise to obvious artistic products. Certain professional specialities, like the tanning of skins, the carding or the dyeing of wool, cannot, however, be detached from the process of production the final product of which – a ceremonial saddle of a carpet – will be a work of art. On the other hand, certain artistic elements – for example the work songs or the badges and special costumes worn on the feast days of the guild – are nearly always associated with the practice of the traditional crafts and constitute a not inconsiderable contribution to the cultural life of Muslim society.

In brief, there are two essential characteristics of Islamic artistic production:

Firstly   : from the spiritual and ethical point of view, it derives essentially from the Koranic Message, the values of which it aims to translate onto the formal plane.

Secondly: from the technical point of view, it rests on the transmission from father to son, or master to apprentice, of unchangeable rules and practices. Such a transmission does not in any way imply stagnation and the automatic repetition of earlier designs. On the contrary, at most times, it has assured a constant source of inspiration to the artists and a stability on the technical level which have favoured the creation of numerous masterpieces which are in no way repetitive. If, at other times, the ancient formulae have become somewhat exhausted as a result of being reproduced, it is necessary to look elsewhere than in the formulae themselves for the cause of this decadence.

(2) The Formal Languages

The time required by the art of Islam to fully develop its personality was relatively very short. It extended over the first 150 odd years after the death of the Prophet (in the 10th year of the Hijrah or 632 of the Christian era) and coincided with the lightning-like expansion of Islam across the Asiatic and Mediterranean worlds as well as with the first decades of the establishment of the Abbasid Caliphate at Baghdad (750 AD).

This growth was the result of contact with the old cultures which Islam encountered and subjugated. Placed at its disposal were the techniques and artistic forms practised by various civilizations, the Hellenistic (and Romano-Byzantine) of Syria, the Sassanid of Persia and Mesopotamia, the Coptic

of Egypt (with its Pharaonic heritage), without mentioning
the numerous local traditions like those of the Berbers of
North Africa or of the Visigoths of Spain, which Islam was able
to sweep along in its wake.

All these elements were placed at the service of the new
community. Often their original forms remained intact, at
least to begin with, after which a selection was operated as
much by the artists themselves, many of whom were converts
to Islam and thus obedient to the new ethical and aesthetic
criteria, as by reason of new needs to which art would hence-
forward have to comply. Amongst these needs those of worship played a predominant role and it was in religious architecture that Islamic art first manifested its faculty for integrat-
ing pre-existing artistic traditions and adapting them to its
own vision and needs. In order to suggest in what sense this
evolution took place, I will take the classical example of the
Grand Mosque of Damascus which was constructed by the
Umayyads at the end of the seventh century AD. At the time
of construction, the Byzantine artists summoned to execute
the glass mosaics on the façades of the court and the walls of
the portico used a style of décor – with thick-leafed trees and
architectural elements done in trompe l'oeil – which was
fashionable in the Eastern part of the Roman Empire and still
reflected the naturalistic tradition of Rome and Greece. The
remarkable fact is that naturalistic motifs like these did not
appear subsequently in religious monuments, whereas the
geometric and vegetal elements of these same mosaics – i. e.
double spirals, rosettes, foliage and garlands – were retained
and soon developed in refined compositions (as on the *miḥrāb*
of Córdoba, scarcely a century later).

In similar vein, the frescoes of the 'desert palaces', those
country-seats built for the Umayyad caliphs, contain numerous representations of human beings: musicians, dancers,
hunters, executed in the Hellenistic or Sassanid style. This art
of the figurative fresco was abandoned fairly quickly and
hardly ever re-appeared except in the form, greatly reduced in
size, of the miniature.

These examples could be multiplied, but what concerns us above all is to see according to what criteria this selection was operated.

The major criterion, which I believe to have already suggested, is the power each work of art should have to recall the Divine Unity, to suggest it in some way, and in all cases, not to distract the attention and senses to the extent that the viewer becomes captivated by illusory appearances. Art should help the soul to concentrate on the essential and not turn it towards the accidental and the transitory.

It is moreover in this preoccupation that one should see the deep-rooted reason for the rejection of figurative representation in Islamic art . This refusal is not founded upon a legal prohibition inscribed in the Koran; but it expresses a repugnance at seeing man substitute himself for the Creator in wishing to imitate natural forms. In itself the creative act of the artist is not reprehensible, quite the contrary, since God Himself in the Koran, uses the example of the potter who moulds clay to characterize His own creative act:

خلق الانسان من
صلصال كالفغار

'He created man of clay like the potter's' (LV: 14).

But such an act runs the risk of engendering in the human artist the illusion of having himself added something to the creation, whence the temptation to pride, which in Islam is considered to be the worst sin of all, since it tends to place the creature at the level of the Creator, or in other terms, to ascribe to God an equal or an associate. Equally, figurative art may have the effect on the observer of making him admire the human genius who, instead of revealing in his work the infinite Richness of Him Who created the prototypes of all things, knows how to reproduce a tree, a flower or the human body in its physical appearance.

Whence the systematic preference of Islamic art for impersonal, linear forms which have a geometrical or mathematical basis. Such is the case with the forms derived from the two branches 'given' by the Revelation which we cited at the beginning of this exposition: psalmody and calligraphy.

The psalmody of the Koran is the sacred art par excellence. There are seven recognized ways of chanting and any one of them requires an apprenticeship of many years. From psalmody are derived numerous manifestations of religious life, such as the call to prayer, the liturgical recitation of litanies – *awrād, aḥzāb* – and the intoning of *mawladiyyāt* (avocations to the praise of the Prophet Muḥammad) and mystical poems. Not less important is the influence of psalmody on the whole of Arab music, that is to say instrumental music – whether it concerns religious music – such as that which is played at the meetings of the mystical brotherhoods – or profane music, the demarcation between the two types being moreover often difficult to establish.

As to calligraphy, its role is equally to make perceptible the eternal beauty of the Koran. After having served to establish, some twenty years after the death of the Prophet, a complete and definitive version of the Book, it has never ceased to spread the text, giving birth to forms and styles of writing the aesthetic qualities of which arouse the admiration even of non-Muslims.

Each script, in playing on the forms, dimensions and proportions of the letters brings more particularly into relief certain Divine Attributes. Thus the Divine Majesty, Rigour and Transcendence are evoked by the vertical strokes, especially that of the *alif,* the symbol of the Unity of the Supreme Principle which stamps its mark on the rhythms of the discourse. Beauty, Gentleness and Immanence are expressed by the horizontal lines, above and below which are written the diacritic and vowel signs, like the notes of a musical score. Finally Perfection and Plenitude are suggested by the rounded forms, such as the *nûn* for example in the style of the Maghrib.

The form of Arabic letters, their hieratic character – above

all in the earliest transcriptions of the Koran – and the proportions which regulate all their outlines lead us to another mode
of artistic expression to which the Arabs were certainly predis-
posed and for which Islam provided the occasion of an
exceptional flowering. I have in mind the language of geometric figures and forms to which also is linked that of numbers.

By means of geometry, the Muslim artists succeeded in
illustrating visually notions as sublime and abstract as that of
tajallī the infinite radiation of the Divine Essence across the
multiplicity of levels of existence. The whole philosophy of
arabesque and tracery, whether it be floral or geometric, as of
polygonal decoration, rests on the idea of an omnipresent
centre which manifests itself where and when it will without
thereby being in any way, in its nature, affected, augmented
or diminished. The explosion of stars on the vault of a cupola
– notably in the mosques of Persia and Turkey – is an illustration of this thesis. As to the friezes of tracery which frame a
door or a prayer niche, or which run under a ceiling, or which
border a carpet, they are, like the march of time which
regulates our lives, the reminder of the guiding thread which
directs and co-ordinates all the worlds and all the beings and
which is none other than the Divine Presence.

Whilst on this subject, I would like to mention that the
linear scheme of arabeseque and entrelacs with its alternation
of complementary motifs and its spatial divisions is very close
to Arabic musical composition where the artist improvises a
whole game of questions and answers.

Likewise, there is a conscious and deliberate analogy between the division of space which is effected by the networks
of polygonal stars and the division of time which is at the base
of psalmody as of Arabic poetry. Each polygonal network is
constructed according to a geometric outline which starts
with the division of the circle into equal parts. Depending on
whether the circle is first divided into three, four or five
segments, the network has for its rhythmical base the equilat-
eral triangle, the square, or the pentagon (the star of five

points), as well as the multiples of these figures: the hexagon or two inverted triangles, the octagon or the star of eight points, etc. Precise symbolic meanings are attached to all these figures and numbers, knowledge of which makes up part of the traditional artistic teaching as is borne out by, among other writings, the letters of the Ikhwān al-Ṣafā,' written in the 4th Century of the Hijrah (10th Century AD) which provide us with valuable information concerning the arts and sciences of the period.

Epilogue

An exposition should have a conclusion. And, authorizing myself on the basis of a field experience acquired with projects for the safeguarding of cultural values and assets, I shall conclude with a warning and an appeal.

Today, in all parts of the Muslim world, numerous craftsmen are abandoning their trades, for want of patronage, to become workers or labourers in industry, or sometimes – if they have the chance – , *chaouch*, that is to say office-boys in an administration; they only do it of necessity, and half-heartedly, because the ancestral crafts are no longer able to support them and their families.

In a world already so impoverished in spiritual values, where the West long since lost its sacred art, can one stand by with indifference and watch the progressive disappearance of an incomparable means of expression? Because the language of Islamic art is, I hope to have shown, of suprahuman inspiration, it is the reflection, in material formed by man, of spiritual truths, the *ḥaqā'iq*, of which man has received the imprint. Making these *perceptible*, the artist leaves them as testimonies of the Divine Concern which is exercised with regard to our world. The whole of Islamic art, in its prestigious monuments as in its more modest creations, bears testimony to the Truth of the Message received fourteen centuries ago by the Prophet Muḥammad. It also demonstrates the efficacity and the vitality of this Message across time and space. Finally, it attracts, by its convincing beauty, those who come into contact with it.

Tamerlane, the Destroyer, who without the least pity was able to exterminate the inhabitants of entire cities, nevertheless spared the guardians of religious science – ʿulamāʾ and fuqahāʾ – and also artists whom he carried off to his capital, Samarkand, to embellish it.

Are we to say that modern states, with their pursuit of technology and comfort, will be shown to be more destructive of traditional values than the armies of Tamerlane? One would like to be able to answer in the negative, more especially as it is false to believe that the improvement of living conditions demands the sacrifice of craftsmen.

Certain leaders of the Muslim community are still aware of the role that an authentic art should continue to play in the Islamic City. May their example be closely followed in the world of Islam so that we may continue to know, by the fruits which are the works of art, the Tree which has produced them and brought them to maturity.

But it is God who is the Master of success!

والله ولى التوفيق

---

[1] Frithjof Schuon, *Understanding Islam*, trans. from French by D.M. Matheson, London, 1963, 1976, 1979; Baltimore Maryland, 1976., chapter four.

[2] Imām Aḥmad, *Musnad.*

Insouciant Birds

Alvin Moore

Birds figure prominently in the symbolism of many different
forms of religion, and there usually are common traits in this
symbolism even if the larger patterns diverge (there is divergence, to be sure, but seldom contradiction). Birds are essential to the structure and meaning of the parable of the
mustard seed in the New Testament, a parable found in each
of the synoptic Gospels – Matthew xiii, 31, 32; Mark iv, 30 -
32; and in briefest form in Luke xiii, 18, 19, as follows:

> To what is the Kingdom of God like, and whereunto
> shall I resemble it? It is like to a grain of mustard seed
> which a man took and cast into his garden, and it grew
> and became a great tree and the birds of the air lodged
> in the branches thereof.

As winged creatures in their usually benign aspect[1], birds
represent the angels, those cosmological degrees or states of
existence beyond form and superior to the human state in
its corporeal modality, but inferior to the Divine. The Greek
aggelos parallels a number of words in the Semitic languages
and in old Persian that have the sense of message, messenger or hireling; and it is the Greek rendering of the Hebrew
mal'akh (Arabic *malak*) which gives the word *angel.* The Old
and New Testaments of the Bible as well as the Koran abound
in references to angels; in these sacred books the reality of
levels of cosmic existence higher than the terrestrial state of
man is a deep and unquestioned belief, almost as if the
existence of the angels were self-evident. Indeed, a sense of

these orders of reality may have been much more evident before the present "solidification" of the world and before human faculties became so throughly engrossed (the word is used advisedly) in externalized and material aspects of existence. The evidence, in fact, indicates that a notion of angelic states as essential links in the "great chain of being" is as old as mankind. Even Aristotle speaks of a primordial revelation to this effect, a divine origin of the belief in a hierarchy of secondary principles (*Metaphysics* xii, 8). Skepticism regarding the angelic states is a deviation, whether among the Saducees of New Testament times or among contemporary modernists.

In this brief study, we propose to survey Christian doctrine on the angels and some of the implications thereof, notably the significance of this belief for the doctrine of the Resurrection. We shall borrow here and there from extra-Christian articulations when these are more profound and more revealing, but only when such expressions are perfectly compatible, parallel and complementary – even as the ancient Hebrews are said to have done in their angelology, particularly during the time of the Babylonian captivity. Christian angelology commonly gives the angels an anthropomorphic coloring, but it could hardly be otherwise, for knowledge is in the knower according to the mode of the knower. Nevertheless, it will be well to bear in mind the statement of René Guénon that whatever is said theologically of the angels and demons can be said metaphysically of those cosmological states which are relatively superior to or inferior to man. The reference to states inferior to man is not so much to inferior and peripheral creatures in our own world, exceptions allowed for what they may symbolize, as to entities dwelling on infra-human levels of the cosmos.

In this review, we follow St Dionysius' *Celestial Hierarchy* and especially St Thomas Aquinas' *Summa Theologica*, section Ia, questions 50 - 64 and 106-113, which contain St Thomas' angelology. Thomas drew most heavily upon Dionysius' *Ce-*

lestial Hierarchy; it is this relatively brief text that he cites most
frequently, though he also drew from other writers whom he
respected, notably St Augustine, St Gregory the Great and St
John Damascene. But the *Celestial Hierarchy* of St Dionysius[2]
is the principal Christian source for doctrine on the angelic
states. In the remarks that follow, citations in the text are
from the indicated questions of the *Summa Theologica* unless
otherwise credited. First, however, let us cite a passage from
Frithjof Schuon, our own contemporary but nevertheless
the peer of an Eckhart and a Dante, whose words would
doubtless receive their full approbation:

> Concerning the angels, it is necessary to distinguish, on
> the one hand those which are the most elevated of
> 'peripheral' or 'passive' beings, and on the other those
> which are aspects or functions of the Spirit and which,
> by this fact, are central and active states *par excellence*;
> they constitute created aspects of the Holy Spirit and
> therefore of God, which ordinary theology obviously
> cannot admit in this form. In Hindu doctrine, these
> 'Angels' are the *Devas* of the *Trimurti*; Islamic doctrine,
> for its part, teaches that the Spirit (*Er-Ruh*, in Sanskrit,
> *buddhi*) – of which the 'aspects' or 'functions' constitute
> precisely the highest Angels (*El-Mala'el* or *El-Mala'ikat
> el-kiram*)– did not have to prostrate himself as did the
> other angels before Adam, and that according to a
> spatial symbolism, he surpasses in immensity all the
> ordinary Angels together; which, moreover, amounts to
> saying that in the universal order, by virtue of inverse
> analogy, the 'center' is greater than the 'periphery'.[3]

At the outset, let us note with Tauler that the ordinary
man does not know the nature of the angels, even as we do
not know ourselves; rather, we know their works in their relationships to us. St Thomas saw in the so-called principle of
plenitude and in that of continuity, ie, the notion of degrees
of reality, demonstrations of the necessary existence of the
angelic orders. Man, as microcosm, occupies a central posi-

tion in his world. In his lower circuit, he touches the mineral, vegetable and animal/sensory orders; as man, he dominates these lesser elements of creation by his rational powers. Though man is a "rational animal", he is potentially much more in virtue of his intellectual powers; for in principle these vastly exceed the scope of reason, *ratio*. Citing St Gregory the Great, St Thomas says "man senses in common with the brutes and understands with the angels." Elsewhere, if memory serves, the Angelic Doctor, who was certainly no friend of unfounded speculation, expressed the view that our rational faculties are, as it were, a failure of intellect – which is certainly not to disparage *ratio*, reason, in its proper place, but rather to disparage the view that would reduce intelligence to reason alone. St Thomas, it may be noted in passing, is considered by many Christians the perfectly rational man.

Now it is by no means alien to human experience that intelligence *per se* can surpass the specifically human mode of human intelligence which is reason. Indeed, this is a matter of common experience in the very form of faith itself as an intellectual virtue; also in our more profound intuitions as, eg, when we grasp the import of a symbol; within reason itself in the axiomatic element in common logic; and *a fortiori* in contemplation in all its degrees. But to return briefly to the principle of plenitude, the chief inference is clear: as the existential reality of the mineral, vegetable, animal/sensory and rational orders is indisputable, so by extension credence must be given to levels of reality above these orders; for we have enough evidence of them that they cannot simply be dismissed. Not only do common men enjoy intimations of an angelic manner of knowing in the higher and more interior reaches of their own intelligence, but some, even in our own dark age, have experienced – however fleetingly – angelic visitations which spilt over into the outer man as ineffable joy, peace and certitude from an unknown or scarcely known interior into the outer man.

The principle of plenitude simply asserts the actual existence, according to their own determining conditions, of all
genuine possibilities of existence. The principle of continuity complements this by affirming that universal existence is
ordered hierarchically, that existence is graded in degrees,
with the angelic states being anterior to the psychic and
corporeal realms both in the ontological hierarchy and in
order of cosmogonic procession. These considerations point
to a traditional unanimity of the three Semitic faiths, Judaism, Christianity and Islam; they affirm that man does not
stand at the pinnacle of all creation though he does stand at
the center – or, more accurately, at one center, that of his
own world.

Angels should not be conceived as corporeal or individualized existences, Christian and other traditional art not-
withstanding. If angelic epiphanies take human form, as well
they may do in missions to men, it is for our benefit, not
theirs; they assume human form when and where this serves
their purpose.

> Angels need an assumed body...on our account, that by
> conversing familiarly with man they may give evidence
> of that intellectual companionship which men may
> expect to have with them in the life to come.... For as in
> Holy Scripture the properties of intelligible things are
> set forth by the likenesses of things sensible, in the
> same way by Divine power sensible bodies are so fash-
> ioned by the angels as fittingly to represent the intelli-
> gible properties of an angel.

It is notable that in angelic epiphanies, the heavenly messengers are awesome and radiant and that they evoke a holy
fear. Even men may evoke something of this on occasion, as
did Stephen when angels drew near to him as he was brought
before the council (Acts vi and vii). His countenance, like
that of Moses, was resplendent with an angelic beauty so that
all those in the Sanhedrin found their eyes fixed upon his
face in spite of their complete disagreement with his utter-

ances.

The angelic ranks exist in graded choirs, a hierarchy of reality, wisdom and beatitude. We know them by names that relate to their nature and function. Essentially the angelic names derive from the Divine Attributes or Qualities which are their prototypes, and it is these latter which determine the character of the angel's contemplation of the Divine. Though there have been differences, the prevailing Christian nomenclature of the angelic ranks has been that of St Dionysius; they are, in descending order: Seraphim, Cherubim, Thrones; Dominations, Virtues, Powers; and Principalities, archangels and angels. Obviously this is a schematic listing and not a precise classification. Only, the entire angelic hierarchy is denominated by the name given to the lowest rank, that nearest man, ie, the angels. But the same can be said of the appellation archangel, for not infrequently the higher angelic ranks may be denominated by the term archangel. For St Dionysius, the hierarchy of the Church is patterned on the angelic hierarchy (see his *Ecclesiastical Hierarchy*).

Angels are creatures in the general sense of this word; they are not uncreate, though in the doctrine of St Thomas they are not of a composite nature but are pure intellectual substances. He does say that they consist of potency and act, God alone being pure act, ie, Essence. Act and potency in the angelic nature relate analogically to form and matter in the physical world. Another great Medieval doctor, Duns Scotus, differed on this point, holding that the angels, too, consist of form and matter; though the matter in question here was clearly conceived as of a more ethereal nature than the *materia secunda* of which man in his physical modalities is fashioned.[4] In any case, let it be noted that matter is primarily potentiality and the "appetite for form", ie, for an idea. Matter should not be thought of as some ill-defined but palpable substance which our senses can register, for in the absence of a formal element there is nothing in matter that

can be known. For St Thomas, the angels are not of a composite nature but are subsistent and hypostasized intelligences, altogether immaterial. The angels are in themselves
beyond the limits of form, ie, form as external contour,
location or mental phantasm. The fact that English and
other Western languages, in certain situations, use the same
word – form – for "shape" and "idea" can lead to confusion if
one is not in the habit of seeing words in their contexts. If a
man, eg, thinks that his lady has a wonderful form, he may
mean only that her presence excites him to passion; if, on
the other hand, he says with Yeats that he loves her "pilgrim
soul", he refers to form in quite another sense. When one
says *informal* or *formless* in reference to a degree of cosmic existence, the reference is to a level superior to all the more
obvious characteristics we associate with terrestrial humanity: an existential degree free from the limitations implicit in
the notion of any kind of physical body, and free even from
those phantasms by which we summon thoughts before our
minds, for as men our mental activity is characterized by
phantasms or mental forms. On the other hand, angels are
formal creatures in the sense that they are manifestations of
a Divine Quality or idea (form) in the Divine Intellect, ie,
the Logos, though this latter is an extended meaning of the
term and not that which is primarily intended when we
distinguish the angelic from the formal levels of existence.

We cannot here "prove" the existence of unembodied
psychic or animic entities, those which the Muslims refer to
as *jinn* (*genie*, as popularly rendered), except to point out
that there is no good reason to doubt the existence of such
creatures; and, further, to point out the dangerous confusion that is becoming ever more common: namely, that of
identifying the psychic with the properly spiritual, which is
reflected in the vocabulary of what remains of religion. We
use the word *soul* to cover both psychic (animic, subtle) and
spiritual realities. The spiritual *per se* is the formless, that
which is not limited by external form as being beyond the

latter. Our most common contact with the genuinely spiritual is through truth, goodness and beauty – beyond the formal aspects of those things by which these qualities are vehicled to us. The psychic, on the other hand, is the intermediary state between the corporeal and the spiritual realms and is still within the formal order, being characterized in its lower levels by fleeting and inchoate phantasms. Moreover, and herein lies the danger, the psychic realm is the area of predilection for the action of demonic forces which are, in effect, confined to the formal order. All traditions are in agreement on the dangers of the psychic realm, and one ignores this at one's great peril.

The traditional exoteric Christian perspective regards humanity in its present familiar existence, along with certain limited extensions of this existence, as a finality[5] and as norm and measure of the universe. A more adequate metaphysical perspective, while denying to the human state none of its proper reality, accords to other existential degrees all *their* due reality. Thus one can quite legitimately emphasize certain aspects of the angelic states which are not commonly presented, and the first such point to make or reiterate is the *informal, formless,* or *supraformal* character of the angelic degrees. This seems to be one thrust of St Thomas' teaching as he contrasts corporeal and incorporeal existence, and demonstrates the necessity of the angelic orders.

There must be some incorporeal creatures. For what is principally intended by God in creatures is good, and this consists in assimilation to God Himself.... God produces the creature by his intellect and will ....the perfection of the universe requires that there should be intellectual creatures. Now intelligence cannot be the act of the body, nor of any corporeal faculty; for every body is limited to here and now. Hence the perfection of the universe requires the existence of an incorporeal creature.... To be circumscribed by essential limits belongs to all creatures both corporeal and incorporeal. Hence

Ambrose says... that 'although some things are not contained in corporeal place, still they are none the less circumscribed by their substance.'

Elsewhere the Angelic Doctor speaks of the difference between material and immaterial existence; in the former, which is contracted by matter, a thing is only that which it is, as a stone is that particular stone and nothing else. But immaterial existences, in the manner of universal causes, are in a manner all things. "...Such things as pre-existed from eternity in the Word of God came forth from Him in two ways: first into the angelic mind; and secondly so as to subsist in their own natures."[6] And St Thomas cites St Gregory's statement that "in that heavenly land, though there are some excellent gifts, yet nothing is held individually", which is as if to say that the angels are beyond individuality. When angels assume a human form (which they may or may not do) in a mission to humans, it is a question of *noblesse oblige*, the greater accomodating itself to the capacities of the lesser. The angels are beyond form and by this fact are rightly called spiritual.

Angels, like men, bear in their natures an image of the Holy Trinity: they *exist*, and they have faculties of *intellect* and of *will*. With all creatures, angels, men or lesser beings, their existence is a function of God's archetypal knowledge; and this knowledge and the creature's possibility are one and the same. Men are too often forgetful of this; but it is not so with an angel, for his existence is a function of the Divine Intellect being consciously present to him and it is this by which he knows himself (cf Eckhart, Sermon *Quasi stella matutina*). This intimacy of the angels with the Divine determines the nobility of their nature and accounts for their awesomeness and majesty before men. In the beatified angels, the angelic intellect regards both good and evil, but their intention is directed to God alone. The angelic will is more untrammeled, freer and more powerful than man's will; angelic love is therefore purer, truer and more intense than man's *caritas* – according to the degree of excellence of the angel, and allowing for exceptions with outstanding saints. Similarly, the angels are mightier in knowledge than men, for in them knowledge is not tied to sensory experience. In St Dionysius' words, the angelic intellect is also more complete than man's and is unfailing; for pure intelligence is always true, and "nothing but what is true can be the object of intelligence." Men achieve their intellectual ends through kinds of movement and process, ie, discursive operations, and in these the element of experience is prominent. But the angelic intellect does not have to resort to these indirect procedures; it uses fewer means than rational men must use[7], eg, the angelic intellect does not have to abstract species from sense data as does human intelligence, but knows by species innate in its own nature.

> In the formless or supraformal world, which is the realm
> of the angelic states, all things are perceived as subsist-
> ing 'in the interior' of the subject, differences among
> the angelic subjects being marked by their modes of
> perception.[8]

The angelic intellect is always in act; it does not understand by reasoning but rather comprehends instantly all that it wills to understand, according to the rank of the angel in the hierarchy of hypostasized intelligences. There are limits to angelic knowledge, however; and these limits, as for example, the need for more numerous ideas in the knowing process, increase and become more restrictive with descending angelic ranks.

Even though the conditions of angelic existence are exceedingly exalted as compared with those determining human existence in this world, the entire angelic hierarchy is of the created or manifested order. The distinction of being uncreate belongs to God alone. Further, the angels are neither comprehensors nor wayfarers, whereas Jesus Christ was both: comprehensor in His Divine nature, and wayfarer in His humanity. Man is wayfarer, though in virtue

of his central state his vocation is to become ultimately comprehensor. The beatified angels are not wayfarers; they are
fixed in virtue and total love of God (according to the measure of their respective natures) from the first instant of their
conversion. But they are not comprehensors either, as not
being fully identified with the Divine Intellect. These state-
ments apply to those angels occupying peripheral or passive
states (see citation from *L'Oeil du coeur*, Frithjof Schuon, p. 3
above); but those in a central state cannot lack, to say the
least, any of the possibilities of metaphysical realization that
are theoretically open to man. For though men are wayfarers
by nature, there exists the theoretical possibility (considering the human race *in toto*) for men[9] to become comprehensors even in this life–a possibility quite unlikely of realization
in these terminal times of the present humanity. And, be it
noted, this a possibility which "official" Christianity, at least
in the west, has forgotten or allowed to lapse; but nevertheless, it is one that is essential to a fully found tradition. To
cite Eckhart again, man's beatitude lies wholly and solely in
the fact that God is knowable and in the realization of this
knowledge[10], and the same is no less true of the angels.

The beatitude of angels and of men, then, lies in the
knowledge of God; but "perfect beatitude is natural only to
God", for being and knowledge and the bliss that stems from
them are perfect only in Him, and in Him are a perfect
unity. Neither knowledge nor being, however, is of the substantive nature of the creature as creature, but are the ends
towards which creatures–men and angels–strive. "Now everything attains its last end by its operation", that operation
which is the particular entelechy of the creature in question.
Man's entelechy, like that of the angels, is knowledge; which
is a manner of saying that man's last end is the knowledge of
all there is to be known, ie, God, and all this implies a gnosis
in which God knows Himself in us; for "only God can know
God." This essential possibility of deification nevertheless
remains open for man because it is at the profoundest root

of his nature and because of the principle that *quisquis Deum intelligit, Deus fit*,[11] or as St Basil said: "the knowledge of God is the communication of immortality."

In the angels, species and hypostasis coincide; ie, a single angelic hypostasis constitutes an entire species. As St Thomas says, there cannot be several distinct whitenesses. Nevertheless, these celestial creatures are extremely numerous:

> ...angels, even inasmuch as they are immaterial substances exist in exceeding great number, far beyond all material multitude....

> There are many blessed armies of the heavenly intelligences, surpassing the weak and limited reckoning of our material numbers.... In angels, number is not that of discrete quantity, brought about by the division of what is continuous, but that which is caused by distinction of forms [ie, ideas or qualities].

Angelic multitude is multitude transposed beyond the discontinuities of material existence. The supraformal creation vastly exceeds in every positive respect the formal orders of existence, ie, the psychic and the corporeal; indeed, Eckhart says of even "the lowest angel in his pure nature: the smallest spark or love-light that ever fell from him would light up the whole world with love and joy!"[12] In humanity, by contrast, species is unitary but individuals are indefinitely numerous–and fragmentary, in what is commonly called "human personality."

Angels enjoy unfailing life, free of generation and corruption and of the permutations of the elements which characterize material existence – including the need for alimentation as we know it. "My meat is to do the will of Him that sent Me", said Christ (Jn iv, 34); and something of the same can be said of the blessed angels. "Their food is the celebration of His glory; their drink, the proclaiming of His holiness; their conversation, the commemoration of God, whose Name be exalted; their pleasure, His worship; and they are created

in different forms and with different powers", according to
the Muslim author Ibn Mājah[13] who also appropriately taught
that the angels are created of light. The angels are free as
regards local motion; hence, the aptness of birds as their
symbols. And they are free of such internal motions as concupiscence and anger. Not being contained, they are local-
ized from our point of view by their acts of understanding
and these acts in regard to our world may become acts of
presence; in this manner they become the container rather
than the contained. Similarly, as it is a question of understanding, angels can quit one place instantly and be instantly
in another; as a Vedic passage puts it, "Intellect is the swiftest
of birds" (quoted by Coomaraswamy). This quite rightly
implies a certain rapprochement between the created Intellect and the created, hypostasized intelligences. Angels, eg,
are the agents of revelation in the Divine economy. Angels
are subject to duration, but it is an aeviternal duration, not
our time which is the measure of the motion of heavenly
bodies, at least in its more external aspects. Some authorities, however, state that there are also certain angelic existences which are momentary and spark-like.

As there is natural knowledge in the angels, so is there
natural love. Both men and angels naturally and properly
seek their own good; this involves enlightened self-love, ie,
insofar as each desires by natural and uncorrupted appetite
that which is the good of their nature and which leads to the
perfection of that nature. Thus the beatified angels and men
in a state of grace naturally love God more than themselves;
for the Divine is the crown of both human and angelic
nature. Unlike men – saints excepted – who are wayfarers *en
route* to perfection (*Deo adjuvante*), the blessed angels love
God perfectly according to the measure of their own nature.
On initially coöperating with grace, the angelic entelechies
are instantly perfected in *gnosis* and *caritas*, again according
to the measure of their nature.

The beatified angels cannot sin, "...because beatitude

consists in seeing God in His essence...[which] is the very essence of goodness." But "so long as nature endures...its operations remain...beatitude does not destroy nature ...it is its perfection", ie, the angelic entelechy remains and the angels retain their faculties of knowledge and volition. As creatures, they are not substantially identical with the Divine Intellect, whatever may be their inner secret.

A few words must be said regarding the fallen angels, though it is not our purpose here to explore theodicy in any detail, for that is not a concern of the parable of the mustard seed. One may note, however, that intellectually, theological accounts of the origin of evil are generally one of the less satisfactory aspects of theology. In the effort to avoid at almost any cost attributing the origin of evil to God, Who by definition is perfect good, theology attributes its radical origin to the highest and finest work of creation, ie, Lucifer, who in his rebellion became Satan. Theologians seem to overlook that this line of argument casts a shadow on Divinity in spite of their best efforts. For where is the principal who remains utterly untouched by the errors of his subordinates, even if these latter are free agents? Metaphysically, however – and we follow Schuon here – we must take into account the "two wills": that of the Godhead ordaining radiation as such; and that of the personal God, Creator, Revealer, Savior and Giver of Law and Grace. To say radiation, manifestation or creation is implicitly to say separation, diminishment, limitation, alterity – even to the extent of the denial of the Principle. Universal Possibility must, on pain of contradiction, include the possibility of its own denial, even though this is a possibility that can be realized only as a tendency or direction.

This said, one must not think that theology has no insights of great value regarding the nature and origin of evil. Theology teaches, eg, that evil has no substantive existence – a particularly important point for theodicy; that sin is contrary to the profoundest nature of man; that the understanding of the fallen angels is darkened by their deprivation of ultimate truth and by their consequent preference for evil; and that the fallen angels have a twofold abode, hell and the air, ie, the subtle realm. Note, too, that orthodox theology perceives the origins of evil as prior to the creation of man; so evil is a datum of the world as we know it, ie, of existence itself in one of its aspects. It is not enough to recall that God described His creation as very good, though this is quite true; one must recall that the earth was cursed, in the Genesis account, because of Adam's sin; that the Lamb was slain from the foundation of the world (Ap xiii, 8); and that Christ said, "Have I not chosen you twelve and one of you is a devil?" (Jn vi, 7). But we are also taught that all the evils that so tragically disfigure the world nevertheless contribute to the total order and equilibrium of the Whole. And metaphysically, we can be certain that evil, however enormous it may seem at a given moment, nevertheless is but a very small segment of reality. Finally, it will not be out of place to mention that a certain ambiguity attaches to most symbols, including that of the birds which can represent – though they do so much less commonly – states inferior to man, certain night birds and carrion eaters, for example.

One theological teaching on the fallen angels contains some notable insights which merit consideration in more detail because of their acute importance for men in the present life. Lucifer's sin is said to be that of pride. One may also see in it a kind of narcissism involving the illusion that a kind of separate reality was a possibility for him. Infatuated with his own glory, he wanted still more, to the extent of wanting to be like God in his, Lucifer's, own nature. "'He sought that to which he would have come had he stood fast'... he sought to have final beatitude of his own power, whereas this is proper to God alone", says St Thomas, quoting St Anselm. It is thus that Lucifer, the light-bearer, became the prince of darkness. All this must be related to the fundamental but much neglected counsel of perfection:

abneget semetipsum (Matthew and Luke) or *deneget semetipsum*
(Mark). "He who would come after Me, let him *deny himself,*
and take up his cross and follow Me" (Mt xvi, 24; Mk viii, 34;
Lk ix, 23). At this point the New Testament joins the Vedanta and more interior teachings of all orthodox traditions
in stressing the need for self-denial, not only in an ethical
and ascetic sense but also and perhaps especially in a conceptual and ontological sense. For self-denial implies a duality in man, one who denies and one who is denied; an Inner
Man who effects the rejection and an outer man with whom
we are counselled not to identify ourselves, an illusory entity,
ever becoming but never possessing his own being. Goethe's
zwei Seelen ... in meiner Brust is one of the last European
echoes of the Medieval *duo sunt in homine* – two souls, between which we must choose if all is to be well.

Each human is given a guardian angel at birth, from the
lower angelic ranks; these encourage, enlighten, guard and
guide men towards the Good. ''I tell you that in heaven their
angels always behold the face of My Father who is in heaven''
(Mt xviii, 10). This statement of Jesus permits us to believe –
salvo meliori judicio – that the doctrine of guardian angels is
the theological manner of stating that the soul is not merely
the "form of the body", as the penny catechism puts it –
though it is that; but that the soul has interior reaches and
expanses of a significance far greater than that of merely
being yoked with a body. Certainly Dante says as much for
those he addresses as: *voi che avete gl' intelletti sani....(Inferno*
ix, 61).

According to words of Christ (Mt xxii, 30), man[14] will be
androgynous in the resurrection: "they shall neither marry
nor be married but shall be as the angels of God in heaven."
Luke (xx, 36) is even stronger: "Neither can they die any-
more, for they are equal to the angels, and are the children
of God, being the children of the resurrection." Men will be
like and even equal to the angels, not by some transmigra-
tion from the human to an angelic state, but by grace and by

the perfection of the nature that is already ours (*al-ḥamd* ^{u} *li-'Llāh*). "Men can merit glory in such a degree as to be equal to the angels in each of the angelic grades...." The Divine Logos is in each creature, angels and men (and animals and plants) in as great a degree as the creaturely nature and worthiness permit (cf Origen, *De principiis* i, 29). Men will be the peers of angels[15]

> ...in incorruption and immortality and incapacity for loss. For the incorruptible nature is not the subject of generation; it grows not, sleeps not, hungers not, thirsts not, is not wearied, suffers not, dies not, is not pierced by nails and spear, sweats not, drops not with blood. Of such kind are the nature of angels and the souls released from the body. For both these are of another kind, and different from these creatures of our world, which are visible and passing.[16]

In the life of Heaven, "there will not be two societies, of men and angels, but only one; because the beatitude of all is to cleave to God alone."

"Cleaving to God alone" implies for some vocations a passage beyond even the highest angelic levels; from this life for some, from some deferred state for others, and for yet others a final reintegration in the *apocatastasis*. But as man occupies a central state and is a direct image of his Divine Principle, he is not called upon to traverse other, even angelic, states in the course of his return to his Fatherland, the Kingdom of God. This journey is, for man, a retracing and a rediscovery of the steps by which he came forth. "Go back the way you came", replied a sage to an inquirer who asked the way to liberation.[17] But it is essentially a question of knowledge, *gnosis*, in which the whole man is the knowing instrument; for intelligence is the central and essential element in the constitution of man. And whether one considers intelligence in angels, men, animals, or even vegetables and minerals – and we follow Schuon again here – it is in essence a question of the One Intelligent. "They shall be inebriated with the plenty of Thy house; and Thou shalt make them drink of the torrent of Thy pleasure. For with Thee is the fountain of life; and in Thy light we shall see light" (Ps xxxv, 9, 10). "The light of Thy countenance, O Lord, is signed upon us" (Ps iv, 7) and "that was the true light which enlighteneth every man that cometh into this world" (Jn i, 9). The human soul, says St Thomas, "...derives its intellectual light from Him...." (*Summa Theologica* I.79.4). The celestial pilgrimage involves the cleansing of one's mirror, vocation, guidance, theory, the virtues, self-denial in the senses mentioned above, plus the concentration that all these imply, along with God-given energies and one's destiny; in short the supression of the limitations which the conditions of a particular state impose on Being/Knowledge/Bliss – or which the latter, the One Intelligent, accepts in the creative process.

This review of Christian doctrine on the angels and its significance for understanding something of the central Christian doctrine of the Resurrection will, we hope, in turn suggest something of the *investigabiles divitias Christi*, the unsearchable riches of Christ Who, as Divine Word or Divine Intellect, is truly *axis mundi* and thereby *axis angelorum* and *axis humanitatis*.[18] It is to the Son, the Divine Word, that the Christian's attention and intention must be directed in all things. St Paul (in Collossians ii) warns against an exaggerated concern for intermediary beings, the angels; for however superior the angelic life may be as compared to the human life we presently know, it is nevertheless only by identifying ourselves with Christ that Christians can hope to reach and ultimately pass beyond the angelic states. Companionship with the angels is doubtless our destiny, but our destination lies beyond. In the words of St Basil: "Man is an animal that has received the command to become God"! – not substantially, to be sure, but essentially. It is Christ, Divine Word, Divine Intellect, Who is the Christian's Alpha and Omega, beginning and end and true Exemplar. In a

period, however, in which conceptions of Jesus Christ are
more and more reduced to the level of terrestrial humanity,
and even an inferior humanity, it is most appropriate to
remind ourselves of the glorious life that is promised as the
inheritance of the Resurrection.

It is this life that is symbolized by the parable of the
mustard seed. Like this minuscule seed, faith (and all it
implies in depth and amplitude), sown in a man's heart,
grows into the axial tree which harbors angels of every degree and their peers, god-like and blessed men. This is the
promise of the synoptic Gospels and of the parable that tells
of the insouciant birds – insouciant because "they neither
sow, nor...reap, nor gather into barns; and [yet] your heavenly Father feeds them" (cf Mt vi, 26). And on what do the
blessed feed? They feed on God Himself. This is the life of
the beatified angels as well as that of men in the Resurrection.
Vita mutatur, non tollitur.

Addendum

St Paul, writing to the Corinthians (I Cor xv) of life *post
mortem* speaks of the *resurrection of the dead* and compares the
present corporeal life to a seed which must fall to the ground
and die and then rise up a new plant, given an appropriate
body by God. Paul goes on to say that there are bodies
celestial and bodies terrestrial, and

> one is the glory of the sun, another the glory of the
> moon, and another the glory of the stars. For star differ-
> eth from star in glory. So also is the resurrection of the
> dead. It is sown in corruption, it shall rise in incorrup-
> tion. It is sown in dishonour, it shall rise in glory. It is
> sown in weakness, it shall rise in power. It is sown a
> natural body, it shall rise a spiritual body. If there is a
> natural body, there is also a spiritual body....flesh and
> blood cannot inherit the Kingdom of God, neither
> shall corruption possess incorruption.

By the high Middle Ages, however, St Thomas Aquinas

could speak of the resurrection of the *body*, of this identical body (*ST* IIIa, supplement, q 79, a 1, 2, 3); and he accentuates this by speaking of sexual differentiation and of the digestive organs being filled with pleasant humors – even though the digestive and generative faculties would not function as in this life. The point of all this with St Thomas seems to have been to stress the integrity of the resurrected state, and doubtless he was voicing the understanding of the Church at that time as well as the empirical thrust of Aristotelianism. Nevertheless, the respective positions of St Paul and of St Thomas represent, at the very least, a clear difference of emphasis; but such differences may eventually issue into different worlds of meaning when one side forgets the anterior meaning.

Dante, writing his description of Paradise at roughly the same time as that of St Thomas, wrote that "many things are lawful there which are not granted to our faculties in this life, thanks to the nature of that place created as proper to mankind" (*Paradiso* i, 55 - 57). Further, "to pass beyond humanity cannot be told in words, but let the example of Glaucus suffice him for whom grace reserves the experience" (ibid, 70 - 72).[19] And in the *Paradiso*, the blessed are identified in part as men or women, according to their earthly roles; but they are much more notable as vehicles of a virtue and of a glory that tends to swallow up individual idiosyncrasy.

The reconciliation of these divergent perspectives, St Paul and Dante as contrasted with St Thomas, is achieved – as so frequently happens – by a luminous and catalytic observation of Frithjof Schuon to the effect that while the blessed in Paradise are still in an individual state, nevertheless there is a rhythmic passage into and out of formless contemplative stations. And this is in perfect accord with Dante's description of his encounters in Paradise, though clearer and more explicit.

[1]Benignity does not imply softness. The point is important because it is necessary to counter false notions of the nature of religion and of religion's demands upon men that have gained such wide currency in the last several centuries in Christianity. Angels, eg, in most of their major aspects, might more appropriately be symbolized by eagles or falcons than by sparrows or canaries – though in the parable here in question small, seed-eating birds are integral to the whole structure.

It may be noted in passing that popular representations of Christ as tender and effeminate and clad in diaphanous garments are repugnant and truly incredible; moreover, they are in effect mortal sins in art for they are mendacious. Jesus Christ, who was in His humanity perfect in virtue, was in no way lacking in heroic and virile characteristics. One may in this connection consider the icons of Christ of noble and even severe countenance that are not uncommon in the Christian East.

[2]In an apparent effort to demolish or diminish the importance of St Dionysius for Christian thought, not a few modern scholars maintain that St Thomas and his peers held Dionysius in such high esteem because they actually believed him to have been the disciple of St Paul. This is reductionism carried to a ridiculous degree, for it is as if to say that St Thomas and the other great Medieval doctors were only historians and that they could not recognize an idea when they encountered one, or that understanding began only with modern critics. The truth seems rather to be that modernists perceive a threat in the writings of Dionysius and others like him, eg, Clement of Alexandria. One would do well to ponder Lk xi, 52: "Woe to you, the doctors of the law, for ye took away the key of knowledge; yourselves did not enter, and those who were entering ye hindered." Note that the Greek word translated as knowledge is *gnoseos*, the genetive singular of *gnosis*.

[3]*L'Oeil du coeur,* 1950 edition, pp 79, 80, footnote.

[4]We cannot elaborate overmuch on these matters here, but it should be noted that for St Thomas *materia prima* or prime matter was the passive principle underlying the material world only, true in this as he most frequently was to an exoteric perspective. In traditional metaphysical and esoteric doctrine, *materia prima* is universally

extended and is the passive principle of the entire universe, for manifestation or creation as such implies the presence of both active and passive principles *in divinis*. We are of God both in our Essence and in our nature. Generally, a key to understanding the metaphysical transposition of theological doctrine is to assume that the latter is universally extended in meaning, though not in form. Theology is, in any case, a particularization of the truly universal, ie, metaphysics. And metaphysics can, in a large sense, operate free of theology; but the latter cannot operate without the light of the former. In the case of Duns Scotus on the angelic nature, he seems to have been the more thoroughly metaphysical, though Scholastic theology particularly in its ontology is truly and splendidly metaphysical.

In discussing the higher angelic states, we get into the difficult realm of levels that are both "created and uncreated", for which see the works of Frithjof Schuon, *passim*.

[5]See Addendum on p. 254.

[6]This important doctrine is particularly relevant to man's "progressive" manifestation from the First Principle; and it clearly implies that man, in certain of his interior dimensions or prolongations, has an "angelic" nature, and ultimately, it implies the doctrine of the Universal man.

[7]But God requires no means whatsoever and knows all there is to be known in absolute simultaneity.

[8] Frithjof Schuon·*Gnosis: Divine Wisdom*, p. 91, note 1.

[9]That is, the being who from our point of view beginning as terrestrial man, has effectively realized in *gnosis* and *in principio* all the possibilities of which he is the microcosmic expression. This implies an integration by knowledge *and* being of the image into the archetype, of the microcosm into the macrocosm, and the universalization of the being in an effective and essential identity with the Principle, the Logos or Divine Intellect. Clearly this is not a matter of individual choice or accomplishment, for "you have not chosen Me, but I have chosen you" and "without Me you can do nothing." Moreover, as long as the servant exists, he "remains the servant and the Lord remains the Lord" in the words of Muḥyī al-Dīn

ibn al-'Arabī; nature, including the external existence of the *jīvan-mukta* in nature, must run its providential course.

The Buddhist sounding terms, comprehensor and wayfarer, are nevertheless eminently Christian, being used by St Thomas in his *Summa Theologica*.

[10]See also the sermon *Quasi stella matutina*, which can be found in many of the collections of Eckhart's works.

[11]"Whoever knows God becomes God." The Latin is a gloss of Abraham Hyacinthe Anquetil-Duperron on *Mundaka Upanishad* iii.2.9, in his Latin translation (from an earlier Persian translation) of the Upanishads, *Oupnek' hat...*, 2 vols, 1801 and 1802, Argentorati (Strasbourg). Cf Matthew xi, 27 (and Luke x, 22): "...no one knoweth the Son, but the Father: neither doth anyone know the Father but the Son, and he to whom it shall please the Son to reveal Him"; and John i, 18: "No *man* hath seen God at any time."

[12]Sermon *Deus caritas est*, in C de B Evans' *Meister Eckhart*, vol I.

[13]Ibn Mājah: cited thus in T. P. Hughes, *Dictionary of Islam* (1885) without further identification, but presumably was Abū ᶜAbd Allāh ibn Yazīd ibn Mājah al-Qazwīnī, early Muslim scholar (AD 824-886/ AH 209-273) and compiler of *aḥādīth*; he also wrote a commentary on the Koran.

[14]Obviously, *man* or *men* in remarks such as these refer to all of humanity, both male and female.

[15]See Addendum on p. 254.

[16]From a fragment of Hippolytus of Rome.

[17]Sri Ramana Maharshi, outstanding saint of South India (d. 1951), to a European visitor. The response was both doctrinally profound and an elegant putdown, depending on the receptivity of the visitor.

[18]The phrase *axis mundi* includes, needless to say, the entire created order of angels, men and every other level of creation. Christian Hermetism taught that there are three natures of Christ, that His cosmic nature is constituted by the created aspect of the existentiating Logos; His Divine and human natures, of course, being the other two (cf Jean Thamar, "Le Zodiaque et la roue des existences", *Etudes Traditionelles*, 1951). Origen, too, spoke of an angelic nature of Christ. Perhaps an echo of this is the appellation

"Angel of the Great Counsel" in the Litany of the Holy Name of Jesus. According to the Fathers, it is the Logos who appears in the epiphanies of the Old Testament, eg, to Abraham, Hagar, Jacob; according to this view, the Old Testament epiphanies of Yahweh were actually those of the Word, for "no man hath seen God at any time" (Jn i, 18). The metaphysical understanding of the doctrine of the two natures, to which the consideration above can be reduced, is that the Universe itself constitutes Christ's possible nature.

[19]"To pass beyond humanity", *trasumanar* in Dante's magnificent expression, evidently meant to pass beyond earthly humanity. Glaucus, in the Greek myth, was a fisherman who ate of a marvelous grass which revived caught fish and he thereby became a sea-God.

Man and Woman

An Evaluation of their Relationship in the Christian Perspective

Philip Sherrard

Any appraisal of the relationship between man and woman in the Christian perspective must begin by recognizing that the distinction of human nature into male and female is in accordance with the wisdom and providence of God. It is not something arbitrary or accidental or that has developed in response to various pressures of a biological, environmental or other relative kind. On the contrary, it is a manifestation of an ultimate mystery hidden in the depths of Divine Life itself. When God created human nature, He created it male and female. But God creates nothing of which the creative causes or principles are not inherent in His own Being. This is to say that the source of the distinction between man and woman lies in the fact that God embraces the principles of masculinity and femininity in Himself. He is Himself male and female. The Divine is androgynous; and, where human nature is concerned, this androgyny of the Divine is polarized in man and woman.

So fundamental indeed is this mystery of God's bisexual nature that echoes and traces of it are to be found on every level of creation, down to that of the most simple and rudimentary forms of life. But of all created beings, man is the most direct expression of the Divine. He is most fully created in the image of God. Hence it is that the principles of masculinity and femininity that co-exist in God are manifest in human nature in the most explicit way. It is as if God wished to see the mystery of His most intimate self revealed, as in a mirror, with as little distortion as possible, and the result was man and woman. It is in man and woman that God perceives the fullest expression of His own glory. His is the secret, non-articulated and formless reality of which the forms of man and woman are the disclosed and articulated images.

At this point it might be asked why, if God is bisexual, does not this bisexuality find its most adequate expression on the human level in the creation, not of two distinct male and female beings, but of a single androgynous figure. Indeed, according to one reading it might be claimed that in the account of creation presented in the opening chapters of Genesis, which provide the starting point for Christian speculation on this theme, such is in fact the original order of things. God creates man – and here 'man' signifies not simply the male sex but human nature in its integrity; and this human nature is bisexual: 'male and female created He them'. But it appears that these dual aspects of human nature – the 'them' in the citation – are still properties of a single being: they are embraced within the single being of Adam.

Still in accordance with Genesis, it would appear that it is only at a subsequent stage of creation that the bifurcation of the sexes takes place and the female is as it were disunited from the male and enshrined in the separate figure of Eve. And the reason given in Genesis for this bifurcation of the original androgynous Adam, and for the separating off of the feminine aspect of human nature in the independent figure of Eve, is not that such polarization of the sexes shows forth God's glory more fully. The reason given is simply the all-too-human one that Adam was alone and lacked a fitting helpmate. This would make it appear that the creation of woman as a separate being has nothing or little to do with God's desire to contemplate more fully the mystery of His most intimate Self in its counterparts on the plane of creation, for He could do this most fully in the single androgynous figure of Adam. It would appear, rather, that the creation of woman as a separated being was not within the original Divine intention, but was a subsequent concession on the part of God to a kind of unforeseen contingency that arose after the creation of Adam. Eve's *raison d'être* lies solely in this insofar as she relates to man as his helpmate. Apart from this, there is no real reason why she should exist.

Many Christian writers have been persuaded by this account of the creation of Adam and Eve in the Book of Genesis to regard woman as a being who is secondary and subordinate to man, who has no reason for her existence apart from man, and who would not in fact have existed had the original man – Adam – been able to preserve his own bisexual nature intact, as God had originally intended that he should. Indeed, some Christian writers have seen in the creation of Eve as a separated identity evidence of a 'fall' that took place within the original creation itself. In this view, the ideal human state is seen as represented by the androgynous Adam, who mirrors in his single being God's own androgyny and so is the Divine image *par excellence*; but for reasons of economy that have to do not so much with God's own desire for self-revelation as with man's created welfare, this ideal state is in practice extrapolated in the forms of two separate human beings, Adam and Eve, who co-exist in paradise. Woman's creation is still regarded as being in accordance with the wisdom and providence of God, and woman is still a revelation or unveiling of the Divine – a theophany – for the simple reason that every created thing possesses a theophanic quality. But in some sense her creation is adventitious, and she is a second best; for, ideally speaking, her creation could be subsumed and transcended in a single created being who unites and reconciles the masculine and feminine aspects of human nature in himself.

Such a conception of the ideal human state has always haunted man, not least of all within the Christian world; and many are those who have set out to attain, or regain a mastery of what they presuppose to be their original bisexual nature, lost through some catastrophe that has tragically cut this nature into two and left each half of it in an abnormal state of destitution and self-exile. And it must be confessed that if God Himself is androgynous, and man is created in the image of God, then it is difficult to see how the destiny of individual man and woman is not most fully achieved when each, severally and independently, does unite and reconcile the sundered masculine and feminine aspects of human nature in a single being.

Yet, as against this conception of the ideal human state, is it not possible to read the Genesis account of the creation of woman in another sense? The word that is used in the opening chapter of Genesis to signify that God sets the seal of His approval on the successive phases of His creation is, in the Greek translation of the Hebrew, the word *kalon*, which primarily denotes the beautiful: 'And God saw that it was beautiful'. The same Hebrew word in the authorized English versions of the text is translated as 'good': 'And God saw it was good'. The Hebrew word itself can, it appears, mean both good and beautiful; but the Greek translation in the Septuagint emphasizes more particularly the aspect of beauty, and the Greek theological tradition has correspondingly seen in the beauty of the created world the manifestation of that Divine Beauty, the desire for whose expression provided as it were the motive force lying behind the original *fiat*: God's desire to reveal His formless and occulted beauty in forms in which He could delight. Hence the fittingness of what He created – the degree to which He recognized that it corresponded to the Divine archetype – was dependent upon its accordance with the inner harmony of His own Being; for it is precisely this harmony which determines the ultimate norms of beauty. When God 'saw that it was beautiful', this seeing was an act of self-recognition by means of which He verified that what he saw was a true and faithful image of His own inner and non-manifest life.

Bearing this in mind, it is surely of great pertinence that the Genesis account of the actual creation of Eve begins with the recognition on the part of God that the presence of the single figure of Adam in paradise was *ou kalon*, 'not beautiful', 'not good' 'And God said: the man alone is not beautiful.' Up to this point, God had seen that all was beautiful, all was good, all was in accordance with the inner harmony of His Being. But at this point something was out of joint and unfitting. Creation was still a distorted or inadequate image of the Divine archetype. It was still in a state of disparity and incompletion; it was still truncated. And this further stage of articulation is accomplished in the creation of Eve.

If this reading of the Genesis narrative is taken into account, then it can be seen that there is nothing whatsoever merely adventitious or second best in the creation of woman. Just as much as man she is the consequence of God's desire to see His Glory displayed on the plane of creation as fully as possible. The bifurcation of God's androgynous nature into two distinct male and female beings is not therefore a tragedy or a fall from an ideal human state into a state that is more imperfect. On the contrary, it is the necessary and only way in which God can put as it were the finishing touch to the Divine work of art in which He is engaged. Failure to put this final touch would have meant leaving it in an arrested and incomplete state. The mastercraftsman would have failed in carrying out His intention, only to be fulfilled by bringing paradigm and artefact into as close a relationship as possible. Only subsequent to the creation of woman could God confirm that the showing forth of the plenitude and richness of human nature in the figures of Adam and Eve was in accord with the inner harmony of His Nature and so was beautiful and good. It is in the mastery of His final touch that the genius of the great Artist is consummated.

It would likewise follow from such a reading of the Genesis narrative that the question which provided the starting-point for this excursus – namely, whether a single androgynous figure might not more adequately reflect God's bisexuality on the human level than two distinct male and female beings – must receive a negative answer. Whatever else may apply in the case of other levels of creation – in the case of the angelic level, for instance, or that of very elementary forms of life – it is clear that where human level is concerned the polarization into the two figures of man and woman represent a fuller manifestation of the Divine than a single androgynous figure. It is as if the two complementary principles that we describe as the masculine and the feminine principles, united and reconciled in God Himself, require this polarization on the human plane if the full potentiality of their creative energies is to be actualized. Each of the two beings stand in a particular relationship to one of these principles, which is its own source of identity, its own *logos* and *sophia*, and which determines its destiny. The differentiation into male and female, far from being a compromise or a concession to human weakness, is intrinsic to the human state as such: it is a condition of the very existence of human nature itself.

This being the case, it may further be said that any endeavour on the part of man to transcend this differentiation through trying to regain what he supposes to be his original bisexual nature represents, not a step towards the perfecting of human nature, but a deviation from it. At best it is mere folly; at worst it is an attempt to go beyond the human norm and to aim at being God Himself. Such an attempt must meet with the fate that attends all such efforts to transcend the level of being on which and for which one is created, and in which one's perfection resides – the fate of which the fall of Lucifer is the paradigm. Correspondingly, any endeavour to suppress this differentiation and to achieve a state of sexual neutrality must also be seen as something that distorts or warps the being concerned, and prevents him or her from ever achieving the end for which he or she is created, his or her unique destiny as a human creature. At least where the Christian tradition is concerned, the norm for what constitutes human life at its deepest and most radiant is provided by paradise, the garden that God planted eastward in Eden, and by the two figures that inhabit it: a man and a woman, both created in the image of God, both created for immortality, yet each clearly to be recognized apart from each other by the predominance in them of the features and qualities, respectively, of masculinity and femininity, which they are to bear with them into eternity as ineradicable and inalienable features and qualities of their uniquely individualized beings. Each of them incarnates in a positive manner an aspect of the Divine; and any attempt on the part of either to deviate from, suppress or eliminate this God-given qualification, with the consequent loss or attenuation of masculinity in man and femininity in woman, represents a step away from perfection and an obstacle to it. Both the bisexual person and the neutral person are parodies of the fully consummated human being.

Yet, if the paradisal situation of man and woman is taken to provide the norm for human beings and an image of how such beings live when they live in accordance with nature and not contrary to nature, then something else of perennial significance is also to be noted. We have seen that, paradoxical as it may at first sight appear, God's Self-determination on the human plane is most fully achieved in the creation, not of a single human being who embraces the principles of masculinity and femininity in himself, but of two individualized beings in each of whom respectively one of these principles predominates; and we have further seen that this predominance of either the masculine principle or the feminine principle is inextricably involved with the eternal destiny of both man and woman. That this is the case is re-affirmed in the Christian tradition by the recognition that

Mary, the Mother of God, bears as fully the features and qualities of womanhood in her state of immortality, in which she is 'higher than the angels', as she did in her sojourn on the earth: no more in heaven than on earth can she by any stretch of the imagination be described as androgynous. Yet, in spite of the fact that she does not combine in her single being the principles of both masculinity and femininity, she has attained the supreme form of human perfection.

How, then, if this is the case, is one to explain what appears to be a discrepancy? When God created human nature in His own image, He created it male and female. Yet a person who most fully realizes the Divine image and achieves the fullest likeness to God that can be attained by a human being does so without any loss or transcendence of sexual differentiation. Surely, it might be thought, whatever the order of things in the terrestrial sphere, this differentiation could be overcome when man attains the state of deification. How otherwise is one to envisage human nature in its totality as being *par excellence* the image of God if individual men and women cannot be other than predominantly male or female even after their deification? And will not individual men and women, even after their deification, be prevented otherwise from attaining anything more than one aspect of the fullness of the Divine which is bestowed on human nature by God when He brings it forth in His own image?

Yet, if the paradisal situation is to provide the norm and model for human life, and if in paradise human nature, male and female in its integrity, is polarized into the individual masculine and feminine beings of man and woman, Adam and Eve, the full picture is still incomplete. For man and woman in paradise, although independent identities each dominantly determined by complementary and even contradictory aspects of the Divine, do not lead their lives in isolation. They lead their lives *in relationship*. And it is precisely in this living by man and woman of their lives in relationship that the mystery of God's bisexual nature is disclosed on the human plane in the most explicit manner. What neither man nor woman can attain as individuals living in isolation, they can attain through living in relationship. Concomitantly, it is in the relationship between man and woman, when this is lived in accordance with the norms of paradise – under the conditions that apply prior to the fall into a state of forgetfulness and ego-centeredness – that the Divine image is most fully achieved on the human plane and the Divine archetype is made most fully manifest. For it is only in and by means of this relationship that the integrity of human nature, created male and female, is integrally represented on the human plane, and so is capable of conforming to the bisexuality of its archetype and of embracing fully both the masculine and the feminine principles. In other words, in their relationship, Adam and Eve typify that primordial plenitude of human nature which each and all may emulate and attain.

This centrality of the relationship between man and woman as the state which both discloses in the fullest possible way the ultimate mystery of Divine Life and provides, when properly understood and lived, the most propitious context for the perfecting of human nature itself, is re-affirmed in the Christian tradition by the fact that the Divine-human event which lies at the heart of this tradition, and which constitutes the gage of its authenticity, takes place within precisely such a context. It is not until Joseph takes Mary into his care, and Mary receives Joseph as her promised spouse, that the Holy Spirit makes His annunciation and the Divine Logos is born in human form. Paradise may be entered, not tomorrow or after one's death, but here and now, provided one fulfils its conditions.

In that case, what are the conditions in accordance with which the primordial human relationship must be lived if it is to fulfil its positive role of bringing man and woman into the fullness of the Divine image and so lead them to a state of perfection? The first thing to be said here is that it must be a relationship of love. This would seem to be so self-evident that it hardly requires any specification. Moreover, it is no more – even if no less – than a condition which should be fulfilled in all human relationships, not simply in that between man and woman. God is love; and insofar as we share in the Divine image, we also share in love and must express it in our activities. What more particularly characterizes the love between man and woman when this is manifest in their paradisal relationship – although the same will apply to its other manifestations – is the recognition that love itself is a Divine Quality and gift and does not belong to man in his own right. Thus when I say 'I love', I am really misappropriating something that is not mine, but which is expressing itself through me. This means that the distinction between sacred and profane love – the love that is paradisal and the love that is not – resides not so much in any qualitative difference in the nature of the love itself as in the qualitative difference in the consciousness of the sacred and profane lover. For the first recognizes that love is a Divine Quality and gift and responds to it accordingly, while the second, in the absence of such recognition, is liable to regard it as little more than expression simply of his own ego, to use or abuse as he thinks fit.

Yet there is more than this. For if the lover recognizes that the love with which and in which he beholds the beloved is a Divine Quality, he will be seeing the beloved in God. He will be seeing her in the light of the love that in its essence is divine. He will not be loving her therefore outside or apart from God. In the fallen – or with the profane type of consciousness – it is quite possible for a man and woman to love each other outside and apart form God, at least where their own awareness and intentions are concerned, and to see each other as beings that have no relationship with God and are quite independent of Him. But in the paradisal state, man and woman love each other in God, aware that it is only by being in God that they can love at all.

Nor is it simply in God that they love each other. For possessing as they do a spiritual form of consciousness, they know that everything that exists is a self-articulation or self-revelation of the Divine. Everything is an unveiling of God, a theophany in which God discloses Himself in His own image. Hence in loving each other what they love is God as He has revealed Himself in each of them to the other. Each becomes an ikon to the other; and because God has revealed Himself as an ikon in the form of the living being who is the beloved, so in loving that being the lover will be loving God. In the ikon, it is God who manifests Himself; and what the man loves in the woman is the mystery she discloses as such an ikon, just as what the woman loves in the man is the mystery that he discloses in a similar way. Each thus discloses for the other that unknown being who is the sacred core of their existence and who Himself aspires to find a birthplace in the hearts of both of them. Nor is there anything idolatrous in this, for neither sees the other apart from or outside God.

Indeed, in this paradisal form of love between man and woman, the real lover – the real subject moving the love within the human lovers – is God Himself, the Lord of Love. The man and woman love God in each other not by or through themselves, but by and through God. Or, rather, in each it is God who loves the other. Such a love is physical, insofar as it is focused on and embraces an incarnate image. Yet it is also spiritual, since it does not want to possess the image but to be reborn in it and transfigured by it. What man and woman do in such a relationship is to invest each other with the concrete form of another living being who promotes in each the aspiration to grow towards the perfection for which both have been created. Their art – for it is an art to which they are committed – is to transfigure each other by arousing the full potentiality of their creative energies, bringing each other in this way ever more intimately into the presence of God. Seeing each other as the manifes-

tation of the Divine Beloved, the Lord of Love, they spiritual-
ize each other's being by raising it beyond its physical or
sensible form to its Divine incorruptible form so that in the
end their contemplation of God in each other becomes the
highest form of contemplation of which human beings are
capable, no less than that of God contemplating Himself in
His own image.

It is in this way, then, and under these conditions that the
relationship between man and woman fulfils its positive role
of bringing them into the fullness of the Divine image and
likeness in which human nature is created and in which the
Divine archetype is most fully made manifest. Such a relationship can achieve this consummation because in it are
engaged two beings each of whom enshrines aspects of the
Divine which the other only possesses in a rudimentary or
stultified form. It should not be necessary to emphasize that
it is not a case of man possessing a monopoly of male characteristics (whatever these may be), while the woman possesses
a monopoly of female characteristics. What is in question is
the predominance of certain aspects of the Divine in each of
the two, to such an extent that two totally non-interchangeable
human beings are produced. Thus it is possible to claim that
while man is distinguished more by qualities of majesty and
impartial judgement, woman is distinguished more by qualities of beauty and a sense of infinite tenderness and compassion. One might say that the corresponding differences are
expressed in the natural world in the distinction between
the mountain and the sea. At a deeper level man may be said
to represent more the non-manifest creative energy of God
and woman more the form in which God eternally reveals
Himself to Himself, His manifest glory and the wisdom 'created before all things'; and this characterization of woman's
prototype might be said to have its homologue in the natural
world in the form of the sun through which the light of the
sun is made manifest.

In this respect woman's prototype – the Eternal Feminine

– enshrines the mystery of the Divine Epiphany, for without the manifestation of His Glory and His Wisdom God's creative energy would remain unknown and unknowable, forever occulted, just as without the sun there would be no sunlight or without Mary the Divine Logos would not have received a human form. Indeed, Mary is able to give birth to God in a human form only by virtue of the fact that on the transcendent spiritual plane her role as Mother of God is fulfilled by the Eternal Feminine, who eternally 'gives birth' to God; for only by symbolizing her Divine prototype could Mary fulfil her role on the human and temporal plane, the plane of history. Every Divine revelation on the plane of history has its origin and prototype on the plane of metahistory, and is but a showing forth of the latter. In short, woman may be said to correspond more to the world of the Soul, not only in the cosmological sense, both as the 'place in which God manifests Himself, and as this manifestation itself, but also in an individual sense, as the aspect of each human being that projects itself on the imagination as a feminine form, the *Anima*. In her essence, she is ' the woman clothed with the sun', the Theotokos who is also the Theophany.

It should be repeated that this characterization of the differences between man and woman, however valid it is, does not in the least mean that man is destitute of the qualities present in a more marked fashion in woman, or *vice versa* . Nor do the differences in question imply any inequality between man and woman, for the prototypes of the qualities of which each is the manifestation and repository have no order of superiority and inferiority but are equally qualities of the Divine Being who is their source. But to ignore such differences in the name of a misconceived egalitarianism is not only to do violence to the particular destinies that man and woman are called upon to fulfil but also, and *a fortiori*, to thwart the realization of the primordial human relationship of which we have been speaking.

It is in fact quite apparent that the realization of this relationship is only too often thwarted in the world of forgetful-

ness and separation in which for most part we live. It is
thwarted perhaps above all because what we have called the
sacred or higher consciousness has been replaced by the
profane or lower consciousness. When the sacred consciousness is operative – when, that is to say, in this relationship the
man and the woman are both spiritually awakened – then it
is in the woman that the man experiences human beauty as
an epiphany of Divine Beauty, and it is in the man that the
woman experiences in human form the Majesty of God.
Similarly with the other qualities which each possesses in a
more marked manner than the other; it is in and through
the other that each becomes capable of experiencing and in-
tegrating qualities which as separate individuals each of them
lacks or has not developed. Indeed, it is only by virtue of
such an interchange of qualities that the relationship between them can grow into the fullness of the Divine image
and likeness. What makes a man and a woman not simply
two isolated individuals each lacking aspects of the integrity
of human nature, but two partners who together achieve
human perfection, is what is added to each in and through
their relationship, in and through what each bestows on the
other. Moreover, this interchange of qualities operates in a
way which as it were doubles each of them, since to the being
of each as it is in and for itself is added the being of each as it
is for the other. Hence in this relationship man and woman
cease in a certain sense to be two individuals: they become
four.

It is at this point that it becomes possible to grasp the true
significance of the scriptural injunction (Gen.I:28), 'Be fruitful and multiply', announced by God to man when He first
created man in His own image 'male and female'. Only too
often literalist interpreters of Christian scripture – of whom,
alas, there are far too many – take these words to mean that
man and woman should produce children in the purely
physical or corporeal sense, and indeed it is in this sense
exclusively that man and woman are exhorted to 'be fruitful
and multiply' in the marriage services of the Christian Church.

How this conclusion is reached, even by these literalist interpreters of Christian scripture, when it is clearly stated in the
Book of Genesis that Adam knew Eve in the carnal sense
only after their expulsion from paradise and that it was only
after expulsion from paradise that they produced children
'according to flesh', is something that these same interpreters tend to pass over in silence. One would have thought that
if a stage towards human perfection is represented by man's
return to the paradisal state, then the last thing one should
exhort him to do is to function in a manner that both is
symptomatic of and consolidates his fallen, non-paradisal
condition. In any case, it is clear that if Adam and Eve produced any progeny in paradise, they were of a kind different
from those produced 'according to the flesh', and were
begotten through a mode of intercourse other than the
carnal mode. In addition, it might be asked how this literalist
exhortation can be made to tally with one of the central
Christian mysteries: that it was *after* Joseph took Mary into his
care, but *before* he knew her in a carnal manner, that she
conceived by the Holy Spirit and bore the Logos of God.
This mystery should disclose for Christian partners a perspective quite other than that insisted on in their marriage
services. However, this is but an only too typical example of
how interpreters of Christian scripture tend, not to spiritual-
ize the natural, but to naturalize the spiritual, thus consum-
mating in their turn the original sin of Adam. The task of
unravelling or resolving the contradictions and confusions
that spring from this naturalizing of things of the spirit – as
in the present case here under consideration – is one that
those who most persist in perpetuating such a sin are the
least likely to undertake.

The true significance of this scriptural injunction may be
approached by way of the Septuagint translation of the phrase
in question. The words that in the English King James version are translated as 'Be fruitful and multiply' are here
translated into Greek as *avxanesthe* and *plithinesthe*, and of

these Greek words the first is patent to the sense of 'grow' or 'become perfect', and the second to the sense of 'make full' or 'increase' not simply in a quantitative manner but also in a qualitative manner. Hence a translation from the Greek into English could read, not 'Be fruitful and multiply', but 'Grow to perfection and increase in spiritual fullness' – though it should be said in passing that no more than Western marriage services does the Orthodox marriage service stress this meaning of the phrase. Read in this light, the phrase accords perfectly with what has been said above about the mutual exchange of qualities in the love relationship between a man and woman leading to human perfection and to their growing into the fullness of the Divine image and likeness.

Moreover, this interchange of qualities between man and woman can be seen as a mutual engendering and begetting that goes far beyond the begetting of children through the body. As Plato puts it, 'our nature longs to beget' (*Symposium*, 206C) and the engendering to which it leads is 'something ever-existent and immortal in our mortal lives' (*Symposium*, 206E), such generation being the only way through which we can attain the immortality in which our life is consummated (*Symposium*, 207D). But while some seek to achieve this immortality in an indirect manner through the begetting of children through the body, there are others 'whose creative desire is of the soul, and who conceive spiritually, not physically, the progeny which it is the nature of the soul to conceive and bring forth' (*Symposium*, 209A); and this generation is the generation of the spiritual or intelligible forms (of beauty, of love) with which God illumines the hearts of those who love Him. That is why the work of love may be described as 'to beget on what is beautiful by means of both body and soul' (*Symposium*, 206B) and why in the end the love between man and woman may be consummated in the vision of 'absolute beauty in its essence, pure and unalloyed' (*Symposium*, 211C). The language is Platonic.

But a vision similar to that which inspires it inspired likewise the language of many Christian authors in the mediaeval world. It must be remembered of course that the mediaeval world was one in which the Christian consciousness was dominated all but exclusively by the male monastic and ascetic spirit in whose perspective earthly woman and feminine beauty, as a whole, feature, not as potential agents of transfiguring grace, but rather as temptations to be avoided at all cost, both in terms of outward social intercourse and in terms of meditation and the inward life. The condemnation and suppression of the role played by the *virgines subintroductae* is perhaps typical of the spirit in question. It goes without saying therefore that the human relationship in which love is recognized to possess a redemptive and transfiguring power is not that between man and woman but that between man and man – not indeed in the erotic sense envisaged by Plato (still less in the modern homosexual sense), but in the sense of a deep spiritual friendship. Hence there is no question of referring it back to the paradigmatic paradisal relationship of Adam and Eve, so that its protagonists are seen to symbolize directly the pre-fallen figures of the primordial human couple. Consequently, this relationship cannot mirror the archetypal androgyny of the Divine with the same integrity as the relationship between man and woman. In this respect, it must as a result fall short of fulfilling the plenitude of the Divine image as this may be fulfilled in the relationship between the two sexually-differentiated beings of man and woman. Indeed, it may be said that, totally valid as it is in its own terms, the vision with which these mediaeval Christian authors invested the union of friends can only disclose its full potentiality when it is transposed to the relationship between man and woman.

For these authors,[1] friendship (*amicitia*) is not merely the highest form of human love. It is a Divine manifestation, the revelation and communication of God Himself. St Augustine called his friend a unique revelation of God present within him. Hence to live in a state of friendship is to live in God or, as Aelred more succinctly puts it, friendship is God (*amicitia Deus est*). As such, friendship is a way of return to paradise, a means of raising oneself to God, of living in Him and of making Him live in us. Such a return to paradise is seen as a new birth, a regeneration in God, a re-integration and re-formation. It is the disclosure of a new heaven and a new earth, the revelation of the beatitude of those who dwell in heaven, and everlasting Sabbath, an entry, here and now, into the promised land and the New Jerusalem, an experience of the paschal resurrection, a return to the source of cosmic harmony and a reconciliation of opposites in an order of tranquillity, rest and peace. The unity of friends reflects the cosmic primal unity of all creation. For Aelred, the mere sight of a friend is a grace that leads one to recollection in God, and the joy of two friends is in God, but in God found and revealed in each other; while for Alcuin the very thought of a friend is like the visitation of the Holy Spirit that may be experienced through prayer. St Augustine sees the goal of the relationship between two friends attained in the union of their souls – or in what Cassian calls their forging of one heart and one soul in two bodies – in the possession of God, in their finding of one another in God.

Thus friendship is a profoundly religious experience, a hierophany or theophany at the heart of the Christian *mysterium*. To be united in love with the beloved is to find oneself returned to oneself, to one's full being. It is a re-attaining of one's paradisal wholeness, an association of the Holy Spirit. The paradise of a friend's love is a revelation of the Divine paradise, a transcending and a transfiguring of man's fallen and mortal state, a rebirth in God. As we have already remarked, the particular ethos in which this relationship of love is conceived and lived by these Christian authors of the mediaeval world restricted it to the association of man with man and hence it cannot fully symbolize with the archetype of the Divine-human relationship, which the plenitude of the Divine image is made manifest. But freed from this restriction and transposed to the relationship between man and woman, the vision that informed this love and the love that inspired this vision can realize their full potentiality. That this vision has not, except perhaps in rare cases, informed the love between man and woman in the post-mediaeval Western world is due partly at least to the fact that it has been so woefully eclipsed in the Christian consciousness itself. Yet, only in its light can the relationship between man and woman be truly consummated. It should hardly be necessary to stress that such consummation can be attained only on condition that the partners concerned continuously and consciously refer what they receive and experience back to its Divine source. They have to recognize that the gifts and graces with which they invest each other, and with which they are invested, are not their own and that they must not seek to possess them or to use them as a means to self-satisfaction or self-aggrandizement. For the vision that their relationship inspires in them would vanish as soon as they failed to acknowledge Who it is that consecrates their love and Whose love it is that validated their lives.

Yet, it is some such failure of acknowledgement that results in the fall from the paradisal state of which the change in consciousness from the sacred to the profane is both the cause and the symptom. To some degree man begins to shift his focus and to see the centre of his being not so much in God, and in the corresponding spiritual essence in himself, as in his own ego and its proclivities. He begins to deny his ontological dependence on God and to seek to be the lord and master of creation in his own right. At the same time, and correspondingly, he is no longer capable of seeing the beauty of woman as an epiphany of Divine Beauty and to contemplate it in this way; he now wants to possess and appropriate it. His love becomes concupiscence and sensual covetousness, and the woman a separate phenomenon that he looks on as though outside and apart from God. Such covetousness places the human spirit in a negative sense beyond good and evil and in the end turns the love between man and woman into little more than a blind search to assuage ego-centered desires: carried along on an insatiable infernal current, man strives in vain to fill the bleak vacuity of his life by pursuing through successive hells unions which, being themselves chimerical, merely exacerbate the mental and moral disequilibrium of which they are expression and of which he is the victim.

This process of profanation of which man is guilty has its counterpart also in woman. Indeed, if anything woman is even more prone than man to esteem things – including her own beauty – in terms of their sensory or aesthetic attraction, in terms of an amoralism and passion that do not take into account any spiritual or qualitative dimension. 'The woman saw that the tree was beautiful to eat, and that it was pleasant to the eyes to look on, and a tree to be desired...': such was the disposition of Eve that led her to violate the Divine Commandment. Cut off in human consciousness from its roots in the Divine, and seen therefore as autonomous, beauty fascinates and destroys. The heavenly Aphrodite, betrayed into the streets and the market-place, assumes the terrible mask of the earthly Aphrodite. Woman becomes the seductress, and the relationship between man and woman an idolatrous cult, with little or nothing ennobling and trans-figuring about it.

To say this is by no means to imply that all such relation-ships in our world are totally deprived of paradisal qualities. Every kind of tenderness, loyalty, endearment, cherishing and forgiveness engendered in the relationship between man and woman as well as the exchange of physical delight, is an echo and intimation of the hidden beatitude man holds at the centre of his being. In this respect, the heavenly Aphrodite may well reveal herself through the violations of her most abandoned earthly counterpart. But given the loss of consciousness of which we have been speaking, with our

consequent failure to see things for what they are and to
treat them accordingly, the relationship between man and
woman does only too often fail to fulfil the role of which it is
capable and which one might say constitutes its fundamental
raison d'être, whatever other subsidiary purposes it may also
serve. Only too often its potentiality is denied or frustrated.
In a sense this is unavoidable so long as men and women
think and act as though they were simply mortal and finite
beings and forget they are immortal beings whose destinies
cannot be fulfilled short of a realization of their spiritual
nature. God is love, and like responds to like. How then can
the God-given love between man and woman be brought to
fruition if they fail to recognize and acknowledge the Divine
in each other? In other words, the failure to realize the full
potentialities of this primal human relationship is made
virtually inevitable by the hopelessly inadequate way in which
men and women regard each other, by their failure to recognize who they are and what their true reality is.

For when we do not see the need for putting down roots
in the eternal, or when we deny that we have the capacity to
do this, what we are actually doing is condemning ourselves
and our activities to eventual disintegration. It is the harmony and rhythm of eternity that hold everything in its
place and permit its growth; and whatever opposes this harmony and rhythm, or cuts itself off from them, will automati-
cally disintegrate in the end. It will disintegrate through its
lack of inherent reality. In spite of appearances, only that
which comes from the source of life, and is directed towards
the source of life, can possess reality in a true and enduring
sense. The rest is but shadow-play, shadow despoiling shadow.
Only that which puts down roots in the eternal can escape
this process of mutual self-destruction and can be sustained
and attain indestructibility. Man has not forfeited the Divine
image in which he is created, even if he fails to live and act in
accordance with it. He can recover what he has lost. He can
reverse the process by which he has reduced his conscious-

ness to the level of profanity. But to do this he has to recognize that in essence he is a spiritual being whose deepest needs and aspirations can be fulfilled only through self-realization in God. Yet, since God is love, this realization can be achieved only through the rebirth of Divine Love in his soul. Hence the crucial role in the whole process of regeneration or redemption that can and should be played by the erotic relationship between man and woman. For the love they bear each other, and the longing for union which it promotes, are the expression both of their need and of their capacity to regain full consciousness of the beatific vision which they possess in the paradise that lies within them: that vision in which they contemplate God in each other and which is fully manifest only in those in whom human life has been transfigured by the beauty of what they behold into a love that is itself Divine.

[1] For fuller account of this whole subject, and for detailed references to all sources cited here, see: Mother Aedele Fiske, 'Paradisus Homo Amicus', in *Speculum*, July 1965, pp. 436-459.

Two Traditions – and Philosophy

Huston Smith

"There is no defending the tradition," Kai Nielsen recently announced. "Systematic analytical philosophy and its Continental cousins along with their historical ancestors must be given up."[1] Hilary Putnam concurs, concluding that "the tradition is in shambles."[2] We hear this admission with increasing frequency these days.

In stark contrast, I find myself wanting to say that the Tradition comes close to being our only philosophical possession that is worth defending. The fact that I capitalize "Tradition," though, makes it clear that we are talking about different things. Nielsen and Putnam are referring to the modern Western philosophical tradition, whereas I am thinking of a Tradition that is perennial, not modern, and primordial in being not distinctively Western. It is the Tradition, often referred to as the Perennial Philosophy, that René Guénon, A. K. Coomaraswamy, Titus Burckhardt, and above all Frithjof Schuon, have reclaimed for twentieth century attention.

The object of this essay is to consider philosophy from the standpoints of these two traditions. That the essay appears in a volume that honors Frithjof Schuon's life and work is appropriate, for I take his magisterial articulation of the Traditionalist position as guide for what I have to say. His writings are difficult, but they use metaphysical exactitude to seize the foundations of one's being in a way that I find unparalleled in modern times.

I begin with the philosophy of the uncapitalized tradition, which for all practical purposes is philosophy as it has been conceived since Descartes disjoined it from theology and launched it on its independent course.

I. Modern Philosophy[3]

Starting from the present and reading that philosophy backwards, I pick up with the disillusionment my opening paragraph led off with. A growing number of pace-setters see no future for the philosophy they have inherited, or at most a minimal one. Modern philosophy seems to have played out its destiny and reached a dead end. Wittgenstein came to see its only real service as therapy, undoing the mental knots philosophy has itself created. Heidegger announced the end of metaphysics, to which Richard Rorty adds "the end of epistemology." And now James Edwards and Bernard Williams are turning down the lights on philosophical ethics with their *Ethics without Philosophy* and *Ethics and the Limits of Philosophy* respectively. What remains after these closures no one seems to know. Rorty and Jacques Derrida propose "conversation" and "play," to which neither sees philosophy as having anything distinctive to contribute. Epitaph-writing, Alasdair MacIntyre observes, has become an accepted philosophical activity.[4]

What has brought all this to pass? The plenary address that Richard Rorty delivered at the 1985 Inter-American Congress of Philosophy in Mexico City provides a useful summary of the proximate answer – i.e., the twentieth century developments that led directly to the cul-de-sac – so I shall use it as my approach to the question.

If nineteenth century philosophy began with Romantic Idealism and ended by worshipping the positive sciences, Rorty points out, twentieth century philosophy began by revolting against a narrowly empiricist positivism and is ending by returning to something reminiscent of Hegel's sense

of humanity as an essentially historical being, one whose activities in all spheres are to be judged not by its relation to
non-human reality but by comparison and contrast with its
earlier achievements and with utopian futures. This return
will be seen as having been brought about by philosophers as
various as Heidegger, Wittgenstein, Quine, Gadamer, Derrida, Putnam and Davidson.[5]

That says a lot in small compass, so let me repeat it, adding
a few particulars. The nineteenth century began with a reaction against the scientism of the Enlightenment, protesting
its claim that mathematical demonstration provides the model
for inquiry and positive science the model for culture. It
ended, though, by swinging back to Enlightenment predilec-
tions and shunting off into literature the counter-Enlighten-
ment sentiments that had given rise to the Romantic Movement and German Idealism. So philosophy entered the
twentieth century allied to science. Experimental science
being outside its province, this meant following Husserl and
Russell into mathematics and logic. Husserl soon deviated
from that program to found a brand-new approach to philosophy, phenomenology, which would replicate science's
apodicticity without using its logic. Heidegger's *Being and
Time* subverted that move and thenceforth continental philosophy renounced both apodicticity and deduction. In
English-speaking countries, though, Russell's slogan that
"logic is the essence of philosophy" persisted, and ability to
follow completeness proofs for formal systems replaced for-
eign languages as a professional requirement.

Even the Anglo-American attempt to 'do philosophy' via
logic eventually abandoned apodicticity, though, for non-
Euclidean geometries showed logic to be flexible; since it
works equally well with whatever primitives we begin with, it
produces nothing that is univocal. In their *Principia Mathematica*, Whitehead and Russell spelled this out by developing
a "logic of relations" to replace the reigning logic of things,
and Cassierer and C. I. Lewis went on to relativize Kant

whose *Critique* had dominated modern epistemology. The human mind is not programmed to see the world in a single way. It sees it in different ways as times and cultures decree.

This drive towards pluralism did not stop with epistemology; it pressed on into ontology. Having satisfied themselves that our minds required nothing of us,* philosophers proceeded to argue that the world does not require anything of us either. Their way of doing this was to go after Plato's essences and Aristotle's substance, for if these exist they could draw the mind up short and thinking would not be indefinitely maleable. Again it is important to see this second rejection – the rejection of the fixity of things to accompany the rejection of the fixity of thought – as motivated by the same determination to stem the tide of the Enlightenment Project in its twentieth century positivistic version, for if there is a way things are it was pretty clear that the twentieth century would take it to be the way the sciences collectively report; the Vienna Circle with its "unfication of science movement" was waiting in the wings with just this recommendation. Rorty brings these two rejections together and shows how central they have been to our century's philosophy. I do not think it far-fetched to see such different books as Carnap's *Logische Aufbau der Welt,* Cassirer's *Philosophy of Symbolic Forms,* Whitehead's *Process and Reality,* C. I. Lewis' *Mind and the World Order,* Langer's *Philosophy in a New Key,* Hartshorne's *The Divine Relativity,* Quine's *Word and Object,* Nelson Goodman's *Ways of Worldmaking,* Putnam's *Reason, Truth and History,* and Davidson's *Essays on Truth and Interpretation* as developments of the anti-Aristotelian and

---

*Chaitin's Theorem, which is so powerful that Godel's Theorem can be derived from it as a corollary, proves that logic cannot tell us anything interesting about objects that are much more complex than the axioms we start with.

anti-substantialist, anti-essentialist implications common to *Principia Mathematica* and to the development of non-Euclidean geometries.

   Once again we should not lose sight of the motivation in all this. Seeing no way in which (in the face of the scientistic temper of our century) it could register a view of reality that could compete with the scientistic one that was gaining ground, philosophy took the next best step. It went after the notion of a single world view period: the notion that there is one univocal, comprehensive way that things actually are; or if there is, that human minds can have any knowledge of what that way is. This meant renouncing what historically had been philosophy's central citadel, metaphysics. Better no metaphysics at all than the one that was threatening to take over.

   But if the "post-Nietzschean deconstruction of metaphysics" excused philosophers from thinking about the world, what should they be thinking about? We saw that during the early, positivistic decades of our century in which philosophers saw science as the royal road to truth, they latched onto logic as the slice of science that they could service. Let the empirical scientists discover synthetic truths; philosophers would monitor the analytic truths that were also needed. In 1951, though, Quine demolished the analytic/synthetic, fact/meaning distinction with his "Two Dogmas of Empiricism." With the analytic rug thus pulled out from under them, philosophers retreated to ordinary language for a preserve of meaning that did not depend on logic yet needed attention. Now, though, the wall around that refuge is being dismantled by Donald Davidson's critique of the distinction between the "formal" or "structural" features of discourse and its "material" ones. The correct theory of meaning, Davidson argues, is one that dispenses with entities called "meanings" altogether. Instead of asking "What is the meaning of an expression?" it asks how the expression functions in its particular linguistic move. With this total de-logicizing and naturalizing of language, the division between it and the rest of life disappears. Instead of a "structure" or body of rules that philosophers can discover and help others to see, or even the multiple structures and rules that Lewis and Cassierer talked about, language now looks like simply another human way of coping with the world.

It really is not surprising, therefore, to find philosophers closing shop, for if logic is not philosophy's essence (Quine) and language is not either (Davidson), the question "What essence remains?" cannot be ducked. We can quibble over whether "essence" is the right word – here Rorty holds that philosophy is not the name of a "natural kind" – but let us come to the point. The deepest reason for the current crisis in philosophy is its realization that autonomous reason – reason without infusions that both power and vector it – is helpless. By itself, reason can deliver nothing apodictic. Working (as it necessarily must) with variables, variables are all it can come up with. The Enlightenment's "natural light of reason" turns out to have been a myth. Reason is not itself a light. It is more than a conductor, for it does more than transmit. It seems to resemble an adapter which makes useful translations, but on condition that it is powered by a generator.

Recognizing reason's contingency, medieval philosophy attached itself forthrightly to theology as its handmaiden. Earlier, Plato too had accepted the contingency and grounded his philosophy in intuitions that are discernible by the 'eye of the soul' but not by reason alone. In the seventeenth century, though, responding to modern science as a powerful new way of getting at truth, philosophy unplugged from theology. Bacon and Comte were ready to replug it immediately, into science, but there were things science still could not lay it's hands on; so philosophy took off on its own. Let reason stand on its own feet. Think of it as a lever that has an Archimedean point built right into it. What that Archimedean point was – Descartes' innate ideas, Kant's

categories of reason, the positivists' sense data? – was hotly
debated, but that reason has a firm foundation was not
seriously doubted.

As long as that assumption remained in place, philosophy
enjoyed a healthy self-image, for it meant that philosophy
was foundational to culture. The components of culture –
science, politics, morality, religion, art, and the rest all make
knowledge claims. It followed therefore, that since philosophers were knowing's experts – epistemology was, after all,
their domain – they were, in an important sense, culture's
arbiters. It was not just their right but their responsibility to
monitor the conceptual foundations of culture's components, validating those that were in order and debunking
those that were not. Kantians and positivists saw themselves
as especially suited for this role, but analytic philosophers
accepted it as well on the strength of their presumed understanding of language, the medium through which thought
proceeds.

It is to Rorty's credit that he has insisted that his profession face up to the pretentions that infused this whole modern self-image, an image that ultimately derives (as we have
seen) from the assumption that reason possesses its own
Archimedean point.* In a dramatic exchange during the
December 1980 meeting of the American Philosophical Association, Rorty pressed his critics to offer examples of
cases "where some philosophical inquiry into the conceptual
foundation of X provided any furtherance of X or anything
else, or even any furtherance of our understanding of X or
anything else." Kai Nielsen tells us that the challenge has not

---

*The current word for this assumption is "foundationalism," and the
extent to which philosophers are now turning against it can be
discerned in Isaac Levi's proposal that "opposition to foundationalism
ought to be the philosophical equivalent of resistance to sin" ("Escape
from Boredom: Edification According to Rorty," in *Canadian Journal
of Philosophy*, Vol. XI, No. 4 [December 1981], p. 509.

been met.

The shattering of a profession's self-image and *raison d'être* is no small matter. It makes it impossible for philosophy to proceed as it has. To quote Kai Nielsen once more, "if philosophy or its successor subject is going to come to anything, it must take a different turn."

What that new turn might be seems to be completely up in the air. I shall not try to predict. Instead, I shall proceed to the second half of this essay and juxtapose to modern philosophy, as sketched, the Traditional philosophy I consider its important alternative. This comes close to being the way philosophy was universally conceived up to the time of Descartes, but I shall tighten that conception to the way philosophy is conceived by the Traditionalist school.

II. Traditional Philosophy

Traditionalists agree with modernists that reason is the philosophical faculty, but they have never supposed that it functions autonomously.* Medieval philosophy, as we have noted, regarded itself as theology's handmaiden, but philosophy can equally be seen as an extension of what Schuon in the footnote just entered refers to as the Intellect, here capitalized to indicate that the word is being employed in a precise and technical sense. The two ways of putting the

---

*Schuon's states the difference as follows: "In the opinion of all profane [in this essay, modern] thinkers, philosophy means to think 'freely', as far as possible without presuppositions, which precisely is impossible; on the other hand, gnosis, or philosophy in the proper and primitive sense of the word, is to think in accordance with the immanent Intellect and not by means of reason alone" (*Sufism: Veil and Quintessence* [Bloomington, IN: World Wisdom Books, 1981], p. 116). This entire essay can be regarded as a meditation on this sentence and its profound import for the understanding of philosophy's past, present, and future.

matter come to the same thing, for theology formalizes and
spreads for public view the truths of the Intellect as these
apply to a given tradition. The Intellect discloses subjectively, to individuals, what theology as the systematic arm of
Revelation spreads objectively before a particular historical
community.

The Intellect is pivotal to the Traditional conception of
philosophy, but it is so different from what the word "intellect" usually suggests that it must be explained.

We can ease into that explanation by noting that there is
something in our mental workings – at this starting point we
need not say what it is – that proceeds differently from
reason.   Reason performs logical operations on items of
information that are in full view and so can be described or
defined.   Through and through, though, we find that our
understanding is floated and furthered by operations that
are mysterious because all that we seem able to know about
them is that we have no idea whatsoever as to how they work.
We have hunches that pay off. Or we find that we know what
to do in complicated situations without being able to explain
exactly how we know.   This ability is unconscious, yet it
enables us to perform enormously complicated tasks, from
reading and writing to farming and composing music.   Ex-
pertise is coming to be recognized as more intuitive than
cognitive psychologists had supposed; these students of learning and behavior are finding that when faced with excep-
tionally subtle tasks, people who "feel" or intuit their way
through them actually have a competitive edge over those
who consciously try to think their way through.   This explains why computer programmers no less than psychologists have had trouble getting the expert to articulate the
rules he follows.   The expert is simply not following rules.
Workers in artificial intelligence are coming to see that
"human intelligence can never be replaced with machine
intelligence because we are not ourselves 'thinking
machines.'...Each of us has, and uses every day, a power of

intuitive intelligence that enables us to understand, to speak, and to cope skillfully with our everyday environment."[7] This intelligence enables us to summarize unconsciously our entire past – all that we have experienced and done – and let that summary affect our future decisions and moves.* Programmers cannot instruct their machines to do this because no one has the slightest idea how we do it ourselves.

This "intuitive intelligence" that cognitive scientists have encountered provides us with an initial glimpse of the Intellect at work. Proceeding from there to philosophy, we find all reputable epistemologists, even modern ones, forced to recognize that *something* besides reason is at work in our knowing. Hume saw this most clearly, and the realization drove him to skepticism for, blind to the Intellect, he saw nothing to vector reason save the passions.[8] His successors resisted that conclusion. Rallying mostly around Kant, they found ways to continue their faith in reason, but the point here is that in doing so they too had to recognize that the mind possesses extra-rational sensibilities. The Germans distinguished *verstehen* and *verstand* from *vernunft*. Romantic philosophers and poets followed Blake in spotting an active imagination that in important respects resembles the Intellect proper, and Heidegger at the close of the day extolled "thinking" over reasoning of the calculative sort.

Thus even modernity, with all its penchant to do so, was unable to fit the entire mind into a rational mold. In the Tradition we find the mind's extra-rational faculties not just admitted but affirmed; they are accorded pride of place. The Vedanta grounds *manas* in *buddhi*, while the Buddhists

---

*A striking example: Japapese chicken sexers are able to decide with 99% accuracy the sex of a chick, even though the female and male genitalia of young chicks are ostensibly indistinguishable. No consciously driven sexing effort could ever approach such accuracy. Aspiring chicken sexers learn only by looking over the shoulders of experienced workers, who themselves cannot explain how they do it.

point to *prajñā* as knowing's supreme capacity. Both of these stand as the Intellect's rough counterparts, but it is the Western tradition that identified that faculty most precisely. Released by Socrates from the tyranny of the obvious, Plato discovered an organ of knowledge which, because it "outweighs ten thousand eyes," he called the Eye of the Soul. This Eye can recall the soul's past, even what it learned in past lives; this is the famous Platonic doctrine of *anamnesis* or recollection.* Aligning it with Aristotle's notion of the Active Intellect as the supraindividual component of the mind which knows (though in individuals only potentially) everything, the Medieval Schoolmen worked the concept of the *Intellectus* into its mature form. It is the mind's foundational faculty, clearly distinguishable from *ratio* which is its emissary.

Ratio works exclusively in the conscious domain, but the Intellect is not thus restricted. Everything possesses it. As Schuon has written,

> If gold is not lead, that is because it "knows" the Divine better. Its "knowledge" is in its very form, and this amounts to saying that it does not belong to it itself, for matter could not know. None the less one can say that the rose differs from the water-lily by its intellectual particularity, by its 'way of knowing' and so by its mode of intelligence. Beings possess intelligence in their form to the extent that they are "peripheric" or "passive" and in their essence to the extent that they are "central," "active" and "conscious.".…
>
> God reveals himself to the plant in the form of the light of the sun. The plant irresistibly turns itself towards the light; it could not be atheistical or impious.

---

*"It is an immediate apprehension of reality, a direct acquaintance. In the *Republic,* Plato frequently [as in 511d and 534a] designates it "intellection" (*noesis*) as distinguished from discursive reason or understanding (*dianoia*) which proceeds through deduction or inference" (Robert Cushman, *Therapeia* [Westport, CT: Greenwood Press, 1958, 1976], p. 81).

The infallible "instinct" of animals is a lesser "intellect," and man's intellect may be called a higher instinct.[9]

This "higher instinct" embraces components of the usual
instinctive sort, but it makes its distinctively human appearance in the conscious domain. There we catch sight of it in
the judgement it exercises on the evidence that reason and
perception lay before it.* This judgement rides our sense of
logic, our capacity for arithmetic, and our discernment of
right and wrong with the sense of justice it produces; these
Intellectual resources are built into the human substance.
In addition, the Intellect can apprehend certain fundamental truths directly, as self-evident; Traditionalists typically
refer to these as Principles. Basic among them is the disjunc-
tion between the Real and the (relatively) unreal, which alternatively goes under the banner of the Absolute/relative,
appearance/Reality, and Noumena/phenomena divides.
Other direct discernments include the requirement that
there be an ontological (not to be confused with mathematical) Infinite, and that it be self-caused, for something cannot
come from nothing any more than a stream can rise higher
than its source, metaphorically speaking.

With these and other deliverances of the Intellect in place,
reason can usefully proceed;** Thus positioned, it lies somewhere between instinct and the Intellect as Schuon has sug-

---

*Vedantins liken *manas* (roughly reason) to lawyers, and *buddhi*
(Intellect) to the judge who weighs the evidence they present and
pronounces a decision.
**Overreacting against the pretenses of Enlightenment rationalism,
"the most 'advanced' of the modernists seek to demolish the very
principles of reasoning, but this is simply fantasy *pro domo*, for man
is condemned to reason as soon as he uses language; unless he wishes
to convey nothing at all. In any case, one cannot assert the impossibility
of asserting anything, if words are still to have any meaning" (F.
Schuon, *Sufism: Veil and Quintessence*, p. 116).

gested. Philosophy is reason working at the highest levels of generality or abstraction. Its function is to use the Intellect's guidelines to order human experience – to help it work its perceptions, feelings, thoughts and intimations into a cosmos. Traditionalists have documented in considerable detail the way Traditional philosophy has done this without violating the significant nuances of the great historical traditions.

In line with the distinction between Intellect and reason, Traditionalists distinguish metaphysics from philosophy. Rather than being a branch of philosophy, metaphysics is for them the articulation of the Intellect's direct discernments – to the extent that this is possible, it must immediately be added, for metaphysics phases into the ineffable. It is *gnosis* in the non-sectarian sense of that word – the *sophia* of the ancient sages, the *sapientia* of the Middle Ages, the Hindus' *jñāna* and the *ma'rifah* or *ḥikmah* of the Muslims. The following schematization may help to fix this technical terminology in place.

Discipline	Object of Inquiry	Faculty of Discernment
metaphysics	Godhead	Intellect
theology	God	faith/Revelation
philosophy	phenomenal world	reason
science	sensible world	senses

The Godhead includes Eckhart's *Gottheit,* Dionysius' *hypertheousios, Nirguṇa Brahman, Śūnyatā,* and the Tao that cannot be spoken. Faith is the subjective response to objective Revelation; it is the capacity to recognize divinely revealed truths as being, in fact, true.

The two lower lines must be considered together. Science is a part of philosophy; it is (as its original designation had it) natural philosophy: reason as it bears on sense deliverances. Philosophy includes natural philosophy but is not restricted thereto. It orders phenomena in their entirety, not just sensible ones, under the guidance of Principles which (as was previously noted) can be derived either indirectly, from the Revelations that theology articulates, or directly from the metaphysical deliverances of the immanent Intellect.

III. Comparisons

If there is no objective way to determine which of the two traditions of this essay has the better hold on philosophy, it is at least clear that it is Tradition that holds the discipline in higher regard. During the modern period this was not clear, for it seemed that by subordinating philosophy to theology, Tradition denied it freedom. Now, though, that the helplessness of the rational mind when left to itself has come to view, this judgement looks out of place, for where footholds are lacking freedom has no meaning. The position modern philosophy has arrived at is there for witness.

It is true that Traditional philosophy is not "queen of the sciences," but as something like prime minister in the rational realm it has a dignified office. And when the reason it employs is grounded in metaphysical principles to the point where philosophy is assimilated to metaphysics, its dignity rises. According to Pythagoras, wisdom is the knowledge of things that are above us; *sophia* is the wisdom of the gods and *philosophia* the wisdom of men. For Heraclitus, the philosopher is one who applies himself to the knowledge of the profound nature of things. For Plato philosophy is the knowledge of the changeless and of Ideas. For Aristotle it is the knowledge of first causes and principles, together with the sciences that issue therefrom. Suffusing all this is the Traditional notion that philosophy requires moral conformity to wisdom. Only he is wise, *sophos*, who lives wisely.[10]

This distinguished view of philosophy would not be possible without confidence in appropriately-grounded reason, its instrument. The modern tradition began with such confidence which even left its mark on an age, the Age of Reason as the eighteenth century *Aufklärung* or Enlightenment was alternatively called, but the first section of this paper traced the crumbling of this confidence when it became clear that unmitigated rationalism does not work – reason is not master in its own house. "It is no longer possible," a typical summarizing statement now tells us, "to deny the influence of the unconscious on the conscious, the role of the preconceptual and nonconceptual in the conceptual, the presence of the irrational – the economy of desire, the will to power – at the very core of the rational."[11] So the two traditions of this essay intersect in recognizing that reason is not autonomous. Only to diverge again immediately, though: modernity into Ricoeur's "hermeneutics of suspicion" and Tradition into the "hermeneutics of belief."* Whereas Tradition holds out the possibility of reason being grounded in the *supra*-rational Intellect, the attachments the modern philosophical tradition now recognizes are, where not neutral, *infra*-rational. A glance back at the statement just quoted makes this plain. Preconceptual and nonconceptual influences on reason are arguably innocent, but the others that are itemized are all suspect. "The unconscious" suggests the id, and Freud's call for its colonization: "where id was, let ego be; it is reclamation, like the draining of the Zuider Zee." "Irrational" is a pejorative in itself, and the parenthetical additions "economy of desire" and "the will to power" spell out why. We think what we want to think, and in ways that will serve our ends. Marx, Nietzsche, and Freud's distrusts of reason, which they somehow lost sight of when they came to proposing their own theories, has deeply permeated the phi-

---

*"Gnosis or pure metaphysics takes certainty as its starting-point, whereas philosophy...in the case of the moderns...has doubt as its starting-point, and strives to overcome this only with the means that are at its disposition and which do not pretend to be more than purely rational" (F. Schuon, *Sufism: Veil and Quintessence, op. cit.,* p. 125).

losophy of the last hundred years.

If we wished to put a good face on this distrust of reason, we could say that epistemology has grown modest. "Virtually every contemporary methodology takes as its starting-point how well we know how little we know," James Cutsinger tells us.[12] So seriously has modernity adhered to Kant's insistence that with respect to everything but sensible objects "the *minimum* of knowledge must suffice,"[13] that to revive even the prospect that our minds are well-endowed we need to ask ourselves two blunt questions. Logically, is it not rather ridiculous to use the mind to place limits on the mind; and psychologically, is it not presumptuous to insist on such limits? Modern philosophers see traditional philosophers as arrogant because of how much they thought they could know, but Cutsinger points out that modernity is not in fact more modest. It simply lodges its arrogance in a different place: in the assurance with which it places limits on human knowledge.[14]

IV. Conclusion

On this issue of noetic confidence turns the question of whether we feel at home in the world or estranged from it. Somewhere in his recent writings Mark Taylor says that the problem modern philosophy has failed to solve is how to get from the subject to the object. Traditional philosophy does not have that problem, for it sees the two as joined from the start: the Intellect is Reality impressing itself upon us. Once again there is no way to prove who is right. Perhaps we have simply reached the point where one by one, individually, each philosopher should ask himself which of the two great allegories of Western philosophy, Plato's Cave or Nietzsche's Death of God, has for him the greater ring of truth.

Perhaps that is where the matter comes to rest, but on behalf of the underdog Cave in this decision it can be noted that philosophy at this juncture is hardly in a position to reject any alternative out of hand. If the Intellect sounds strange to its ears, it should remember that it has no agreed-on criterion of rationality with which to dismiss the concept. Similarly with the metaphysical project in general; epistemology has given it a hard time, but now that epistemology is itself in shambles, even metaphysics' most shrill detractors are calling for some attention to "how things, in the broadest possible sense of the term, hang together, in the broadest possible sense of the term" (Wilfred Sellars). As they turn to that issue, philosophers will do well to keep in mind two points that Alasdair MacIntyre made to the Pacific Division of the American Philosophical Association in 1987.

First, the way philosophers have taken to incorporating the history of their discipline contributes in itself to the absence of a shared understanding as to what philosophy should now be up to. Typically, says MacIntyre,

> we select out from the texts of our intellectual forbearers what would be accounted philosophy now, disregarding its inseparability from those parts of what [those texts] accounted philosophy....We also detach what we take to be distinct and isolable topics from the systematic metaphysical contexts in which our predecesors' discussions of these topics were embedded. At the level of elementary instruction this is achieved by anthologizing authors into snippets, at more advanced levels by the fragmentation of systems into more or less piecemeal treatments of particular problems. What these institutionalized patterns and habits enable us to avoid is confrontation with the systematic claims of the major philosophies of the past.[15]

MacIntyre's other point was a plea to his colleagues not to underestimate the magnitude of the challenge those systematic claims of past philosophies present. For what they say to current philosophy in effect is "either accept this overall standpoint...or do better by finding or inventing a superior system of thought."

Where is the superior system of thought that provides grounds for disregarding the Traditional system that Frithjof Schuon has devoted his life to reminding the world of?

[1]"Scientism, Pragmatism, and the Fate of Philosophy," *Inquiry,* 29, p. 278. I have converted Nielsen's rhetorical questions into straightforward assertions.

[2]"After Empiricism," in John Rajchman and Cornell West (eds.), *Post-Analytic Philosophy*, New York: Columbia Unviersity Press, 1985, p. 49.

[3]Portions of this section follow closely my paper, "The Crisis in Philosophy," *Behaviorism,* 16:1 (Spring 1988).

[4]"Philosophy: Past Conflict and Future Direction," *Proceedings and Addresses of the American Philosophical Association,* Supplement to 61/1 (September 1987), p. 81.

[5]*Proceedings of the American Philosophical Association.* vol.59 (July 1986), p. 748.

[6] Kai Nielsen's summary of the occasion in an as yet unpublished paper, "The Withering Away of the Tradition."

[7]Hubert and Stuart Dreyfus, *Mind over Machine,* New York: The Free Press. 1986, p. xiv.

[8]His pronouncement that "reason is the slave of the passions" sent shock-waves through the philosophic world, for it was an affront to the foundational faith of modernity to be told that belief is "more properly an act of the sensitive than of the cogitative part of our natures" (*A Treatise on Human Nature,* p. 183).

[9]*The Essential Writings of Frithjof Schuon,* edited by Seyyed Hossein Nasr, Amity, NY: Amity House, 1986, pp. 114-15.

[10]Paraphrased from F. Schuon, *Sufism: Veil and Quintessence* Bloomington, IN: World Wisdom Books, pp. 115-116.

[11]From the General Introduction to Kenneth Baynes, James Bohman, and Thomas McCarthy (eds.), *Philosophy: End or Transformation?* Cambridge: MIT Press, 1987, p. 4.

[12]"Towards a Method of Knowing Spirit," *Sciences Religieuses/ Studies in Religion,* 14/2 (Spring 1985), p. 150.

[13]*Religion Within the Limits of Reason Alone* (New York: Harper & Row, 1960), p. 142n.

[14]"We seem intent, not on overcoming, or even suppressing, but

on dignifying our weaknesses and deficiencies, that is, our obvious and universally admitted subjective imprisonment and self-enclosure, as if they were a strength," Cutsinger continues. "For though we confess our limitations and doubts, we refuse to acknowledge any personal responsibility for them, claiming instead that they are endemic to the human condition. This claim gives us comfort, no doubt – confirms and encourages our satisfaction with our situation – and results, however ironically, in a kind of smugness or pride. We are after all the first of our race to face up to the fact of our limits. Of course we have assumptions, and, yes, they are mostly unexamined. But so are those of other men, nor is it possible to live without them." From unpublished paper, "He That Is Not Against Us Is for Us."

[15] *Op. cit.,* p. 82.

A PRAYER

London, June 10th, 1987.

June 18th will be attracting very many people, including myself, in prayers for your welfare in all senses, both "physical" and "metaphysical". May God's grace be with you! There must needs be an ending in this life, but, in another sense, there is endless beginning. There is nothing else I can add from this corner of the world.

Please receive my prayers.

Marco Pallis

This prayer for Frithjof Schuon was written by the late Marco Pallis just before his 92nd birthday. ·

FRITHJOF SCHUON

Bibliography

Contents

Books in German

Leitgedanken zur Urbesinnung, Zürich, Orell Füssli Verlag, 1935

Sulamith (poems), Bern, Urs Graf Verlag, 1947.

Tage- und Nächtebuch (poems), Bern, Urs Graf Verlag, 1947.

Das Ewige im Vergänglichen (translation by Titus Burckhardt of *Regards sur les mondes anciens*), Weilheim, Oberbayern, Otto Wilhelm Barth Verlag, 1970.

Von der inneren Einheit der Religionen (translation by the author of *De l'Unité transcendante des religions*), Interlaken, Ansata-Verlag, 1979.

Den Islam Verstehen – Eine Einführung in die innere Lehre und die mystische Erfahrung einer Weltreligion (translation of *Comprendre l'Islam* by Irene Hoening and Harald von Meyenburg), Otto Wilhelm Barth Verlag, 1988.

Urbesinnung – Das Denken des Eigentlichen (revised edition of *Leitgedanken zur Urbesinnung*), Freiburg-im-Breisgau, Aurum Verlag, 1989.

Articles in German

"Zum Verständnis des Islam", *Kairos* (Salzburg), Number 2, 1959.

"Religio Perennis", *Antaios* (Stuttgart), 1966.

"Keine Tätigkeit ohne Wahrheit", *Zeitschrift für Ganzheitsforschung* (Vienna), Volume 15, Number III, 1971.

"Wesen und Amt des geistigen Meisters", *Zeitschrift für Ganzheitsforschung*, Volume 17, Number 11, 1973; also in INITIATIVE 65, Freiburg-im Breisgau, Herderbücherei, 1986.

"Von den Gottesbeweisen", *Zeitschrift für Ganzheitsforschung*, Volume 18, Number III, 1974.

"Verstehen und Glauben", *Zeitschrift für Ganzheitsforschung,* Volume 19, Number II, 1975.

"Der Widerspruch des Relativismus", *Zeitschrift für Ganzheitsforschung,* Volume 19, Number III, 1975.

"Wirklicher und scheinbarar Rationalismus", *Zeitschrift für Ganzheitsforschung,* Volume 19, Number IV, 1975.

"Von den Formen der Kunst", *Zeitschrift für Ganzheitsforschung,* Volume 21, Number III, 1977.

"*Sophia Perennis*", in *Wissende, Verschwiegene, Eingeweihte* (*Hinführung zur Esoterik*), INITIATIVE 42, Freiburg-im-Breisgau, Herderbücherei, 1981.

"Der Mensch als Bild" (translated from the French by Hans Küry), in INITIATIVE 46, 1982.

"Das Geheimnis der prophetischen Substanz" (translated from the French by Hans Küry), in INITIATIVE 50, 1982.

"Der Sinn für das Heilige" (translated from the French by Roland Pietsch), in INITIATIVE 67, Freiburg-im-Breisgau, Herderbücherei, 1986.

"Das Werk", in *René Guénon – eine Einführung in sein Werk,* Braunschweig, Aurum Verlag, 1990.

Books in French

De Quelques aspects de l'Islam, Paris, Chacornac, 1935.

De l'Unité transcendante des religions, Paris, Gallimard, 1948; second edition (revised and with additional chapter), Paris, Editions du Seuil, 1979; third edition (with addition), Paris, Editions Maisonneuve & Larose, 1989.

L'Oeil du coeur, Paris, Gallimard, 1950; second edition (revised), Paris, Dervy-Livres, 1974.

Perspectives spirituels et faits humains, Paris, Cahiers du Sud, 1953.

Sentiers de gnose, Paris, La Colombe, 1957.

Castes et races, Lyon, Derain, 1957; second edition (revised), Paris, Dervy-Livres, 1979.

Les Stations de la sagesse, Paris, Buchet/Chastel-Corrêa, 1958

Images de l'Esprit, Paris, Flammarion, 1961.

Comprendre l'Islam, Paris, Gallimard, 1961; second edition, Paris, Editions du Seuil, 1976, and many later impressions.

Regards sur les mondes anciens, Paris, Editions Traditionnelles, 1965.

Logique et transcendance, Paris, Editions Traditionnelles, 1970.

Forme et substance dans les religions, Paris, Dervy-Livres, 1975.

L'Esotérisme comme principe et comme voie, Paris, Dervy-Livres, 1978.

Le Soufisme: voile et quintessence, Paris, Dervy-Livres, 1980.

Christianisme/Islam, Milan, Archè; Paris, Dervy-Livres, 1981.

Du Divin à l'humain, Paris, Le Courrier du Livre, 1981.

Sur les traces de la Religion pérenne, Paris, Le Courrier du Livre, 1982.

Approches du phénomène religieux, Paris, Le Courrier du Livre, 1984.

Résumé de métaphysique intégrale, Paris, Le Courrier du Livre, 1985.

Avoir un centre, Paris, Maisonneuve & Larose, 1988.

Racines de la condition humaine, Paris, Les Editions de la Table Ronde, 1990.

Les Perles du pèlerin, Paris, Les Editions du Seuil, 1990.

Articles in French

"L'aspect ternaire de la Tradition monothéiste", *Voile d'Isis* (Paris), June, 1933.

"*Shahādah et Fātihah*", *Voile d'Isis,* July, 1933.

"L'Oeil du coeur", *Voile d'Isis,* November, 1933.

"Réflexions sur le symbolisme de la pyramide", *Voile d'Isis*, February, 1934.

"Transgression et purification", *Voile d'Isis*, June, 1934.

"*Imān, Islām et Ihsān*", *Voile d'Isis*, August-September, 1934.

"Christianisme et Islàm", *Voile d'Isis*, August-September, 1934.

"La demonstration des voies", *Voile d'Isis*, August-September, 1934.

"Poèmes soufis de Mohyiddin Ibn Arabī", translation and notes by Frithjof Schuon, *Voile d'Isis*, August-September 1934.

"De l'Oraison", *Voile d'Isis*, March 1935.

"*Rāhima-hu'Llāh*" (on the Shaikh al-ᶜAlawī), *Cahiers du Sud* (Paris) (Marseille), August-September, 1935.

"*Ed-Dīn*", *Etudes Traditionnelles*, March, 1936.

"Du Sacrifice", *Etudes Traditionnelles*, April, 1938.

"Du Christ et du Prophète", *Etudes Traditionnelles*, August-September, 1938.

"Considérations générales sur les fonctions spirituelles", *Etudes Traditionnelles*, November-December, 1939.

"Les dimensions conceptuelles", *Etudes Traditionnelles*, January, 1940.

"L'intégration des éléments psychiques", *Etudes Traditionnelles*, February, 1940.

"De l'Exotérisme", *Etudes Traditionnelles*, March, 1940.

"Prédestination et volonté libre", *Etudes Traditionnelles*, April, 1940.

"Communion et invocation", *Etudes Traditionnelles*, May, 1940.

"La Vierge noire de Czenstochowa", *Etudes Traditionnelles*, May, 1940.

"De l'Alliance", *Etudes Traditionnelles*, June, 1940.

"Transcendance et universalité de l ésotérisme", *Etudes Traditionnelles*, October-November, 1945.

"La question des formes d'art", *Etudes Traditionnelles*, January-February, 1946.

"De la connaissance", *Etudes Traditionnelles*, May and July-August, 1946.

"Qu'est-ce que l'élite intellectuelle?", *Etudes Traditionnelles*, October-November, 1946.

"Des modes de la réalisation spirituelle", *Etudes Traditionnelles*, April-May, 1947.

"*En-Nūr*", *Etudes Traditionnelles*, June, 1947.

"Fatalité et progrès", *Etudes Traditionnelles*, July-August, 1947.

"Christianisme et Bouddhisme", *Etudes Traditionnelles*, January-August, 1948.

"Mystères christiques", *Etudes Traditionnelles*, July-August, 1948.

"Le sens spirituel du travail", Etudes Traditionnelles, September, 1948.

"Aperçus sur la tradition des Indiens de l'Amérique du Nord", *Etudes Traditionnelles*, March, April-May, June, and October-November, 1949.

"De l'"humilité", *Etudes Traditionnelles*, March, April-May, and June, 1950.

"L'énigme Ramakrishna-Vivekananda", *Etudes Traditionnelles*, July-August and September, 1950.

"Amour et connaissance", *Etudes Traditionnelles*, January-February, 1951.

"L'Oeuvre" (de René Guénon), *Etudes Traditionnelles*, July-November, 1951.

"Définitions (en ce qui concerne René Guénon)", *France-Asie* (Saïgon), January, 1953.

"Les vertus spirituelles selon Saint François d'Assise", *Etudes Traditionnelles*, April-May, 1953.

"Des stations de la sagesse", *France-Asie* (Saïgon), June-July, 1953.

"Caractères de la mystique passionnelle" (de Saint Jean de la Croix), *Etudes Traditionnelles*, July-August and September, 1953.

"Nature et arguments de la foi", *Etudes Traditionnelles*, December, 1953.

"Le Yoga comme principe spirituel", in *Yoga: Science de l'homme integral*, edited by Jacques Masui, Paris, Cahiers du Sud, 1953.

"Introduction", in *Les Rites secrets des Indiens Sioux* by Black Elk, Paris, Payot, 1953.

"Principes et critères de l'art normatif", *France-Asie* (Saïgon), March, 1954.

"L'âme de la caste", *Etudes Traditionnelles*, March and April-May, 1954.

"Orthodoxie et intellectualité", *Etudes Traditionnelles*, July-August and September, 1954.

"Que peut donner l'Orient à l'Occident?", *France-Asie* (Saïgon), December, 1954.

"De la 'Prière sur le Prophète'", *Etudes Traditionnelles*, June, 1955.

"Le sens des races", *Etudes Traditionnelles*, January-February, 1956.

"Y a-t-il une 'mystique naturelle'?", *Etudes Traditionnelles*, April-May, 1956.

"Vicissitudes des tempéraments spirituels", *France-Asie* (Saïgon), June-July, 1956.

"La gnose, langage du Soi", *Etudes Traditionnelles*, July-August, 1956.

"L'Esprit symboliste", *Etudes Traditionnelles*, June, 1957

"Aperçus sur le Shinto", *Etudes Traditionnelles*, October-November and December, 1957.

"Signification spirituelle du Prophète", *France-Asie* (Saïgon), September 1958.

"Généralités sur le Koran", *Etudes Traditionnelles*, March-April, 1960.

"Symbolisme et alchimie des sentiments", *Etudes Traditionnelles*, September-October, 1960.

"Une Métaphysique de la nature vierge", *Etudes Traditionnelles,* September-October, 1960.

"L'homme dans l'univers" *Etudes Traditionnelles,* November-December, 1960.

"Réflexions sur le sentimentalisme idéologique", *Etudes Traditionnelles,* January-February, 1961.

"La croix 'temps-espace' dans l'onomatologie koranique", *Etudes Traditionnelles,* January-February and March-April, 1961.

"Trésors du Bouddhisme", *France-Asie/Asia* (Tokyo), May-June, 1961.

"Sur les traces de Maya", *Etudes Traditionnelles,* May-June, July-August and September-October 1961.

"Chute et déchéance", *Etudes Traditionnelles,* July-August and September-October, 1961.

"Vérités et erreurs sur la beauté", *Etudes Traditionnelles,* March-April, 1962.

"Le mystère du Bodhisattva", *Etudes Traditionnelles,* July-August and September-October, 1962.

"Remarques sur un problème eschatologique", *Etudes Traditionnelles,* May-June, 1962.

"Les cinq Présences divines", *Etudes Traditionnelles* July-August and September-October, 1962.

"Dialogue entre Hellénistes et Chrétiens", *Etudes Traditionnelles,* November-December, 1962.

"L'Homme et la certitude", *Etudes Traditionnelles,* January-February, 1963.

"L'Argument de la Substance", *Etudes Traditionnelles,* March-April, 1963.

"Le rythme ternaire de l'esprit", *Etudes Traditionnelles,* May-June, 1963.

"Des preuves de Dieu", *Etudes Traditionnelles,* July-August and September-October, 1963.

"Chamanisme Peau-Rouge", *Etudes Traditionnelles,* July-August,

September-October and November-December, 1963.

"Regards sur les mondes anciens", *Etudes Traditionnelles*, January-February and March-April, 1964.

"Le Serviteur et l'union", *Etudes Traditionnelles*, May-June, 1964.

"Le Délivré et l'image divine", *Etudes Traditionnelles*, July-August and September-October, 1964.

"Propos sur la naïveté", *Etudes Traditionnelles*, November-December, 1964.

"*Religio perennis*", *Etudes Traditionnelles*, January-February, 1965

"Quelques difficultés des textes sacrées", *Etudes Traditionnelles*, May-June and July-August, 1965.

"Note sur Jung", in "Cosmologie et science moderne" by Titus Burckhardt, *Etudes Traditionnelles*, May-June-July-August, 1965, page 146.

"Le Commandement suprême", *Etudes Traditionnelles*, September-October, 1965.

"Usurpations du sentiment religieux", *Etudes Traditionnelles*, December, 1965.

"Remarques sur le symbolisme du sablier", *Etudes Traditionnelles*, January-February, 1966.

"L'imposture du psychologisme", *Etudes Traditionnelles*, March-April, 1966.

"Le message koranique de Seyyidnâ Aïssa", *Etudes Traditionnelles*, May-June, 1966.

"Synthèses des Pâramiṭas", *Etudes Traditionnelles*, July-August and September-October, 1966.

"Nature et fonction du maître spirituel", *Hermès* (Paris), 1967.

"Le Démiurge dans la mythologie nord-américaine", *Etudes Traditionnelles*, January-February, 1967.

"Note sur l'élément féminin dans le Mahâyana", *Etudes Traditionnelles*, March-April, 1967.

"Des concomitances de l'amour de Dieu", *Etudes Traditionnelles*, May-June, 1967.

"L'impossible convergence", *Etudes Traditionnelles*, September-October, 1967.

"L'Hyperbolisme dans la rhétorique arabe", *Etudes Traditionnelles*, January-February, March-April, May-June and July-August, 1968.

"La Sagesse virginale", *Etudes Traditionnelles*, March-April, May-June and July-August, 1968.

"Quelques aperçus sur le phénomène mohammédien", *Etudes Traditionnelles*, September-October and November-December, 1968.

"La Danse du soleil", *Etudes Traditionnelles*, September-October and November-December, 1968.

"Remarques critiques sur des thèses acharites", *Etudes Traditionnelles*, January-February, March-April, May-June, and July-August, 1969.

"Le voeu de Dharmakara", *Etudes Traditionnelles*, September-October, 1969.

"A propos d'un paradoxe de la Divine Comédie", *Etudes Traditionnelles*, November-December, 1969.

"Comprendre et croire", *Etudes Traditionnelles*, January-February, 1970.

"En marge des improvisations liturgiques", *Etudes Traditionnelles*, March-April, 1970.

"La dialectique orientale et son enracinement dans la foi", *Etudes Traditionnelles*, September-October and November-December, 1970.

"La marge humaine", *Etudes Traditionnelles*, September and November 1970, January, February, March-April and May-June, 1971.

"Rumeurs, médisances et vérités", *Etudes Traditionnelles*, January-February, 1971.

"Remarques sur des rois de France", *Etudes Traditionnelles*, July-August, 1971.

"Remarques sur l'énigme du Koan", *Etudes Traditionnelles*, January-February, 1972.

"Les deux Paradis", *Etudes Traditionnelles*, March-April, 1972

"Images d'Islam", *Etudes Traditionnelles*, May-June, July-October and November-December, 1972.

"Le double écueil", *Etudes Traditionnelles*, March-April 1973.

"Atmâ-Mâyâ", *Etudes Traditionnelles*, May-August 1973.

"Remarques sur la Sounna", *Etudes Traditionnelles*, September-October, 1973.

"Le Mystère des deux natures", *Etudes Traditionnelles*, November-December, 1973.

"Paradoxes de l'expression spirituelle", *Revue Philosophique* (Paris), 1974.

"La question des théodicées", *Etudes Traditionnelles*, March-April, 1974.

"A propos des reliques", *Etudes Traditionnelles*, September-October, 1974.

"Le fruit défendu", *Etudes Traditionnelles*, April-June, 1975.

"Un homme de la Tradition" (interview), *Question de...* (Paris), No. 8, 3rd Quarter, 1975.

"Critériologie élémentaire des apparitiones célestes", *Sophia Perennis* (Tehran) Vol. I, No. 2, Autumn, 1975; *Etudes Traditionnelles*, January-March, 1976.

"Le problème de la possibilité", *Sophia Perennis*, Vol. II, No. 1, Spring 1976.

"Le mystère du voile", *Sophia Perennis*, Vol. II, No. 2, Autumn, 1976.

"Le Paradis comme théophanie", *Etudes Traditionnelles*, January-March, 1977.

"La religion du coeur", *Sophia Perennis*, Vol. III, No. 1, Spring, 1977.

"Alternances dans le monothéisme sémitique", *Etudes Traditionnelles*, April-September, 1977.

"Le problème des divergences morales", *Etudes Traditionnelles*, October-December, 1977.

"Les degrés de l'art", *Sophia Perennis*, Vol. III, No. 2, Autumn, 1977.

"L'enigme de l'épiclèse", *Etudes Traditionnelles*, January-March, 1978.

"Conséquences découlant du mystère de la subjectivité", *Sophia Perennis*, Vol. IV, No. 1, Spring, 1978; *Etudes Traditionnelles*, April-June, 1979.

"Etre homme, c'est connaître", *Sophia Perennis*, Vol. IV, No. 1 Spring, 1978.

"Il n'y a pas de droit sacré à l'absurdité", *Etudes Traditionnelles*, April-June, 1978.

"Nature et rôle du miracle", *Etudes Traditionnelles*, October-December, 1978.

"Le sens du sacré", *Etudes Traditionnelles*, January-March, 1979.

"Refuser ou accepter le message", *Etudes Traditionnelles*, July-September, 1979, October-December, 1979, January-March, 1980.

"L'ésotérisme quintessentiel de l'Islam", *Etudes Traditionnelles*, April-September, 1980.

"Le jeu des Hypostases", *Etudes Traditionnelles*, October-December, 1980.

"L'idée du 'meilleur' dans l'ordre confessionnel", *Etudes Traditionnelles*, January-March, 1981, April-June, 1981, July-September, 1981.

"Les deux problèmes", *Etudes Traditionnelles*, October-December, 1981.

"*Sedes Sapientiae*", *Etudes Traditionnelles*, January-March, 1982.

"Le mystère de la Substance prophétique", *Etudes Traditionnelles*, April-June, 1982, July-September, 1982.

"L'Intuition décisive", *Etudes Traditionnelles*, October-December 1982.

"Sur les traces de la notion de l'éternité", *Etudes Traditionnelles*, January-March 1983.

"Le problème des délimitations dans la spiritualité musulmane", *Etudes Traditionnelles*, April-June, 1983.

"Ambiguïté de l'élément émotionnel", *Etudes Traditionnelles*, July-September, 1983.

"Anonymat des vertus", *Etudes Traditionnelles* (Paris), October-December 1983.

"Failles dans le monde de la foi", *Etudes Traditionnelles,* January-March, 1984.

"Le mystère du visage hypostatique", *Etudes Traditionnelles*, April-June 1984.

"Notes sur le vêtement des Indiens Peaux-Rouges", *Etudes Traditionnelles*, July-September 1984.

"Quelques critiques", (de l'oeuvre de René Guénon), in *Les Dossiers H: "René Guénon"*, L'Age d'Homme, Lausanne, 1984.

"A propos de quelques critiques", (de l'oeuvre de René Guénon), *Etudes Traditionnelles*, October-December, 1984 (feuillet complémentaire).

"A propos d'une image" (de René Guénon), *Etudes Traditionnelles*, October-December, 1984 (feuillet complémentaire).

"Note sur René Guénon", in *René Guénon, Les Cahiers de l'Herne*, Paris, 1985.

"Primauté de l'intellection", *Connaissance des Religions*, (Nancy), Vol. 1, No. 1, June, 1985.

"Degrés et dimensions du théisme", *Connaissance des Religions*, Vol. 1, No. 2, December, 1985.

"David, Shankara, Honen", *Connaissance des Religions*, Vol. 1, No. 3, December, 1985.

"Tour d'horizon d'anthropologie intérgrale", *Connaissance des Religions*, Vol. 1, No. 4, March, 1986.

"'Notre Père qui êtes aux cieux'", *Connaissance des Religions*,

Vol. 2, No. 1, June, 1986.

"Avoir un centre" (première partie), *Connaissance des Religions*, Vol. 2, No. 2, September 1986.

"Avoir un centre" (suite et fin), *Connaissance des Religions*, Vol. 2, No. 3, December, 1986.

"A propos d'une ambiguïté onto-cosmologique", *Connaissance des Religions*, Vol. 2, No. 4, March, 1987.

"L'homme en face du Souverain Bien", *Connaissance des Religions*, Vol. 3, No. 4, March, 1988.

"Dimensions salvatrices", *Connaissance des Religions*, Vol. 4, No. 1/2, June-September, 1988.

"Mahâshakti", *Connaissance des Religions*, Vol. 5, No.1, June, 1989.

"De l'intelligence", *Connaissance des Religions*, Vol. 5, Nos. 2/3, September-December, 1989.

"De l'intention", *Connaissance des Religions*, Vol. 5, No.4, March, 1990.

"Le jeu des masques", *Connaissance des Religions*, Vol.6, Nos. 2-3, September – December, 1990.

Books in English

The Transcendent Unity of Religions (translated by Peter Townsend), London, Faber, 1953; revised edition, Wheaton, Illinois, TPH Quest, 1984.

Spiritual Perspectives and Human Facts (translated by Macleod Matheson), London, Faber, 1954; second impression, London, Perennial Books, 1970; new translation (by P. N. Townsend), London, Perennial Books, 1987.

Gnosis: Divine Wisdom (translated by G. E. H. Palmer), London, John Murray, 1959; second impression, London, Perennial Books, 1978.

Language of the Self (translated by Marco Pallis and Macleod

Matheson), Madras, Ganesh, 1959.

Stations of Wisdom (translated by G. E. H. Palmer), London, John Murray, 1961; second impression, London, Perennial Books, 1980.

Understanding Islam (translated by Macleod Matheson), London, Allen & Unwin, 1963, and many later impressions; Baltimore, Penguin Books, 1972; London, Unwin & Hyman, 1986.

Light on the Ancient Worlds (translated by Lord Northbourne), London, Perennial Books, 1965; Bloomington, Indiana, World Wisdom Books, 1984.

In the Tracks of Buddhism (translated by Marco Pallis), London, Allen & Unwin, 1968; Unwin & Hyman, 1989.

Dimensions of Islam (translated by Peter Townsend), London, Allen & Unwin, 1969.

The Sword of Gnosis (edited by Jacob Needleman) (principal contributor to), Baltimore, Penguin Books, 1974; second edition, London, Arkana, 1986.

Logic and Transcendence (translated by Peter Townsend), New York, Harper & Row, 1975; second impression, London, Perennial Books, 1984.

Islam and the Perennial Philosophy (translated by J. Peter Hobson), London, World of Islam Festival Publishing Company, 1976.

Esoterism as Principle and as Way (translated by William Stoddart), London, Perennial Books, 1981; Bloomington, Indiana, 1982.

Sufism: Veil and Quintessence (translated by William Stoddart), Bloomington, Indiana, World Wisdom Books, 1981.

Castes and Races (translated by Marco Pallis and Macleod Matheson), London, Perennial Books, 1982.

From the Divine to the Human (translated by Gustavo Polit and Deborah Lambert), Bloomington, Indiana, World Wisdom Books, 1982.

Christianity/Islam – Essays on Esoteric Ecumenism (translated by Gustavo Polit), Bloomington, Indiana, World Wisdom Books,

1985.

The Essential Writings of Frithjof Schuon (edited by Seyyed Hossein Nasr), Warwick, New York, Amity House, 1986.

Survey of Metaphysics and Esoterism (translated by Gustavo Polit), Bloomington, Indiana, World Wisdom Books, 1986.

In theFace of the Absolute, Bloomington, Indiana, World Wisdom Books, 1989.

The Feathered Sun, – Plains Indians in Art and Philosophy, Bloomington, Indiana, World Wisdom Books, 1990.

To have a Center, Bloomington, Indiana, World Wisdom Books, 1990.

Pearls of the Pilgrim, Bloomington, Indiana, World Wisdom Books, forthcoming.

Roots of the Human Condition, Bloomington, Indiana, World Wisdom Books, forthcoming.

Images of Primordial and Mystic Beauty, Bloomington, Indiana, World Wisdom Books, forthcoming.

Articles in English

"Christianity and Islam", *Triveni* (Madras), Vol. VIII, 1935; *The Arab World* (New York), Vol. 1, No. 3, 1945.

"Concerning Forms in Art", in *Art and Thought* (Festschrift in Honour of Ananda K. Coomaraswamy), London Luzac, 1947.

"The Stations of Wisdom", *Asia* (Saigon), Vol. III, No. 10, September, 1953.

"The Sacred Pipe of the Red Indians", *Asia*, Vol. III, No. 12, November, 1953.

"Yoga as a Spiritual Principle", *Asia*, Vol. IV, No. 15, December, 1954.

"The Nature and Arguments of Faith", *Islamic Quarterly* (London), Vol. II, No. 3, October, 1955.

"Understanding the Koran", *Islamic Quarterly*, Vol. V, No. 1, April, 1958.

"Studies in Shinto", *France-Asie/Asia* (Tokyo), Vol. XVII, No. 164, November-December, 1960.

"Invocation of the Divine Name", *Kalyana Kalpataru* (Gorakhpur, Uttar Pradesh, India), October, 1961.

"Treasures of Buddhism", *The Middle Way* (London), Vol. XXXVI, No. 3, November, 1961.

"Some Notes on the Shamanism of North America", *Tomorrow* (London), Vol. II, No. 4, Autumn, 1963.

"Reflections on Ideological Sentimentalism", *Tomorrow*, Vol.12, No. 1, Winter, 1964.

"The Ancient Worlds in Perspective", *Tomorrow*, Vol. 12, No. 2, Spring, 1964.

"Truths and Errors concerning Beauty", *Tomorrow*, Vol. 12, No. 4, Autumn, 1964.

"Dialogue between Hellenists and Christians", *Tomorrow*, Vol. 13, No. 1, Winter, 1965.

"The Delivered One and the Divine Image", *Tomorrow*, Vol. 13, No. 2, Spring, 1965.

"Some Observations on a Problem of the Afterlife", *Tomorrow*, Vol. 13, No. 3, Autumn, 1965.

"The Symbolist Outlook", *Tomorrow*, Vol. 14, No. 2, Spring, 1966.

"The Psychological Imposture", *Tomorrow*, Vol. 14, No. 2, Spring, 1966.

"Some Observations on the Symbolism of the Hourglass", *Tomorrow* (London), Vol. 14, No. 3, Summer, 1966.

"The Demiurge in North American Mythology", *Tomorrow*, Vol. 14, No. 4, Autumn, 1966.

"Keys to the Bible", *Studies in Comparative Religion* (London), Vol. 1, No.1, Winter 1967; also in *The Sword of Gnosis*.

"Nature and Function of the Spiritual Master", *Studies in*

Comparative Religion, Vol. 1, No. 2, Spring, 1967; *Journal of Oriental Research* (Madras), Vols. XXXIV-XXXV, 1964-1966.

"The Impossible Convergence", *Studies in Comparative Religion,* Vol. 1, No. 4, Autumn, 1967.

"The Sun Dance", *Studies in Comparative Religion,* Vol. 2, No. 1, Spring, 1968.

"Usurpations of Religious Feeling", *Studies in Comparative Religion,* Vol. 2, No. 2, Spring, 1968.

"The Wisdom of the Virgin", *Studies in Comparative Religion,* Vol. 2, No. 3, Summer, 1968.

"His Holiness and the Red Indian", in *Sankara and Shanmata,* Madras, 1969.

"Dilemmas in Theological Speculation", *Studies in Comparative Religion,* Vol. 3, No. 2, Spring, 1969; *Islamic Quarterly,* Vol. XVII, Nos. 1 & 2, January and June, 1973.

"Understanding and Believing", *Studies in Comparative Religion,* Vol. 3, No. 3, Summer, 1969; also in *The Sword of Gnosis* .

"No Activity without Truth", *Studies in Comparative Religion,* Vol. 3, No. 4, Autumn, 1969; also in *The Sword of Gnosis.*

"On the Ancient Wisdom in Africa", *Studies in Comparative Religion,* Vol. 3, No. 4, Autumn, 1969 (under F. S.).

"Dharmakara's Vow", *Studies in Comparative Religion,* Vol. 4, No. 1, Winter 1970.

"Concerning a Paradox in the Divine Comedy", *Studies in Comparative Religion,* Vol. 4, No. 2, Spring, 1970.

"The Spiritual Virtues according to St. Francis of Assisi", *Studies in Comparative Religion,* Vol. 4, No. 3, Summer, 1970.

"On the Margin of Liturgical Improvisations", *Studies in Comparative Religion,* Vol. 4, No. 4, Autumn, 1970; also in *The Sword of Gnosis.*

"Oriental Dialectic and its Roots in Faith", *Studies in Comparative Religion,* Vol. 5, No. 1, Winter, 1971.

"Remarks on the Enigma of the Koan", *Studies in Comparative*

Religion, Vol. 5, No. 2, Spring, 1971; also in *The Sword of Gnosis.*

"The Human Margin", *Studies in Comparative Religion,* Vol. 5, Nos. 3 & 4, Summer and Autumn, 1971; also in *The Sword of Gnosis.*

"Remarks on some Kings of France", *Studies in Comparative Religion,* Vol. 6, No. 1, Winter, 1972.

"Man and Certainty", *Studies in Comparative Religion,* Vol. 6, No. 2, Spring, 1972.

"Realization", *Studies in Comparative Religion,* Vol. 6, No. 2, Spring, 1972.

"The Two Paradises", *Studies in Comparative Religion,* Vol. 6, No. 3, Summer 1972.

"Remarks on the Sunna", *Studies in Comparative Religion,* Vol. 6, No. 4, Autumn, 1972.

"Concerning the Proofs of God", *Studies in Comparative Religion,* Vol. 7, No. 1, Winter, 1973.

"The Contradiction of Relativism", *Studies in Comparative Religion,* Vol. 7, No. 2, Spring, 1973.

"Atmā-Māyā", *Studies in Comparative Religion,* Vol. 7, No. 3, Summer, 1973.

"The Double Pitfall", *Studies in Comparative Religion,* Vol. 7, No. 4, Autumn, 1973.

"The Problem of the Theodicies", *Studies in Comparative Religion,* Vol. 8, No. 1, Winter, 1974.

"The Mystery of the Two Natures", *Studies in Comparative Religion,* Vol. 8, No. 2, Spring, 1974.

"Form and Substance in the Religions", *Studies in Comparative Religion,* Vol. 8, No. 3, Summer, 1974.

"The Seeds of a Divergence", *Studies in Comparative Religion,* Vol. 8, No. 4, Autumn, 1974.

"Comment on Jung", in "Cosmology and Modern Science" by Titus Burckhardt, in *Sword of Gnosis,* page 177. Also in *Mirror of the Intellect* by Titus Burckhardt (Quinta Essentia, Cambridge,

England; State University of New York, Albany; 1987), pages 66-67.

"Letter on Existentialism", *Studies in Comparative Religion*, Vol. 9, No. 2, Spring, 1975.

"On Relics", *Studies in Comparative Religion*, Vol. 9, No. 3, Summer, 1975.

"What Sincerity is and is not", *Studies in Comparative Religion*, Vol. 9, No. 4, Autumn, 1975.

"The Three Dimensions of Sufism", *Studies in Comparative Religion*, Vol. 10, No. 1, Winter, 1976.

"Celestial Apparitions", *Studies in Comparative Religion*, Vol. 10, No. 2, Spring, 1976.

"Foundation of an Integral Aesthetics", *Studies in Comparative Religion*, Vol. 10, No. 3, Summer, 1976.

"The Degrees of Art", *Studies in Comparative Religion*, Vol. 10, No. 4, Autumn, 1976.

"The Problem of Sexuality", *Studies in Comparative Religion*, Vol. 11, No. 1, Winter, 1977.

"The Mystery of the Veil", *Studies in Comparative Religion*, Vol. 11, No. 2, Spring, 1977.

"Alternations in Semitic Monotheism", *Studies in Comparative Religion*, Vol. 11, No. 3, Summer, 1977.

"Consequences Flowing from the Mystery of Subjectivity", *Studies in Comparative Religion*, Vol. 11, No. 4, Autumn, 1977.

"Aspects of the Theophanic Phenomenon of Consciousness", *Studies in Comparative Religion*, Vol. 12, Nos. 1 & 2, Winter-Spring, 1978.

"A Belated but Still Timely Word about the Encyclical *Populorum Progressio*", *Studies in Comparative Religion*, Vol. 12, Nos. 1 & 2, Winter-Spring, 1978.

"Travel Meditations", *Studies in Comparative Religion*, Vol. 12, Nos. 1 & 2, Winter-Spring, 1978.

"Paradoxical Aspects of Sufism", *Studies in Comparative Religion*,

Vol. 12, Nos. 3 & 4, Summer-Autumn 1978.

"Hamlet", *Studies in Comparative Religion*, Vol. 12, Nos. 3 & 4, Summer-Autumn, 1978.

"The Quintessential Esoterism of Islam", *Studies in Comparative Religion*, Vol. 13, Nos. 1 & 2, Winter-Spring, 1979.

"To be Man is to Know", *Studies in Comparative Religion*, Vol. 13, Nos. 1 & 2, Winter-Spring, 1979.

"*Sophia Perennis*", *Studies in Comparative Religion*, Vol. 13, Nos. 3 & 4, Summer-Autumn, 1979.

"The Characteristics of Passional Mysticism", *Studies in Comparative Religion*, Vol. 13, Nos. 3 & 4, Summer-Autumn, 1979.

"Outline of a Spiritual Anthropology", *Studies in Comparative Religion*, Vol. 14, Nos. 1 & 2, Winter-Spring, 1980.

"Concerning the Notion of Eternity", *Studies in Comparative Religion*, Vol. 14, Nos. 3 & 4, Summer-Autumn, 1980.

"*Sedes Sapientiae*", *Studies in Comparative Religion*, Vol. 14, Nos. 3 & 4, Summer-Autumn, 1980.

"Islam and the Consciousness of the Absolute", *Studies in Comparative Religion*, Vol. 15, Nos. 1 & 2, Winter-Spring, 1983.

"A Message on North American Indian Religion", *Studies in Comparative Religion*, Vol. 15, Nos. 1 & 2, Winter-Spring, 1983.

"The Ambiguity of Exoterism", *Studies in Comparative Religion*, Vol. 15, Nos. 3 & 4, Summer-Autumn, 1983.

"The Ambiguity of the Emotional Element", *Studies in Comparative Religion*, Vol. 15, Nos. 3 & 4, Summer-Autumn, 1983.

"Dimensions of Omnipotence", *Studies in Comparative Religion*, Vol. 16, Nos. 1 & 2, 1984.

"The Primacy of Intellection", *Studies in Comparative Religion*, Vol. 16, Nos. 3 & 4, 1985.

"Summary of Integral Metaphysics", *International Philosophical Quarterly* (New York), Vol. 26, No. 2, June, 1986.

322   FRITHJOF SCHUON

"The Spiritual Significance of the Substance of the Prophet",
in *Islamic Spirituality* (edited by Seyyed Hossein Nasr), New
York, Crossroad, 1987.

"Transgression and Purification", *Avaloka* (Grand Rapids,
Michigan), December, 1990.

"The Perennial Philosophy", in *The Unanimous Tradition* (edited
by Ranjit Fernando), Institute of Traditional Studies, Colombo,
Sri Lanka, forthcoming.

Books in Italian

Dell'Unità trascendente delle Religioni (translated by N. and S.
Dallaporta Xidias), Bari, Laterza, 1949; *Unità trascendente delle
Religioni* (translated by G. Jannaccone and M. Magnini),
Rome, Edizioni Mediterranee, 1980.

L'Uomo e la Certezza (translated by G. Cantoni), Turin, Borla,
1967.

Comprendere l'Islam (translated by G. Jannaccone and M.
Magnini), Milan, Archè, 1976.

Le Stazioni della Saggezza (translated by N. Dallaporta Xidias),
Rome, Edizioni Mediterranee, 1981.

Il Sufismo: Velo e Quintessenza (translated by G. Jannaccone),
Rome, Edizioni Mediterranee, 1982.

L'Occhio del Cuore (translated by S. Dallaporta Xidias), Rome,
Edizioni Mediterranee, 1982.

L'Esoterismo come Principio e come Via (translated by G.
Jannaccone), Rome, Edizioni Mediterranee, 1984.

Forma e Sostanza nelle Religioni (translated by M. Magnini),
Rome, Edizioni Mediterranee, 1984.

Sulle tracce della Religione perenne (translated by G. Jannaccone),
Rome, Edizioni Mediterranee, 1988.

Dal Divino all'Umano (translated by G. Jannaccone), Rome,
Edizioni Mediterranee, 1989.

Cristianesimo/Islam (translated by G. Jannaccone), Rome, Edizioni Mediterranee, in preparation.

Sguardi sui Mondi antichi (translated by N. Floridia, D. Nason, and C. Ranghiero), Rome, Edizioni Mediterranee, in preparation.

Articles in Italian

"Del Cristo e del Profeta", *Rivista di Studii Iniziatici* (Naples), Vol. XX, Nos. 4-6, July-December, 1946.

"Del Sacrificio", *Rivista di Studii Iniziatici*, Vol. XXI, Nos. 1-3, January-July, 1947 and Vol. XXI, Nos. 4-5 August-October, 1947.

"Il Significato spirituale del lavoro", *Rivista di Studii Iniziatici*, Vol. XXI, Nos. 4-5, August-October, 1947.

"I Modi della Realizzazione spirituale", *Rivista di Studii Iniziatici*, *Vol.* XXI, Nos. 6, November-December, 1947.

"Fatalità e Progresso", *Rivista di Studii Iniziatici*, Vol. XXII, No. 1, January-June, 1948.

"Misteri Cristici", *Rivista di Studii Iniziatici*, Vol. XXII, numbers 4-6, July-December, 1948.

"Cristianesimo e Buddhismo", *Rivista di Studii Iniziatici*, Vol. XXIII, nos. 1-3, January-June, 1949.

"Della Conoscenza", *Rivista di Studii Iniziatici*, Vol. XXIII, Nos. 4-6, July-December, 1949.

"Vedanta e Vedantisti", *Rivista di Studii Iniziatici*, Vol. XXIV, Nos. 1-3, January-June 1950 and Vol. XXIV, Nos. 4-6, July-December, 1950.

"Il Demiurgo nella Mitologia nord-americana", in *L'Aquila e il corvo nel Mondo degli Uomini rossi* by Antonio Medrano and Frithjof Schuon, with an introduction by E. Castore, Parma, Edizioni di AR, 1979.

Books in Spanish

De la unidad transcendente de las religiones, Buenos Aires, Anaconda, 1949; (new translation by Manuel García Viñó), Madrid, Heliodoro, 1980.

Sobre los mundos antiguos (translated by Jesús García Varela), Madrid, Taurus, 1980.

El esoterismo como principio y vía (translated by Manuel García Viñó), Madrid, Taurus, 1982.

Tras las huellas de la religión perenne (translated by Esteve Serra), Palma de Mallorca, José de Olañeta, 1982.

Castas y razas (translated by Francesc Gutiérrez y Esteve Serra), Palma de Mallorca, José de Olañeta, 1983.

Comprender el Islam (translated by Esteve Serra), Palma de Mallorca, José de Olañeta, 1987.

Perlas del pelegrino (compiled by Thierry Béguelin and translated by Esteve Serra), Palma de Mallorca, 1990.

Articles in Spanish

"A propósito de una paradoja de la Divina Comedia", *Graal* (Madrid), 1977.

"Del misterio de la subjectividad", *Cielo y Tierra* (Barcelona), No. 1, 1982.

"La espiritualidad de San Francisco de Asís", *Cielo y Tierra*, No. 3, 1982-1983.

"Rechazar o aceptar la Revelación", *Cielo y Tierra*, No. 12, 1985.

Books in Portuguese

Da Unidade Transcendente das Religiões (translated by F. G. Galvão), São Paulo, Livraria Martins Editôra, 1953; revised and newly translated edition, Lisbon, Publicações Dom Quixote, in preparation.

O Esoterismo como Princípio e como Caminho (translated by Setsuko Ono), São Paulo, Editora Pensamento, 1987.

Compreender o Islão (translated by Emanuel Lourenço Godinho), Lisbon, Publicações Dom Quixote, 1989.

Islã: O Credo e a Conduta (translated and edited by Roberto S. Bartholo, Jr. and Arminda Campos); contains "Islã" (a section from *Understanding Islam)* and "O Esoterismo quintessencial do Islã" by Frithjof Schuon. Rio de Janeiro, Editora Imago, 1990.

Articles in Portuguese

"Cristianismo e Budismo", *Thot* (São Paulo), No. 54, 1990.

Books in Swedish

Tidlös Besinning i besinninglös Tid - ur Frithjof Schuons Werk (extracts from the writings of Frithjof Schuon), selected and translated by Kurt Almquist, Stockholm, Natur och Kultur, 1973.

Books in Greek

Kammia Drastêriotêta choris tên Alêtheia ("No Activity without Truth") kai *Oi Ekdêloseis tês Theias Archês* ("Manifestations of the Divine Principle") (translated by G. Paigês), Athens, Bibliothèque "Sphinx", 1981.

Books in Arabic

فريدهوف شووان – حتّى تفهم الاسلام – دار المتعّده للنشر، بيروت، ١٩٨٠

Ḥatta nafhama'l-islām (translation of *Understanding Islam* by
Ṣalāḥ al-Ṣāwī and Seyyed Hossein Nasr) Dâr al-Muttaḥidah li'l-
Nashr (The United Publishing House), Beirut, 1980.

Books in Persian

تفهم حقائق اسلام

Tafahhum-i ḥaqāq-i islām
(Understanding Islam)

Articles in Persian

١ – ''ودانتا''، مجلة مهر، بهار ١٣٤٣ ، ص ٣٦ – ٤٣ (ترجمة سيد حسين نصر).

٢ – ''اصول ومعيار های هنر جهانی''، مطالعاتی درهنردينی، ١، تهران، انتشارات سازمان
جشن هنر شيران ١٣٤٩ (ترجمة سيد حسين نصر).

Articles in Urdu

‏'' انسان اوریقین ''، روایت، ا، لاهور ۱۹۸۳ ص ۱۸۱ – ۱۸۸

Books in Malay/Indonesian

Memahami Islam (translation of *Understanding Islam* by Anas Mahyuddin), Penerbit Pustaka Bandung, 1983.

Titik Pertemuan Agama-Agama (translation of *The Transcendent Unity of Religions*), Jakarta, 1986.

Notes on Contributors

Nasr, Seyyed Hossein – University Professor of Islamic Studies
at George Washington University; of Iranian origin
and formerly professor at Tehran University. Author
of *Knowledge and the Sacred* and editor of *The Essential
Writings of Frithjof Schuon.*

Stoddart, William – Life-long British devotee of the perennial
philosophy. Translator of several books by Frithjof
Schuon. Author of *Sufism – The Mystical Doctrines and
Methods of Islam,* and editor and translator of *Mirror of
the Intellect* by Titus Burckhardt.

Almqvist, Kurt – Swedish philosopher and author; editor and
translator of *Tidlös Besinning i besinninglös Tid – ur
Frithjof Schuons Werk.*

Borella, Jean – French Catholic philosopher and professor of
philosophy at the University of Nancy; author of *La
Charité profanée* and *Le Sens du surnaturel.*

Canteins, Jean – French traditionalist writer and scholar, and
adviser to *Connaissance des Religions.* He is the author of
La Voie des Lettres and *Miroir de la Shahāda.*

Chittick, William – American professor of religion and Islamic
studies at the State University of New York at Stony
Brook and author of *The Sufi Path of Love* and *The Sufi
Path of Knowledge.*

Coomaraswamy, Rama – American surgeon and theologian.
Catholic traditionalist. Author of *The Destruction of the
Christian Tradition* and co-editor of *Selected Letters of
Ananda Coomaraswamy.*

Cutsinger, James – American professor of religion at the
University of South Carolina and author of *The Form of
Transformed Vision.*

Du Pasquier, Roger – Swiss scholar, journalist and specialist in
Islam. The author of *Découverte de l'Islam* and *L'Islam
entre tradition et révolution.*

Hani, Jean – French theologian and traditionalist; author of *La Divine liturgie* and *Le Symbolisme du temple chrétien.*

Kelly, Bernard – (1907-1958) – English Catholic author and Thomist philosopher. Frequent contributor to *Blackfriars, The Life of the Spirit,* and *Dominican Studies.*

Küry, Hans – (1906-1987) German Swiss philosopher and author; translator into German of some of Schuon's writings; contributor to the *Zeitschrift für Ganzheitsforschung* (Vienna) and author of *Der wissende Tod* (Interlaken, 1982).

Lindbom, Tage – Swedish thinker and writer, author of *The Tares and the Good Grain.*

Lings, Martin – English traditionalist and scholar. Author of *A Sufi Saint of the Twentieth Century, What is Sufism?, Ancient Beliefs and Modern Superstitions,* and *The Eleventh Hour.*

Michon, Jean-Louis – French specialist in Sufism and Islamic art; author of *Le Soufi marocain Ahmad ibn 'Ajiba et son mi'raj* and *L'Autobiographie (fahrasa) du Soufi marocain Ahmad ibn 'Ajiba (1747-1809).*

Moore, Alvin – American traditionalist and translator. Co-editor of *Selected Letters of Ananda Coomaraswamy.*

Pallis, Marco – (1895-1989) – Born in England of Greek parents. Correspondent of René Guénon and Ananda Coomaraswamy. Friend, for over 40 years, of Frithjof Schuon. Author of *Peaks and Lamas, The Way and the Mountain,* and *A Buddhist Spectrum.*

Sherrard, Philip – English professor of Greek thought. Author of *The Rape of Man and Nature* and *The Sacred in Life and Art;* co-translator of the *Philokalia.*

Smith, Huston – American philosopher and historian of religion and former professor at M.I.T. and Syracuse University. Author of *Forgotten Truth* and *Beyond the Post-Modern Mind.*